"Femininity,"
"Masculinity,"
and
"Androgyny"

"Femininity," "Masculinity," and "Androgyny"

A Modern Philosophical Discussion

Edited by

MARY VETTERLING-BRAGGIN

1982

LITTLEFIELD, ADAMS & COMPANY

Dedicated to the memory of Eunice Belgum

Copyright © 1982
by
LITTLEFIELD, ADAMS & CO.
81 Adams Drive, Totowa, N.J. 07512

Library of Congress Cataloging in Publication Data
Main entry under title:

"Femininity," "masculinity," and "androgyny."

(Littlefield, Adams quality paperback; 399)
Bibliography: p.
1. Women—Psychology. 2. Men—Psychology.
3. Sex differences (Psychology) 4. Androgyny
(Psychology) I. Vetterling-Braggin, Mary.
HQ1206.F44   305.3   81-19365
ISBN 0-8226-0399-3 (pbk.)   AACR2

Printed in the United States of America

Contents

General Introduction

One of the few topics of central concern to those interested in women's studies that philosophers have, historically speaking, said a great deal about is that of so-called psychological sex differences. Since the fifth century B.C., philosophers have provided extensive theories to the effect that males and females have what they view as opposite psychological sex trait differences; males, we have been told, are "masculine," females "feminine."

While this thesis appears to be relatively straightforward, the idea that males are "masculine" and females "feminine" is subject to radically different interpretations. What some have meant by it makes it a tautology. What others have meant makes it normative, rather than descriptive, in import. What yet others have meant makes it descriptive, but not empirically testable in practice. And what yet others have meant makes it debatably empirically testable in practice, although it is not clear that the claim ever has been or could be tested with complete objectivity. Since how the thesis is interpreted does make a significant difference as to whether it is true, false, or indeterminably true or false, various notions of sex and gender in the literature of so-called psychological sex differences are presented and discussed in Part I of this volume. Part II represents an overview of those theories which take the descriptive thesis to be true and provide explanations for the link claimed to exist between sex and gender.

The authors in Part III, however, discuss the serious methodological difficulties of any attempt to confirm the thesis or to justify any of the different explanations suggested for the claimed link between sex and gender even when it is merely presupposed rather than demonstrated to exist. There it is argued that *if* one commits oneself to the thesis in the absence of definitive evidence in its favor, there may be overriding ethical grounds for selecting "nurture" explanations over "nature" ones.

Part IV asks what an ideal society might look like if there is no real connection between sex and psychological gender or if there is such a connection but it is a "breakable" one. There it is suggested that although an "androgynous" ideal is not without its difficulties, if properly construed, it merits renewed consideration at this time.

I am grateful to Joyce Trebilcot of Washington University, St. Louis, for working with me through some of the more difficult philosophical implications of some significant feminist materials. Patrick Grim of the State University of New York at Stony Brook reviewed the introductions to each section and offered extensive and helpful critical philosophical and stylistic comments. Lastly, I am indebted to Adele Laslie of Lehigh University and John Wieboldt of Littlefield, Adams and Co. for having repeatedly and cheerfully provided the encouragement necessary for the completion of the project; and to my children for having patiently tolerated one of their favorite but neglectful agents for the duration of the project.

Part I
Notions of Sex and Gender

Introduction

Virtually all sex difference theorists presuppose that for the overwhelming majority of us, each is either a "female" (a "woman") or a "male" (a "man") in some biological sense of these terms.[1] This is our *sex,* to be distinguished from our *gender:* "feminine" or "masculine."[2] Virtually all sex difference theorists also affirm some link between sex and gender[3] and argue that this link needs explanation. But are all "females" "feminine," all "males" "masculine?"

The answers to this question clearly depend on how we more carefully specify sex and gender. These notions have been by no means universally construed in the same way. It is thus crucial for the reader of sex difference theory first to come to grips with any author's notion of sex and gender before she or he can understand the thesis with which the author begins. A theorist who implicitly or explicitly *defines* "sex" in terms of "gender," or vice versa, will effectively link "sex" and "gender" by trivial definitional fiat, forcing a conclusion by linguistic sleight of hand rather than by empirical investigation.[4] Such a trap must be avoided if we are to answer the question prompted by the thesis of the sex difference theorist in any significant sense.

Let us take a closer look at some of the most common attempts at specifying "sex" and "gender."

A. NOTIONS OF "SEX"

A number of criteria have been advanced for classifying a person as either "female" or "male" on the basis of biological traits. None of these, however, is entirely free of counterexamples.

1. Hormonal Criteria

Hormonal criteria classify a person as either "female" or "male" based on the amount of androgen and estrogen in the body of that person. Those persons with higher estrogen than androgen ratings are called "female," those with higher androgen than estrogen ratings are called "male." Such criteria, however, fail in those (rare) cases where unusually high amounts of estrogen are produced by the testes and adrenals in males and unusually high amounts of androgen are produced by the ovaries in females. More frequently, the criteria fail when males (females) are injected with large doses of estrogen (androgen) for a variety of reasons (in preparation for transsexual surgery on men and women, or, up until recently, for the prevention of milk production in those who have just become mothers and who do not wish to lactate).

2. Anatomical Criteria

At least two different types of criteria have been advanced for classifying a person as either "female" or "male" on the basis of certain features of a person's anatomy. *Genital* criteria assign sex based on primary anatomical characteristics ("maleness" is assigned to persons with testes, "femaleness" to persons with ovaries). *Morphological* criteria classify persons as either "female" or "male" on the basis of secondary anatomical characteristics (a person with a penis, scrotum, prostate or deep voice, for example, is called "male," a person with a clitoris, vulva, uterus, vagina, or high voice, for example, "female").

Since it is now medically possible to alter both a person's primary and secondary anatomical characteristics, both types of criteria face exceptions. But it is fair to say that of the two types, genital criteria are more valuable since fewer people lack primary anatomical characteristics than lack secondary ones.

3. *Chromosomal Criteria*

Chromosomal criteria classify a person as "female" when a chromosomal XX pattern is present and as "male" when an XY chromosomal pattern is present. Some, but very few, known cases in which XXY or XXYY constellations have appeared in humans are the only known counterexamples to chromosomal criteria for sex. For that reason, some current theorists, such as Janice Raymond, take chromosomal patterns for determining a person's sex to be the most reliable criteria currently available to us.[5]

The importance of determining just what criteria are being presupposed by any given sex difference theorist cannot be overemphasized to the reader of sex differences literature. For those authors who are affirming some link (causal or otherwise) between sex and gender, it makes a difference whether gender is being linked to hormonal, anatomical, or chromosomal features of persons; it is possible for a person to be a "female" in an anatomical sense of the term, but a "male" in the chromosomal sense. Moreover, since many authors conflate sex and gender, it is important to be wary of sex classification from the start. Let us now turn to some of the more common notions of gender.

B. NOTIONS OF "GENDER"

In common usage, a person's gender is often characterized as either "feminine" or "masculine," although what is meant by these terms varies from author to author. We shall try to capture here only the two major senses of the terms as commonly used in sex difference research.

The claim that a person is either "feminine" or "masculine" is often tantamount to a claim that the person exhibits certain psychological traits. Here the terms in quotes are being used *descriptively*. A sex difference theorist might describe a person as "feminine," for example, if the theorist thought that the person had any or all of the following psychological traits (P-traits):

> gentleness
> modesty
> humility
> supportiveness
> empathy

Group X $\left\{\begin{array}{l}\text{compassionateness} \\ \text{tenderness} \\ \text{nurturance} \\ \text{intuitiveness} \\ \text{sensitivity} \\ \text{unselfishness}\end{array}\right.$

Or the theorist might classify a person as "masculine" if the theorist thought that person to have any or all of the following P-traits:

Group Y $\left\{\begin{array}{l}\text{strength of will} \\ \text{ambition} \\ \text{courage} \\ \text{independence} \\ \text{assertiveness} \\ \text{aggressiveness} \\ \text{hardiness} \\ \text{rationality or the ablity to think logically,} \\ \quad \text{abstractly and analytically} \\ \text{ability to control emotion[6]}\end{array}\right.$

The P-traits the sex difference theorist claims a person has are to be distinguished from the behavior traits (B-traits) on the basis of which the theorist judges the presence of the P-traits in that person. For example, the theorist might claim that John has the P-trait aggressiveness because John has the B-trait of engaging in an unusually large number of fist fights. Or that Susan has the P-trait nurturance because she is the primary rearer of her children. The reason that this distinction should be noted by the reader (as PATRICK GRIM and SARAH HOAGLAND point out in Part III) is that the assignment of P-traits to individuals on the basis of B-traits is often biased; different B-traits are sometimes selected as indicating the presence of certain P-traits in women from those B-traits selected as indicating the presence of those same P-traits in men. Thus, for example, a sex difference theorist might classify a woman as "nurturant" because she often takes care of children whereas that same theorist might not classify a man as "nurturant" who also frequently takes care of children.

However, the claim that a person is either "feminine" or "masculine" can also be tantamount to the claim that not only does the person exhibit psychological traits from Group X or

Group Y but it is good or proper that the person does. In this case, the terms are being used *prescriptively*. Since it is very rare for prescriptive sex difference theorists to hold that it is good for a male to have a P-trait from Group X or that it is good for a female to have a P-trait from Group Y, such theorists, rather than demonstrate, presuppose, that sex and gender are linked; in those cases where a woman (man) appears to have a P-trait from Group Y (Group X), the theorist can fail to assign "masculinity" ("femininity") to the woman (man) on the belief that it is not good for her (him) to have the traits in question.

In the above accounts of sex and gender, it is easy to see that those sex criteria which rely on chromosomal differences suffer from the fewest number of counterexamples and that descriptive accounts of gender appear least likely to tempt the theorist to presuppose (as opposed to demonstrate) a positive answer to the key question at hand. (This is not, however, to deny that other problems may occur with descriptive accounts; these problems will be discussed in Part III.) But the paucity of psychological sex difference theories which do rely on chromosomal criteria for sex and descriptive accounts of gender will immediately strike the reader of primary sources in the field.

Some examples of sex difference theories which apply the term "feminine" to women and examples of the psychological traits often assumed to be central to the notion of the "feminine" are discussed by ANNE DICKASON in Part I. It is important to notice that sex difference theorists are concerned primarily with the ascription of "masculinity" and "femininity" to *persons,* since what they want to explain is the connection they affirm between a person's being a certain sex and a person's exhibiting certain psychological traits but not others. The meanings of these terms are to be distinguished from the meanings these terms might have when applied to other sorts of things (such as psychological traits themselves, behavioral traits, certain types of jobs or sports). Questions about the "masculinity" and "femininity" of these latter sorts of things will be raised in Part IV.

NOTES

1. This assumption is not entirely unproblematic. However, the problems with it will be carefully noted and spelled out in what follows.

Some are discussed at length by Glorianne M. Leck in "Philosophical Concerns About Gender Distinction," SISCOM Proceedings (1975) and by Glorianne M. Leck and Bonnie McD. Johnson in their "Philosophical Assumptions of Research on Gender Difference or: Two-By-Two and We'll Never Break Through," unpublished ms. available from Glorianne Leck, Department of Philosophy of Education, Youngstown State University, Youngstown, Ohio 44555.

2. For the time being it will be presupposed, along with the preponderance of the literature on the subject, that there are no philosophical problems with referring to a person's gender as "feminine" or "masculine." This presupposition will, however, be challenged in Part III of this work. To remind the reader of possible problems, the terms will appear in quotes wherever they occur.

3. At the time of this writing, I am aware of no printed publication by a sex difference theorist which flatly denies that there are at least some statistically significant psychological differences between the sexes. It is only in comparatively modern times that psychologists have tried to demonstrate that there are such differences (see, for example, Maccoby and Jacklin) and, as will be pointed out in Part III, these "demonstrations" are often fraught with methodological difficulties.

4. There is in common usage a sense of the term "feminine" ("masculine") which *means* "being of the female (male) sex." There is also in common usage a sense of the term "female" ("male") which *means* "being of the feminine (masculine) gender." However, to use these terms in these senses when engaging in sex difference research is in effect to link sex with gender merely by definition. Making this simple error has not, by the way, been limited to non-philosophers. See, for example, the writings of Rousseau and Nietzsche.

5. The above distinctions between the various notions of "sex" in the literature on sex difference are spelled out and discussed by Janice Raymond in her *The Transsexual Empire* (Boston: Beacon Press, 1979), pp. 6–8. She is, in turn, explicating the various notions as originally noted by John Money in his "Sex Reassignment as Related to Hermaphroditism and Transsexualism," which can be found in *Transsexualism and Sex Reassignment,* ed. Richard Green and John Money (Baltimore: Johns Hopkins University Press, 1969), pp. 91–93. Money also refers to definitions of "sex" in terms of the law, but we shall not be concerned with these definitions in this volume. In addition, he points out that sex is often defined in terms of psychological gender, but for the reason cited in footnote 4, I have followed Robert Stoller in clearly distinguishing between sex and psychological gender. See Stoller's *Sex and Gender* (New York: Science House, 1968), pp. viii and ix.

6. This list of traits often used in applying the terms "masculine" and "feminine" to persons was compiled and presented for another purpose by Mary Anne Warren in her *The Nature of Woman* (Point Reyes, Calif.: Edgepress, 1980), p. 17. It is not exhaustive (for example, it does not contain many of the overly negatively-valued psychological traits sometimes associated with the terms), but is merely exemplary of the sorts of traits usually selected. The reader might suspect that the justification for selecting the traits from Group X (often called "passive" traits) as criteria for applying "femininity" to persons and the traits from Group Y (often called "active" traits) as criteria for applying "masculinity" to persons will necessarily lead to some kind of circularity. Indeed, if the theorist's justification for the selection is that all and only females exhibit traits from Group X and that all and only males exhibit traits from Group Y, the theorist is open to the charge of already having answered the question "Are sex and gender linked?" in advance of showing that they are. However, this is not the only justification to which the theorist might appeal. He or she could, for example, maintain that what is being reflected in dividing up the lists in this way is merely the common usage or ordinary meanings of the terms "masculine" and "feminine." But once again, although circularity need not be reflected at this juncture, there may be other problems with applying the labels on the basis of lists divided up in this way (to be discussed in Part III).

Anne Dickason

The Feminine as a
Universal

Throughout the history of ideas, few concepts have been so influential, yet so elusive, as that known as "the feminine." The concept appears well defined as early as the third century B.C. in both Western and Eastern thought; the Pythagorean Table of Opposites and the dualisms of Yin-Yang express similar divisions of nature clustered arouund "masculine" and "feminine" characteristics.[1] Recent scholarship has widely investigated the legal, economic, and religious status of women in various societies; and current research is exploring the biological and psychological characteristics of women and men in order to see if there are any innately feminine and masculine traits. But it is obvious from the level of current debate that final answers are not yet available on this question. There is, in fact, much contradictory evidence.

"Accidentalists" believe that all masculine and feminine qualities are nonessential properties of what it means to be a man or a woman. They argue that both men and women are primarily shaped by the surrounding culture, and that neither sex is born with any sex-linked psychological characteristics. Studies that show upbringing rather than gender as the molder

Reprinted from *Feminism and Philosophy,* Mary Vetterling-Braggin, Jane English and Frederick Ellison, eds. (Totowa, N.J.: Littlefield, Adams and Co., 1977), pp. 79–100, by permission of the publisher and author.

of identity in hermaphrodite individuals are cited to support this position,[2] which is further upheld by sociological data on the enormous variety of sex-role assignments found among different cultures.[3] Many feminists are in sympathy with the accidentalists' position, thinking that they must abandon traditional conceptions of masculine and feminine behavior and attitudes if equality is to be achieved.

"Essentialists" take the counter position, and believe in definite, universal masculine and feminine characteristics. They cite studies that link the presence of male sex hormones to increased aggressive behavior,[4] and they emphasize the agreement among cultures on feminine and masculine identification.[5] According to this theory, psychosexual neutrality at birth is a misconception; the concepts of feminine and masculine contain specific qualities that are independent of cultural differences. The essentialist position varies greatly in interpretation from outright mysogynism ("feminine is inferior") to more willing acceptance ("separate but equal"). Relatively few feminists support this position, though some feel forced into it by what they see as the weight of the arguments. Others accept it more easily, claiming that the traditional evidence has been unfairly interpreted; they believe that the natural superiority of women rather than second-class status is indicated by the research involved.

In the midst of the controversy generated by this problem lies the fact that there has been no thorough consideration of the concept of "feminine" itself. There are many modern theories regarding the masculine and the feminine. These vary from the biological explanation of Charles Darwin to the sociological thesis of J.J. Bachofen; from the economic analysis of Robert Briffault to the psychological theories of Sigmund Freud; from the mythic interpretations of C.G. Jung and Erich Neumann to the anthropological research of Margaret Mead. Basically, Darwin, Bachofen, Freud, Jung and Neumann provide arguments often used by essentialists, while Briffault and Mead give foundations for the accidentalists. When we examine all of these views we find little agreement on the origins of the concept of the feminine, yet a surprising consistency on what the feminine is. We also find that although ideas about feminine characteristics are not universal enough to be considered necessary, they do occur often enough to seem more than coincidental. This paper is concerned with whether the disclosed commonality can be explained without reverting to the necessity of essentialism. It is my thesis that such an explanation is possible, if we look at the logical foundations of the theories themselves. To do this, I will first give a brief presentation of each view, and then analyze them all.

I. DARWIN

The first modern theory of the feminine and masculine appears in Charles Darwin's discussion of evolution. Darwin thought that in addition to the primary influence of natural selection (the survival of the fittest) there is another influence on the development of a species, that of sexual selection. Less rigorous than natural selection, since the result is not death for the individual but the production of fewer offspring, sexual selection depends not on external conditions, but on the struggle of (usually) males for females.[6] Such small advantages as better weapons for driving away other males, more attractive ornaments, and more appealing odors will attract the most vigorous females, who breed earliest; and these traits will be transmitted to the young.[7]

If such variations are of no service to either sex, they will not be accumulated and increased by sexual or natural selection. Nevertheless, they may become permanent if the exciting cause acts permanently; and in accordance with a frequent form of inheritance they may be transmitted to that sex alone in which they first appeared. In this case the two sexes will come to present permanent, yet unimportant, differences of character.[8]

An example of this is different colors worn by males and females of the same species; the differences are unimportant in the sense that they are not necessary for survival, since females without brilliant plumage survive as well as males who possess it. In this way masculine and feminine traits could become sex-linked.

This theory, combined with careful observation of the animal world, led Darwin to draw analogous conclusions about men and women. "Man is more courageous, pugnacious and energetic than woman, and has more inventive genius."[9] The greater size and courage of men "are all due in chief part to inheritance from his half-human male ancestors."[10] Even with regard to the differences in mental powers between men and women, he says, "it is probable that sexual selection has played a highly important part."[11] Presumably, women chose to mate with men who were braver and more intelligent, thus perpetuating those qualities. And males developed these traits both through competing with other males for a female and through fighting females of equal dominance that they could overpower. Gradually the human male gained the power of selection, unlike the lower animals where the female chooses her mate. When this transition occurred, males then chose females who possessed more submissive qualities.[12] Darwin notes that it is fortunate that there is some equality in the transmission of traits, "otherwise it is probable that man would have become as superior in mental endowment to women, as the peacock is in ornamental plumage to the peahen."[13]

Darwin unabashedly draws many of his conclusions about innate temperament from nonhuman life; he concludes that some difference is "at least probable from the analogy of the lower animals which present other secondary sexual characteristics."[14]

No one disputes that the bull differs in disposition from the cow, the wild-boar from the sow, the stallion from the mare, and, as is well known to the keepers of menageries, the males of the larger apes from the females. Woman seems to differ from man in mental disposition, chiefly in her greater tenderness and less selfishness . . . Woman, owing to her maternal instincts, displays these qualities towards her infants in an eminent degree; therefore it is likely that she would often extend them towards her fellow creatures. Man is the rival of other men; he delights in competition, and this leads to ambition which passes too easily into selfishness. These latter qualities seem to be his natural and unfortunate birthright. It is generally admitted that with women the powers of intuition, of rapid perception, and perhaps of imitation, are more strongly marked than in man; but some, at least, of these faculties are characteristic of the lower races, and therefore of a past and lower state of civilization.[15]

Darwin thus believes in the traditional attributes of masculine and feminine, and explains their origin in terms of biological development; these traits were considered more attractive by the opposite sex and so were preserved through the process of evolution. Since the power of selection eventually settled on the human male, his choice of feminine traits was reflected in the offspring.

II. BACHOFEN

During the time that Darwin was developing his theory of biological evolution, J.J. Bachofen formulated his theory of cultural evolution through the doctrine of mother-right. After careful examination of myths, mortuary symbolism, and primitive societies, Bachofen concluded that each human society without exception passes through three stages. The first, the tellurian, is characterized by motherhood without marriage, the absence of agriculture, and abusive sexual treatment of women. In this primary phase women are important because of their maternal role; they establish kinship, and the feminine powers of fruitfulness and nourishment are called forth in religious rites. But, Bachofen believes, during the tellurian phase women are subject to man's uncontained lust. Eventually women revolt, demanding a more settled, monogamous life. This second stage is the lunar, and brings with it marriage and agriculture; as women insist upon a more gentle life, societies discover more peaceful occupations. It is at this time that men begin to recognize their biological relationship to children. This comprises the second, higher stage of mother-right. As fathers acquire almost exclusive rights over their children, society moves into the solar period of human development; this is the third and final phase, that of father-right. Here, division of labor arises and individual ownership of property gains importance. Bachofen considers father-right the highest stage of culture, and views mother-right as an essential prelude.

Mother-right is an important stage for several reasons:

> The relationship which stands at the origin of all culture, of every virtue, of every nobler aspect of existence, is that between mother and child; it operates in a world of violence as the divine principle of love, of union, of peace. Raising her young, the woman learns earlier than the man to extend her loving care beyond the limits of ego to another creature, and to direct whatever gift of invention she possesses to the preservation and imporvement of this other's existence. Woman at this stage is the repository of all culture, of all benevolence, of all devotion, of all concern for the living and grief for the dead.[16]

The matriarchal principle, the feminine, is thus inherently universal; it provides the idea of inclusiveness in a broad family. "It is the basis of the universal freedom and equality so frequent among matriarchal peoples, of their hospitality, and of their aversion to restrictions of all sorts."[17] Bachofen believes that this comes because of the lack of an idea of paternity; if no one recognizes the biological connection between men and their children, then everyone sees all others as brothers and sisters. The maternal principle is subject to matter and the phenomena of natural life; it feels harmony with the universe and is keenly aware of pain and death. Because it was women who demanded an end to the primary stage, women were first drawn to a purer ethical view. But father-right overcomes this because "the triumph of paternity brings with it the liberation of the spirit from the manifestations of nature, a sublimation of human existence over the laws of material life."[18]

Bachofen, like Darwin, believes that the characteristics we term feminine and masculine are imbedded in our human nature; to Bachofen, the feminine begins with the maternal relationship and develops by influencing the cultural growth of society along a particular, universal path. Women are more inclusive, passive, and nurturing as a result of their role as mother; these qualities influence society for a while, bringing it to a more advanced stage, but eventually these qualities give way to the narrower but more successful concepts coming from patriarchy.

III. BRIFFAULT

Robert Briffault was influenced by Bachofen, but provided a more neutral explanation for the prominent occurrence of patriarchy. Like Darwin, Briffault looks first to the animal world for explanatory models. But what Briffault finds is that instead of the male being smarter and braver, "the female is the more cautious, wary, ingenious, and sagacious; while the male is reckless, incautious, and often stupid in comparison."[19] To Briffault, it is the female, not the male, who forms the nucleus of the animal family; the mother and her offspring are the family. "The male, instead of being the head and supporter of the group, is not an essential member of it, and more often than not is altogether absent from it."[20] Thus, Briffault feels that animal life can provide us with valuable clues about the innate characteristics of male and female, but that the traits we find are often nearly opposite from those cited by Darwin. Further, when Briffault looks to primitive societies, he finds:

There is not among primitive men and women the disparity in physical power, resourcefulness, enterprise, courage, capacity for endurance, which are observed in civilized societies and are often regarded as organic sexual differences. To a very large extent those differences in physical and mental capacity are the effect, rather than the cause, of that divergence in the avocations of men and women which has taken place in the course of cultural and social development.[21]

The reason for this divergence is economic, Briffault believes, and does not rest on physical advantages. He discovers that in

primitive societies there is nothing corresponding to the domination of one sex by the other which characterizes later, patriarchal
societies. But, unlike Bachofen, he does not see the transition
from matriarchy to patriarchy as a universal, necessary pattern.
Whereas Bachofen sees this transition as a result of the development of human nature toward the spiritual, Briffault ties it to
economic changes which are frequent, but not necessary. So
long as men are hunters, women remain gatherers; men may
contribute the raw materials, but women actually make the
products of household industry, for example, pottery and
baskets. Women are in charge of administration as well. In such
societies women remain important for the economy, contributing independently to the society, and are not subject to the
rule of men. But when men cease to be hunters and develop
domesticated cattle, society becomes patriarchal due to the concentration of wealth in the hands of men. Here women's
economic importance drastically declines. Pastoral society is
"without exception . . . stringently patriarchal and moreover ex-
tensively polygamous."[22]

When agriculture is introduced at this later stage, rather than
directly after the hunting and gathering mode, the importance of
women continues to decrease. Briffault said that "the loss of
woman's economic value as a worker abolished the purpose for
which the association of individual marriage, such as it is found
in primitive societies, originally arose."[23] This results in an inversion of the original, biological sex roles and makes women
compete for men, for example, through beauty. Primitive
woman has little need to cultivate charm and attraction; but in
pastoral life "her value is as an attractive sexual asset."[24] According to Briffault, those characteristics we call masculine and
feminine are not found in the corresponding sexes in the animal
world. Females, not males, possess courage and intelligence and
ward off danger. And he finds that as long as primitive societies
remain hunting-gathering groups, it is the women who are considered wise, and often strong and courageous as well. The
"feminine" attributes in women develop only when males acquire superior economic power, usually through their prior
association as hunters with animals. No longer having economic
importance, women must cultivate other qualities if they are to
survive in the society.

But any society, our own included, would at once lose its patriarchal
character founded upon masculine economic dominance, were the

forms of industry and wealth-production to revert to the dimensions of household industry.[25]

To Briffault, our image of the feminine comes from economic dominance, not biological or psychological characteristics, and would disappear if the economic structure were to change, giving women more power.

IV. FREUD

With Sigmund Freud, the discussion of masculine and feminine moves to a new, internal plane. Freud's discussion of women has long been scathed by feminists, for reasons easily seen, but it should be pointed out that Freud himself asserted that "it is not always easy to distinguish between what is due to the influence of the sexual function and what to social training."[26] Like Darwin and Briffault, Freud sees some clues to the nature of feminine and masculine in the animal world, though he is not certain this carries enough force.

In an early writing Freud states that autoerotic sexuality in young girls might be said to be "of a wholly masculine character."[27]

Indeed, if we were able to give a more definite connotation to the concepts of 'masculine' and 'feminine,' it would even be possible to maintain that libido is invariable and necessarily of a masculine nature, whether it occurs in men or in women and irrespectively of whether its object is a man or a woman.[28]

He explains the reason for this in a footnote added later:

'Masculine' and 'feminine' are used sometimes in the sense of activity and passivity, sometimes in a biological, and sometimes, again, in a sociological sense. The first of these three meanings is the essential one and the most serviceable in psychoanalysis. When, for instance, libido was described in the text above as being 'masculine,' the word was being used in this sense, for an instinct is always active even when it has a passive aim in view. The second, or biological, meaning of 'masculine' and 'feminine' is the one whose applicability can be determined most easily. Here 'masculine' and 'feminine' are characterized by the presence of spermatozoa or ova respectively and by the functions proceeding from them. Activity and its concomitant phenomena (more powerful muscular development, aggressiveness, greater intensity of libido) are as a rule linked with biological masculinity; but they are not necessarily so, for there are animal species in which these qualities are on the contrary assigned to the female. The third, or sociological, meaning receives its connotation from the observation of actually existing masculine and feminine individuals. Such observation shows that in human beings pure masculinity or femininity is not to be found either in a psychological or a biological sense. Every individual on the contrary displays a mixture of the character-traits belonging to his own and the opposite sex; and he shows a combination of activity and passivity whether or not these last charcacter-traits tally with his biological ones.[29]

Here Freud reveals his ambiguity; on the one hand, the identification of male as active and female as passive seems verified by observation of animal or cellular life; on the other hand, Freud recognizes that this is far from a universal identification. Freud writes later, "even in the sphere of human sexual life, one soon notices how unsatisfactory it is to identify masculine behavior with activity and feminine with passivity."[30] But if Freud was not able to discover the origins of our behavior, if he could not find a clear biological basis of our characterizations of feminine and masculine, he was nonetheless able to describe the nature of these images which he thought we possess. Although the origin of the feminine might have been unknown to Freud, its essence was not.

He believed that women, unlike men, must make two important transformations in order to achieve adult sexuality; the erogenous zone must change from the clitoris to the vagina, and the love object must change from the mother to the father. These difficulties mean that it is harder for a girl to become a woman than it is for a boy to become a man; the female faces a sterner, more indirect task. But even in the child the feminine reveals itself:

The little girl is as a rule less aggressive, less defiant, and less self-sufficient; she seems to have a greater need for affection to be shown her, and therefore to be more dependent and docile. . . . One gets the impression, too, that the little girl is more intelligent and more lively than the boy of the same age; she is more inclined to meet the external world halfway, and, at the same time, she makes stronger object-cathexes.[31]

And in mature women we find additional characteristics:

We attribute to women a greater amount of narcissism (and this influences their object-choice) so that for them to be loved is a stronger need than to love. Their vanity is partly a further effect of penis-envy, for they are driven to rate their physical charms more highly as a belated compensation for their original sexual inferiority.[32]

It must be admitted that women have but little sense of justice, and this is no doubt connected with the preponderance of envy in their mental life; for the demands of justice are a modification of envy. . . . We say also of women that their social interests are weaker than those of men, and that their capacity for the sublimation of their instincts is less.[33]

Freud notes that while a man of age thirty in analysis is usually relatively young, a woman of the same age "frequently staggers us by her psychological rigidity and unchangeability;" it is "as though, in fact, the difficult development which leads to femininity had exhausted all the possibilities of the individual."[34]

Freud does assert that "the anatomical distinction between the sexes must, after all, leave its mark in mental life;"[35] and in this way it seems that he would like his theory of what is masculine and feminine to carry some universality. He is often criticized as if he were writing about human nature itself, about how men and women are innately, rather than about how the masculine and feminine are currently expressed. But careful reading of his works does not support this view. For he also believes that psychology cannot solve the "riddle of femininity" until biology can explain how sexual division came about in life itself; since this has not been done, the full nature and importance of the feminine and masculine cannot be known. It is at least possible, to Freud, that cultural influences might someday be seen as more important than he thinks.

V. JUNG AND NEUMANN

C.G. Jung, once a student of Freud, developed his own theory of the masculine and feminine. Whereas Freud was interested in personal conflicts and in the desires people acquire while very young, Jung formulated the concept of a collective unconscious, which each of us possesses and which contains the constant images or archetypes of a universal psychic life. Jung believed that we have access to this collective unconscious through myths, dreams, and art. When we examine these for repetitive features, we find portrayals of the feminine and masculine which clarify the meaning of these concepts. Jung does not look to the animal world for an explanatory model, and he does not discuss why these differences of masculine and feminine arose; like Freud, he is interested in describing what content the concepts have, and how they are expressed in human life. He states that

Every man carries within him the eternal image of woman, not the image of this or that particular woman, but a definite feminine image. This image is fundamentally unconscious, an hereditary factor of primordial origin engraved in the living organic system of the man, an imprint or 'archetype' of all the ancestral experiences of the female, a deposit, as it were, of all impressions ever made by woman—in short, an inherited system of psychic adaptation. Even if no woman existed, it would still be possible, at any given time, to deduce from this unconscious image exactly how a woman would have to be constituted psychically. The same is true of the woman: she too has her inborn image of man.[36]

In man this archetype is the anima; in woman, the animus. Lovers project this image upon their beloved, and this often keeps them from seeing the beloved's true nature. It is a general human characteristic to do this, "but in woman it is given a particularly dangerous twist because in this respect she is not naive and it is only too often her *intention* to let herself be convinced by (the man's projected feelings)."[37] This is because of her feminine qualities. Jung believes that consciousness and activity are masculine attributes, while unconsciousness and passivity are feminine; but through the anima and animus each person contains something of the opposite sex. It is possible to "live out the opposite sex in oneself," for a man to live in his feminine part and a woman to live in her masculine part, but if this is done, "one's real individuality suffers."[38] This happens because people try to negate their true male or female nature, and want to pretend that such an essence does not exist.

The basic difference Jung sees between feminine and masculine is that "woman's psychology is founded on the principle of Eros, the great binder and loosener, whereas from ancient times the ruling principle ascribed to man is Logos."[39] Women are interested in feelings, psychic relatedness, and completeness, while men are drawn to logic, objectivity, and perfection. "To a woman it is generally more important to know how a man feels about a thing than to know the thing itself."[40] But while these characteristics are true of outer attitudes, "in the soul it is the other way round: inwardly it is the man who feels, and the woman who reflects."[41] "Hence a man's greater liability to total despair, while a woman can always find comfort and hope; accordingly, a man is more likely to put an end to himself than a woman."[42]

What Jung has done is to concretize and universalize particular attitudes toward the world as "feminine" and "masculine," yet offer an explanation of individual variations within each sex. For example, it is possible for a woman to be only feminine, but she is likely to seem shallow and to be only a mirror for men's projections onto her; once she attains some consciousness, she cannot return to this state. From then on she must accept the masculine element within her, integrating it into her feminine personality; she must accept her own rationality and assertiveness, and not try to bury them in the guise of only wanting to be a "man's woman." Only then will she be able to achieve relatedness, to be a feminine woman in the fullest sense.

Erich Neumann took many of these ideas from Jung, and discussed them in more literary, less psychoanalytic terms. He carries Jung's theory about masculine and feminine personal identification even further:

It is in this sense that we use the terms 'masculine' and 'feminine' throughout the book, not as personal sex-linked characteristics, but as symbolic expressions. When we say masculine or feminine dominants obtrude themselves in certain stages, or in certain cultures or types of person, this is a psychological statement which must not be reduced to biological or sociological terms. The symbolism of 'masculine' and 'feminine' is archetypal and therefore transpersonal; in the various cultures concerned, it is erroneously projected upon persons as though they carried its qualities. In reality every individual is a psychological hybrid. Even sexual symbolism cannot be derived from the person, because it is prior to the person. Conversely, it is one of the complications of individual psychology that in all cultures the integrity of the personality is violated when it is identified with either the masculine or the feminine side of the symbolic principle of opposites.[43]

Neumann retains Jung's identification of the feminine with "unconsciousness-darkness-night" and the masculine with "consciousness-light-day." This holds true regardless of sex: that is, unconsciousness is feminine in men or women. Neumann believes, like Bachofen and Briffault, that society has moved from the matriarchal to the patriarchal with its increasing reach toward the conscious phase of objective, rational thought. The masculine is concerned with the ego, with "the qualities of volition, decision, and activity as contrasted with the determinism and blind 'drives' of the preconscious, egoless state."[44]

Neumann then considers the path the feminine follows in its emergence from this preconscious state. Unlike Freud, who emphasizes genital sexuality and feelings toward the parents, Neumann sees the journey in strikingly different terms. The myth of Amor and Psyche provides him with an ideal model. Psyche, a beautiful mortal, is given in marriage to a husband she never sees and does not know; he is, in fact, the god Eros. Psyche takes a lamp one night, and tries to glimpse him; but a drop of oil spills from the lamp, waking Eros, who flies away. Psyche then must accomplish several tasks in order to be united with Eros again. Neumann states:

The fundamental situation of the feminine, as we have elsewhere shown, is the primordial relation of identity between daughter and mother. For this reason the approach of the male always and in every case means separation. Marriage is always a mystery, but also a mystery of death. For the male — and this is inherent in the essential opposition between masculine and the feminine — marriage, as the matriarchate recognized, is primarily an abduction, an acquisition — a rape. When we concern ourselves with this profound mythological and psychological stratum, we must forget cultural development and the cultural forms taken by the relationship between man and woman and go back to the primordial phenomenon of the sexual encounter between them. It is not hard to see that the significance of this encounter is and must be very different for the masculine and the feminine. What for the masculine is aggression, victory, rape, and the satisfaction of desire — we need only take a look at the animal world and have the courage to recognize this stratum for man as well — is for the feminine destiny, transformation, and the profoundest mystery of life.[45]

Neumann describes what it is about the sexual encounter that provides such meaning for the feminine. Both women and men seek ego-stability, or personal identity.

Among men this stability is manifested as endurance of pain, hunger, thirst, and so forth; but in the feminine sphere it characteristically takes the form of resistance to pity. This firmness of the strong-willed ego, concentrated on its goal, is expressed in countless other myths and fairy tales, with their injunctions not to turn around, not to answer, and the like. . . . The feminine is threatened in its ego stability by the danger of distraction through 'relatedness,' through Eros.[46]

Psyche in her tasks comes to a donkey-driver, a corpse, and elderly weaving-women, all of whom ask for her help. But she has been instructed, "be thou not moved with pity . . . for it is not lawful."[47] The feminine must always keep in mind the distant goal and not give way to the close-at-hand. Like Jung, who believes that the feminine aims at completion, Neumann states that "the conception of the archetypal feminine as a unity is one of woman's fundamental experiences."[48] It is the collective, the group, the bringing together that characterizes the feminine; the masculine is tied to the individual, the self. But in order to attain this unity, "the feminine must develop toward and beyond the masculine, which represents consciousness over against the unconscious."[49] For either man or woman to become whole, both masculine and feminine elements must be accepted. And when this is done, love is possible. It is the experience of love that makes sexual union a "transformation" for the feminine, and, through the feminine, for the masculine as well. Psyche has, in effect, taught Eros to love, and this makes her divine.

VI. MEAD

We can see now that all of these writers, with the exception of Briffault, agree that there is some unified concept to which "the feminine" refers, even if they do not agree on its origins. It was not until Margaret Mead's anthropological research that this idea was seriously undermined. In *Sex and Temperament* Mead describes three societies: the Arapesh, whose ideal is mild, responsive men and women; the Mundugumor, whose ideal prescribes violent, aggressive men and women; and the Tchambuli, whose ideal is dominant women and dependent men. Her conclusion is:

If those temperamental attitudes which we have traditionally regarded as feminine — such as passivity, responsiveness, and a willingness to cherish children — can so easily be set up as the masculine pattern in one tribe, and in another be outlawed for the majority of women as well as for the majority of men, we no longer have any basis for regarding such aspects of behavior as sex-linked.[50]

The history of the social definition of sex differences is filled with such arbitrary arrangements in the intellectual and artistic field, but because of the assumed congruence between physiological sex and emotional endowment we have been less able to recognize that a similar arbitrary selection is being made among emotional traits also. We have assumed that because it is convenient for a mother to wish to care for her child, this is a trait with which women have been more generously endowed by a carefully teleological process of evolution. We have assumed that because men have hunted, an activity requiring enterprise, bravery, and initiative, they have been endowed with these useful attitudes as part of their sex-temperament.[51]

Mead thus believes that cultural definitions of masculine and feminine vary considerably. Her explanation for this is that among all societies there are some disparities in individual temperament; some people are more aggressive, while others are restrained, and some people are brave, while others are more cautious. For various reasons, often relating to economic and geographic circumstances, societies come to value these temperaments differently. They educate the children accordingly, encouraging some behavior and not other. To Mead, there must be both "aggressive" and "passive" human dispositions, but assigning these universally as "masculine" and "feminine" is an illegitimate step. She believes that "we are forced to conclude that human nature is almost unbelievably malleable."[52] "Standardized personality differences between the sexes are of this order, cultural creations to which each generation, male and female, is trained to conform."[53] Our concept of the feminine had origins in specific cultural conditions, and we must not assume that other images of the feminine are identical or even similar; in fact, they may be nearly opposite.

VII. ANALYSIS

Having seen these basic theories on the origin and nature of the feminine, we can take up the first basic question of this paper: Is the feminine a universal? Philosophy from the time of the Greeks has been interested in whether general objects of thought exist, and if they do, whether they have real existence independent of the mind. When Plato asked "What is virtue?" and "What is beauty?" he was asking for "a single and essential form common to all things of the same kind, by virtue of which they are things of the same kind."[54] Debate on the nature of the feminine has polarized around two common theories of universals: essentialists believe that there is one essence, or universal property, which characterizes every concept of the feminine, and accidentalists deny this, asserting that there is no one concept of the feminine, but rather that there are many varying images. It has become increasingly clear through research such as Mead's that the answer to the question of whether the feminine is a Platonic universal must be "no." It seems, as a matter of fact, that there is enormous variety throughout the world on what is masculine and what is feminine.

But, returning to the second question of this paper: Is there some general agreement on the nature of the feminine, even if the feminine is not a universal? Judging from the major theories we have considered, the answer must be "yes;" most of the writers agree that there is some essence of the feminine, and they also usually agree with each other on the qualities that this essence contains.

This raises our third major question: Is some explanation of this general agreement possible without reverting to essentialism? And here again, I believe, the answer must be "yes." When we recall the positions presented above, it seems more than coincidental that so many of them find a universal feminine and can agree almost completely on its nature (if not its origins).

Before proceeding, we must separate two issues which are easily confused.[55] The historical problem of the origin and nature of concepts of the feminine is one question; the logical problem of the basis of theories about the feminine is another. The former problem is being considered by the writers we have presented; they examine various types of evidence and present diverse speculations on, for example, the biological purpose of sexual differentiation, or what notions the Greeks had of masculine and feminine. But one facet of their arguments on the historical problem intrigues me here. Darwin, Bachofen, Freud, Jung and Neumann each occasionally admit, as we have seen, that there are some counter-examples that their theories cannot explain. Often this is an example in the animal world or a primitive society that does not comply with what the theory re-quires—for example, an instance where the male is passive and the female is aggressive. Why, I wonder, were such skilled scien-tists and scholars so drawn to universality, given the problem of exceptions? Why did they not settle for a claim of generality, and leave their conclusions more open-ended? Why did they believe so strongly that this is the way the feminine must be (Darwin and Bachofen), or, at any rate, always is (Freud, Jung and Neumann)?

I believe that if we look at Briffault and Mead we can find at least a clue for answering these questions. Briffault is at times ambivalent on the conclusions we can draw from the examples of animal life, and portions of his position can be given an essen-tialist slant. But the area where he is the most convincing on the importance of non-human behavior is in his analysis of sexual encounters. He states, "Nowhere do we know of the male using compulsion towards the female. The family group of animals is the manifestation of a correlation of instincts, not of a process of physical domination."[56] The model of sexual activity among animals is one of female receptivity; she decides with whom she will mate. Briffault believes that this mode is maintained in primitive societies where women still have economic power; it is not until patriarchy that the bride-price is instituted. The rise of patriarchy brings with it an "inversion of the biological and primitive relations between the sexes;"[57] through this inversion the rule of female receptivity is abandoned, and male dominance takes over. Thus Briffault does not consider the male-dominance model as having any basis in either animal life or primitive society.

Margaret Mead also analyzes the sexual relationship, and comes to a similar conclusion:

Many writers on the sexes and the human family lay great emphasis upon the fact that the human male is capable of rape. This is an abrupt and startling way of putting something that is actually much subtler. In the human species the male is capable of copulating with a relatively unaroused and uninterested female. We have no evidence that suggests that rape within the meaning of the act — that is, rape of a totally unwilling female — has ever become recognized social practice.[58]

There is, she believes, a shift from female to male readiness between the primates and humans; but rape itself "is a very different act from any behavior that can be postulated for the small groups of creatures who at the dawn of our history were just inventing social patterns."[59] I think this is a telling point; the two more liberal theories believe it is not correct to construe the sexual relationship as one where the male "has his way" with the female, for either animals or primitive human society.

But in Darwin, Bachofen, Freud, Jung and Neumann, this is not true. Each of these writers assumes a picture of primitive sexuality where man forces himself on woman. They do not offer arguments on why they think this is true, and yet I feel that they use it as the basis for much broader conclusions. This assumption presupposes the very point the theories are designed to prove: that men are aggressive and women are passive. By accepting without justification the male-dominance model for primitive human relationships, each of these theories then claims on the basis of this model that men are by nature assertive and independent, while women by nature are passive and dependent. This unjustified model is used to attribute these qualities to the whole personality. The model assumes, by extension, that "man defines, woman conforms," that the masculine structures the feminine in a non-reciprocal way.

In Darwin, this presupposition of male dominance in primitive human life is seen in the theory of sexual selection:

Man is more powerful in body and mind than woman, and in the savage state he keeps her in a far more abject state of bondage than does the male of any other animal; therefore it is not surprising that he should have gained the power of selection.[60]

The competition of women for men through beauty and feminine charms is not the result of recent economic or social conditions to Darwin, but has ancient biological origins. Because of his superior strength, man could choose any woman; the traits in her he favored were passed on to female offspring and are those we now call feminine. This process of selection was not two-way because a man could mate with any woman he wanted and did not need to be willingly accepted by her.

In Bachofen, the assumption is expressed in the idea that during the first stage women were "defenseless against abuse by men"[61] and only in the second level of mother-right did their position improve. Bachofen brings back this image of male force in the third, patriarchal stage. When patriarchy succeeds, it is because the spiritual, self-oriented male aspect rises over the material, group-oriented female existence. In the highest phase of civilization, masculine force takes on a more psychological character, as man acts as a restrictive foil to woman's universality. The masculine provides the human species with its highest goal and final direction, and so limits the power of the feminine. It shapes the feminine, yet finds itself when it is unfettered by feminine limits.

Freud expresses the presupposition of primitive male dominance when he discusses sex in this way:

The male sexual cell is active and mobile; it seeks out the female one, while the latter, the ovum, is stationary, and waits passively. This behavior of the elementary organisms of sex is more or less a model of the behavior of the individuals of each sex in sexual intercourse. The male pursues the female for the purpose of sexual union, seizes her and pushes his way into her.[62]

Woman's passivity is passive in relation to something, and this something is the activity found in the male; this activity can be observed in human behavior, in animal groups, in the sexual act, and even microscopically in the sexual cells themselves. Because of this, Freud feels that men find their adult sexuality more directly. A woman needs to transfer her erogenous zone and the love-object, and she is consequently more easily influenced by external factors. Women, as passive, are more receptive and malleable. They are more influenced by men, more defined by men, than men are by women.

In Jung and Neumann the assumption occurs again. Erich Neumann's interpretation of primitive sexual encounters has been given above. Because Jung and Neumann identify the feminine with unconsciousness and the masculine with consciousness, the masculine gives form and structure to the feminine but receives a subjective loosening in return. Both the masculine and the feminine are considered equally valuable, but the model of male definition of the female is still held. The masculine limits the feminine by providing objectivity and rationality; it tries to contain the darkness of the unconscious. Yet the masculine is itself only liberated, not confined, by what the feminine brings to it.

In conclusion, our investigation of the concept of the feminine has revealed several things. There does not seem to be any one quality which all images of the feminine must have; in this way we found that the feminine is not a Platonic universal. But there has been much traditional agreement among theories of the feminine on what characteristics are included in the concept. We found that this agreement can be explained without appealing to essentialism if we examine how the theories of the feminine themselves were constructed. Those writers (Darwin, Bachofen, Freud, Jung and Neumann) who assume male dominance as the model of primitive human sexual relations seem to carry this model, by analogy, into all other personality traits of men and women; these authors accept or imply essentialist conclusions. But those writers (Briffault and Mead) who deny this model more easily accept wide cultural variations in concepts of the feminine. "The Eternal Feminine draws us on," judging from our analysis of these theories, only when we presuppose that early sexual encounters were the result of male force and female unwillingness, and when we then use this as a model for all female and male traits.

NOTES

1. Aristotle, in the *Metaphysics* (986a, 25–30), states that the Pythagoreans organized the ten principles in this way: in the Monad were male, limit, odd, one, right, resting, straight, light, good, and square; in the Dyad were female, unlimited, even, plurality, left, moving, curved, darkness, bad, and oblong. The Chinese constructed the characteristics according to Yin: female, negative, passive, weak, destructive, earth, completion; and Yang: male, positive, active, strong, constructive, heaven, beginning (Wing-tsit Chan, *A Source Book in Chinese Philosophy* [Princeton: Princeton University Press, 1963], pp. 244–248.

2. John Money, "Psychosexual Differentiation," in *Sex Research: New Developments,* John Money, ed. (New York: Holt, Rinehart & Winston, 1965), pp. 10–11.

3. Margaret Mead, *Sex and Temperament* (New York: William Morrow, 1935), pp. 279–280.

4. Corine Hutt, *Males and Females* (Harmondsworth, England: Penguin, 1972), pp. 118–119.

5. C.G. Jung, *Civilization in Transition* (New York: Pantheon, 1964), pp. 117–118.

6. Charles Darwin, *The Origin of the Species* (1859; New York: Mentor Books, 1958), p. 94.

7. Charles Darwin, *The Descent of Man* (1871; New York: D. Appleton, 1895), pp. 210–214.

8. *Ibid.,* p. 224.

9. *Ibid.,* p. 557.

10. *Ibid.,* p. 563.

11. *Ibid.*

12. *Ibid.,* p. 597.

13. *Ibid.,* p. 565.

14. *Ibid.,* p. 563.

15. *Ibid.,* pp. 563–564.

16. J.J. Bachofen, *Myth, Religion, and Mother Right* (Princeton: Princeton University Press, 1967), p. 79.

17. *Ibid.,* p. 80.

18. *Ibid.,* p. 109.

19. Robert Briffault, *The Mothers* (New York: Macmillan, 1931), p. 21.

20. *Ibid.,* p. 23.

21. *Ibid.,* p. 159.

22. *Ibid.,* p. 245.

23. *Ibid.,* p. 249.

24. *Ibid.,* p. 253.

25. *Ibid.,* p. 176.

26. Sigmund Freud, "The Psychology of Women," in *New Introductory Lectures on Psychoanalysis* (New York: W.W. Norton, 1933), p. 180.

27. Sigmund Freud, "Three Essays on the Theory of Sexuality," in *The Complete Psychological Works,* vol. 7 (London: Hogarth, 1953), p. 219.

28. *Ibid.*

29. *Ibid.,* pp. 219–20.

30. Freud, "Psychology of Women," p. 157.

31. *Ibid.,* p. 160.

32. *Ibid.,* p. 180.

33. *Ibid.,* p. 183.

34. *Ibid.,* p. 184.

35. *Ibid.,* p. 170.
36. C.G. Jung, *The Development of Personality* (New York: Pantheon, 1954), p. 198.
37. Jung, *Civilization in Transition,* p. 117.
38. *Ibid.,* p. 118.
39. *Ibid.,* p. 123.
40. *Ibid.,* p. 125.
41. C.G. Jung, *Psychological Reflections,* Jolande Jacobi, ed. (Princeton: Princeton University Press, 1970), p. 110.
42. *Ibid.*
43. Erich Neumann, *The Origins and History of Consciousness* (New York: Pantheon, 1954), p. xxii.
44. *Ibid.,* p. 125.
45. Erich Neumann, *Amor and Psyche* (New York: Pantheon, 1956), pp. 62–63.
46. *Ibid.,* pp. 112–113.
47. *Ibid.,* p. 48.
48. *Ibid.,* p. 129.
49. *Ibid.,* p. 130.
50. Mead, *Sex and Temperament,* p. 279.
51. *Ibid.,* p. 286.
52. *Ibid.,* p. 280.
53. *Ibid.*
54. *The Encyclopedia of Philosophy,* vol. 8, Paul Edwards, ed. (New York: Macmillan, 1967), p. 195.
55. I am indebted to Dr. Jann Benson for valuable discussion on this point.
56. Briffault (above, n. 19), p. 20.
57. *Ibid.,* p. 249.
58. Margaret Mead, *Male and Female* (New York: William Morrow, 1949), p. 203.
59. *Ibid.,* p. 204.
60. Darwin, *Descent of Man,* p. 597.
61. Bachofen (above, n. 16), p. 94.
62. Freud, "Psychology of Women," p. 156.

Part II
Nature, Nurture, Both . . .

Introduction

The amount of literature offering explanations for so-called psychological sex differences is staggering; the list provided in the "Further References" section at the end of this volume represents merely a sample of what is available. This literature dates from as early as the fifth century B.C. and continues to be steadily produced. To understand the history of the subject then, it might be helpful to begin by classifying various explanations into three very general types: a) nature theories, b) nurture theories, and c) theories combining elements of both nature and nurture theories.

A. NATURE THEORIES

Paradigm nature theorists — sometimes called "biological determinists" or "essentialists" — are in agreement that all and only women are "feminine" and all and only men are "masculine." They also agree that the terms "men" and "women" are to be defined in terms of biological characteristics. But they may disagree as to how "masculine" and "feminine" are to be defined. Here theorists may each emphasize different traits among those we listed as groups X and Y in the Introduction to Part I. Some may take nurturance and supportiveness as definitional of "femininity," for example, paying little attention to other traits. Others may emphasize intuitiveness and sensitivity, with little attention to nurturance. On some definitions, an individual who is both aggressive and intuitive may be classified as "masculine" because aggressiveness is emphasized as a "masculine" trait and intuitiveness is not considered crucial. In other definitions, aggressiveness might be less emphasized and that same individual might be labelled "feminine" on the grounds of intuitiveness.

Nature theorists also offer an explanation of the proposal that all and only women are "feminine" and all and only men are "masculine" by appealing to general laws asserting a causal relationship between a person's having a certain biological makeup and exhibiting certain psychological traits. For example, a nature theorist might say that all women are "feminine" because high estrogen levels result in nurturance. But of course *which* biological features are taken to be important cause disagreement among nature theorists.

Blatant counterexamples to theories which attribute "femininity" only to females and "masculinity" only to males—women who primarily exhibit traits from Group Y (Indira Ghandi or Golda Meir, for example) or men who primarily exhibit traits from Group X (the entertainer Tiny Tim, for example)—are either completely ignored or ruled out as "deviant" cases. (SARAH HOAGLAND makes this point in Part III.) Aquinas, for example, admits that some women have the ability to reason (which he classifies as a "masculine" trait), but rules such cases as exceptionally rare.[1] Nietzsche admits that there are some women who do not want to bear children, but rules them out as counterexamples to his theory because he thinks that such persons are not "real" women to begin with.[2] So, although in principle, nature theories should be empirically testable (counterexamples could be provided which prove the theories false), in practice nature theorists tend to make such theories untestable by refusing to count any apparent exception as "really" a man or "really" a woman.

There are at least two general areas of disagreement among those who believe that differences in the biological construction of males and females cause differences in psychological traits. One area of disagreement is over whether the biological differences between women and men are subject to change (i.e., whether they can be eliminated or mutated). Some (Aristotle, Aquinas, Kant, Rousseau, Tiger, Goldberg, Nietzsche, Schopenhauer) take biological (and thus the biologically-caused psychological) differences to be universal and eternal. Aristotle says,

Again, the male is by nature superior, and the female inferior; and the one rules, and the other is ruled; this principle, of necessity, extends to all mankind.[3]

Steven Goldberg says that male aggression toward and dominance of women is universal and immutable because he believes this aggression is caused by male hormones, which he presupposes to be unalterable features of men's bodies.[4] But others (Firestone, Holliday, Atkinson) take the view that biological features of persons can be mutated or eliminated due to the medical possibility (now realized, although not at the time of their writing) of eliminating or altering some of the very biological features in question.

Another source of disagreement among nature theorists lies in the value judgments they make about the psychological differences they find between males and females. Aristotle, Aquinas, Nietzsche, Goldberg, and Schopenhauer, for example. consider women to be inferior to men because of the inferiority they assign to the psychological traits they claim to be exhibited by women. (Schopenhauer speaks of "the *sexus sequoir*—the second sex inferior in every respect to the first."[5]) A second group of nature theorists (Montagu, Solanas, Davis, Gilder) regard women as superior to men, and yet a third group (Marolow and Davis, Rousseau, Kant) argues that although there are biologically-caused psychological differences between men and women, it does not follow that either males or females are in any way superior. About this Rousseau says,

These resemblances and differences must have an influence on the moral nature; this inference is obvious and it is confirmed by experience; it shows that vanity of the disputes as to the superiority or equality of the sexes; as if each sex, pursuing the path marked out for it by nature, were not more perfect in that very divergence than if it more closely resembled the other. A perfect man and a perfect woman should not more be alike in mind than in face, and perfection admits of neither less nor more.[6]

Among those who are convinced that there are biologically-caused psychological differences between women and men it is not uncommon to find those who argue that because there are, society is justified in reserving certain behavioral roles for women and others for men (Goldberg, Lucas). JOYCE TREBILCOT, however, argues that whether or not there are biologically-caused psychological differences has little bearing on the question of whether society should reserve certain labor roles for females and others for males. (PATRICK GRIM argues for the same thesis, although on different grounds, in Part III.) Trebilcot's argument concerns only biologically-caused *psychological* differences, and thus leaves open the question of whether other biologically-caused *behavioral, physical, or physiological* differences between the sexes might provide grounds for society's reserving certain work or sport roles for men and others for women. This latter question will be touched upon in Part V.

It is important to note that it has yet to be shown that there is in fact even one psychological trait which all and only women share, or which all and only men share. So nature theories have to be taken with at least the following grain of salt: if whatever psychological differences there are between the sexes are only statistically significant, then biological features exhibited universally by males or universally by females will not alone account for the differences; either some feature(s) other than these biological ones or some feature(s) in addition to these biological ones must be forthcoming to explain any exceptions.

B. NURTURE THEORIES

Paradigm nurture theorists (sometimes also called "accidentalists") agree with nature theorists insofar as they argue that there is a link between sex and gender and that the link needs explanation. However, they disagree with nature theorists in that nurture theorists deny both that sex and gender are universally correlated and that differences in biological features of persons' bodies can explain the statistically significant differences they find in the psychological traits of men and women. Rather, say the nurture theorists, differences in gender can only be explained by appealing to factors "outside the body" or "environmental" factors.

Paradigm nurture theorists flatly deny that all and only men are "masculine," all and only women "feminine," where "masculine" and "feminine" are defined in terms of the traits outlined as groups X and Y in the Introduction to Part I. Margaret Mead, after studying three primitive societies (the Arapesh, the Mundugumor, and the Tschambuli), found both Arapesh sexes "feminine," both Mundugumor sexes "masculine," and the female Tschambuli "masculine," the male Tschambuli "feminine" in those senses of the terms. The fact that gender (so defined) is not universally correlated with sex, she concludes, is sufficient to show that a person's biology cannot be the cause of a person's gender (so defined):

If these temperamental attitudes which we have traditionally regarded as feminine — such as passivity, responsiveness, and a willingness to cherish children — can so easily be set up as the masculine pattern in one tribe, and in another be outlawed for the majority of men, we no longer have any basis for regarding such aspects of behavior as sex-linked.[7]

Robert Briffault agrees:

There is not among primitive men and women the disparity in physical power, resourcefulness, enterprise, courage, capacity for endurance, which are observed in civilized societies and are often regarded as organic sexual differences. To a very large extent those differences in physical and mental capacity are the effect, rather than the cause, of that divergence in the avocations of men and women which has taken place in the course of cultural and social development.[8]

Nurture theorists do not deny that there are differences in gender traits between the sexes in *any given society* or that these differences require explanation. Rather, what they deny is that these differences can legitimately be called "masculine" or "feminine" in the way some *in our society* use the terms. These theorists are quite willing to speak of individuals as "masculine" or "feminine," not on the basis of supposed universal traits, but on the basis of traits selected as "feminine" or "masculine" by the society under study. For Mead and Briffault, males and females do exhibit differences in "gender" (in this society-relativized sense of the term) and for them these differences require explanation by appealing to socioeconomic factors which can and do change with time.

One area of disagreement among nurture theorists is over what the ultimate environmental causes of sex differences are in any given society. All agree that environmental factors — in particular, social conditioning — provide a sufficient account of differences. But some (Lenin, Jennes, Hamilton, Guettel, Gieles, Bebel, Reed) argue that the economic structure of a given society is the ultimate cause, whereas others emphasize other social factors, such as matriarchal or patriarchal social structures. Bachofen, Morgan, and McLennan, view societies as advancing from stages of matriarchy to current — and in their view superior — stages of patriarchy; Sir Henry Maine viewed all — even the earliest Roman, Hebrew, and Hindu — societies as patriarchal; and the Vaertings argue that matriarchy and patriarchy have alternated with one another throughout the history of societies. JANE DURAN discusses in greater detail some areas of agreement and disagreement among nurture theorists and she points the way to philosophically questionable aspects of some nurture theories.

C. BOTH

Were every sex difference theory easily classifiable into a clear-cut "nature" or "nurture" category, the debate between nature and nurture theorists would be relatively straightforward. Unfortunately, it is not possible to so-classify even many of the most well-known and widely-read of sex difference theorists.

One could hold within the confines of one and the same theory that some psychological differences between the sexes are biologically caused and others are the result of environmental factors. Or, some sex differences are biologically caused in childhood, but those remaining in adulthood are environmentally caused. Or, some are biologically-caused sex differences, but the biological factors are overridable by environmental ones such as parenting. And so on. As OWEN FLANAGAN illustrates, the writings of Sigmund Freud seem to contain elements of both "nature" and "nurture" theories. Other examples of theories which seem to combine aspects of both nature and nurture viewpoints include those of Barber, Bardwick, Bonaparte, Davis, Darwin, De Castillejo, Deutsch, Fox, Harding, Holliday, Janeway, Jung, Lewis, Maccoby and Jacklin, Marx, Money and Ehrhardt, Neumann, Scott-Maxwell, Stern, Stoller, Thompson, Wilson, Westermark, and Woolf.

Do we have sufficient knowledge at this time to adjudicate between these opposing points of view? Will we ever? Or is the nature/nurture debate essentially *unresolvable?* Let us turn to these and related questions in Part III.

NOTES

1. St. Thomas Aquinas, *Summa Theologica,* trans. the Fathers of the English Dominican Province, vol. II (New York: Bensiger Brothers, 1947), p. 1931, Part II, Question 155, Article 1.
2. Friedrich Nietzsche, *Ecce Homo,* trans. Walter Kaufman and R.J. Hollingdale (New York: Vintage Books, 1967), p. 266.

3. Aristotle, *The Politics,* Chapter V, relevant passages are reprinted in *Sex Equality,* ed. Jane English (Englewood Cliffs, N.J.: Prentice-Hall, 1977), p. 25.
4. Steven Goldberg, *The Inevitability of Patriarchy,* relevant passages are reprinted in *Sex Equality,* op. cit., p. 197.
5. Arthur Schopenhauer, "On Women," in his *Studies in Pessimism: A Series of Essays,* trans. J. Baily Saunders (London: Swan Sonneschein and Co., 1893), p. 115.
6. Jean Jacques Rousseau, *Emile,* relevant passages are reprinted in *Sex Equality,* op. cit., p. 43.
7. Margaret Mead, *Sex and Temperament in Three Primitive Societies* (New York: William Morrow, 1935), p. 279.
8. Robert Briffault, *The Mothers* (New York: Macmillan, 1931), p. 21.

Joyce Trebilcot

Sex Roles:
The Argument from Nature

I am concerned here with the normative question of whether, in an ideal society, certain roles should be assigned to females and others to males. In discussions of this issue, a great deal of attention is given to the claim that there are natural psychological differences between the sexes. Those who hold that at least some roles should be sex roles generally base their view primarily on an appeal to such natural differences, while many of those advocating a society without sex roles argue either that the sexes do not differ in innate psychological traits or that there is no evidence that they do.[1] In this paper I argue that whether there are natural psychological differences between females and males has little bearing on the issue of whether society should reserve certain roles for females and others for males.

Let me begin by saying something about the claim that there are natural psychological differences between the sexes. The issue we are dealing with arises, of course, because there are biological differences among human beings which are bases for designating some as females and others as males. Now it is held by some that, in addition to biological differences between the sexes, there are also natural differences in temperament, in-

---

Reprinted in full from *Ethics,* 85 (1975), pp. 249–255 by permission of Joyce Trebilcot and the University of Chicago Press. © 1975 by the University of Chicago. All rights reserved.

terests, abilities, and the like. In this paper I am concerned only with arguments which appeal to these psychological differences as bases of sex roles. Thus I exclude, for example, arguments that the role of jockey should be female because women are smaller than men or that boxers should be male because men are more muscular than women. Nor do I discuss arguments which appeal directly to the reproductive functions peculiar to each sex. If the physiological processes of gestation or of depositing sperm in a vagina are, apart from any psychological correlates they may have, bases for sex roles, these roles are outside the scope of the present discussion.

It should be noted, however, that virtually all those who hold that there are natural psychological differences between the sexes assume that these differences are determined primarily by differences in biology. According to one hypothesis, natural psychological differences between the sexes are due at least in part to differences between female and male nervous systems. As the male fetus develops in the womb, the testes secrete a hormone which is held to influence the growth of the central nervous system. The female fetus does not produce this hormone, nor is there an analogous female hormone which is significant at this stage. Hence it is suggested that female and male brains differ in structure, that this difference is due to the prenatal influence of testicular hormone, and that the difference in brains is the basis of some later differences in behavior.[2]

A second view about the origin of allegedly natural psychological differences between the sexes, a view not incompatible with the first, is psychoanalytical. It conceives of feminine or masculine behavior as, in part, the individual's response to bodily structure. On this view, one's more or less unconscious experience of one's own body (and in some versions, of the bodies of others) is a major factor in producing sex-specific personality traits. The classic theories of this kind are, of course, Freud's; penis envy and the castration complex are supposed to arise largely from perceptions of differences between female and male bodies. Other writers make much of the analogies between genitals and genders: the uterus is passive and receptive, and so are females; penises are active and penetrating, and so are males.[3] But here we are concerned not with the etiology of allegedly natural differences between the sexes but rather with the question of whether such differences, if they exist, are grounds for holding that there should be sex roles.

That a certain psychological disposition is natural only to one sex is generally taken to mean in part that members of that sex are more likely to have the disposition, or to have it to a greater degree, than persons of the other sex. The situation is thought to be similar to that of height. In a given population, females are on the average shorter than males, but some females are taller than some males, as suggested by Figure 1. The shortest members of the population are all females, and the tallest are all males, but there is an area of overlap. For psychological traits, it is usually assumed that there is some degree of overlap and that the degree of overlap is different for different characteristics. Because of the difficulty of identifying natural psychological characteristics, we have of course little or no data as to the actual distribution of such traits.

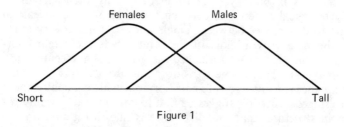

Figure 1

I shall not undertake here to define the concept of role, but examples include voter, librarian, wife, president. A broad concept of role might also comprise, for example, being a joker, a person who walks gracefully, a compassionate person. The genders, femininity and masculinity, may also be conceived as roles. On this view, each of the gender roles includes a number of more specific sex roles, some of which may be essential to it. For example, the concept of femininity may be construed in such a way that it is necessary to raise a child in order to be fully feminine, while other feminine roles—teacher, nurse, charity worker—are not essential to gender. In the arguments discussed below, the focus is on sex roles rather than genders, but, on the assumption that genders are roles, much of what is said applies, *mutatis mutandis,* to them.

A sex role is a role performed only or primarily by persons of a particular sex. Now if this is all we mean by "sex role," the problem of whether there should be sex roles must be dealt with as two separate issues: "Are sex roles a good thing?" and

"Should society enforce sex roles?" One might argue, for example, that sex roles have value but that, even so, the demands of individual autonomy and freedom are such that societal institutions and practices should not enforce correlations between roles and sex. But the debate over sex roles is of course mainly a discussion about the second question, whether society should enforce these correlations. The judgment that there should be sex roles is generally taken to mean not just that sex-exclusive roles are a good thing, but that society should promote such exclusivity.

In view of this, I use the term "sex role" in such a way that to ask whether there should be sex roles is to ask whether society should direct women into certain roles and away from others, and similarly for men. A role is a sex role then (or perhaps an "institutionalized sex role") only if it is performed exclusively or primarily by persons of a particular sex *and* societal factors tend to encourage this correlation. These factors may be of various kinds. Parents guide children into what are taken to be sex-appropriate roles. Schools direct students into occupations according to sex. Marriage customs prescribe different roles for females and males. Employers and unions may refuse to consider applications from persons of the "wrong" sex. The media carry tales of the happiness of those who conform and the suffering of the others. The law sometimes penalizes deviators. Individuals may ridicule and condemn role crossing and smile on conformity. Societal sanctions such as these are essential to the notion of sex role employed here.

I turn now to a discussion of the three major ways the claim that there are natural psychological differences between the sexes is held to be relevant to the issue of whether there should be sex roles.

I. INEVITABILITY

It is sometimes held that if there are innate psychological differences between females and males, sex roles are inevitable. The point of this argument is not, of course, to urge that there should be sex roles, but rather to show that the normative question is out of place, that there will be sex roles, whatever we decide. The argument assumes first that the alleged natural differences between the sexes are inevitable; but if such differences are inevitable, differences in behavior are inevitable; and if differences in behavior are inevitable, society will inevitably be structured so as to enforce role differences according to sex. Thus, sex roles are inevitable.

For the purpose of this discussion, let us accept the claim that natural psychological differences are inevitable. We assume that there are such differences and ignore the possibility of their being altered, for example, by evolutionary change or direct biological intervention. Let us also accept the second claim, that behavioral differences are inevitable. Behavioral differences could perhaps be eliminated even given the assumption of natural differences in disposition (for example, those with no natural inclination to a certain kind of behavior might nevertheless learn it), but let us waive this point. We assume then that behavioral differences, and hence, also role differences, between the sexes are inevitable. Does it follow that there must be sex roles, that is, that the institutions and practices of society must enforce correlations between roles and sex?

Surely not. Indeed, such sanctions would be pointless. Why bother to direct women into some roles and men into others if the pattern occurs regardless of the nature of society? Mill makes the point elegantly in *The Subjection of Women:* "The anxiety of mankind to interfere in behalf of nature, for fear lest nature should not succeed in effecting its purpose, is an altogether unnecessary solicitude."[4]

It may be objected that if correlations between sex and roles are inevitable, societal sanctions enforcing these correlations will develop because people will expect the sexes to perform different roles and these expectations will lead to behavior which encourages their fulfillment. This can happen, of course, but it is surely not inevitable. One need not act so as to bring about what one expects.

Indeed, there could be a society in which it is held that there are inevitable correlations between roles and sex but institutionalization of these correlations is deliberately avoided. What is inevitable is presumably not, for example, that every woman will perform a certain role and no man will perform it, but rather that most women will perform the role and most men will not. For any individual, then, a particular role may not be inevitable. Now suppose it is a value in the society in question that people should be free to choose roles according to their individual needs and interests. But then there should not be sanctions enforcing correlation between roles and sex, for such sanctions tend to force some individuals into roles for which they have no natural inclination and which they might otherwise choose against.

I conclude then that, even granting the assumptions that natural psychological differences, and therefore role differences, between the sexes are inevitable, it does not follow that there must be sanctions enforcing correlations between roles and sex. Indeed, if individual freedom is valued, those who vary from the statistical norm should not be required to conform to it.

II. WELL-BEING

The argument from well-being begins with the claim that, because of natural psychological differences between the sexes, members of each sex are happier in certain roles than in others, and the roles which tend to promote happiness are different for each sex. It is also held that if all roles are equally available to everyone regardless of sex, some individuals will choose against their own well-being. Hence, the argument concludes, for the sake of maximizing well-being there should be sex roles: society should encourage individuals to make "correct" role choices.

Suppose that women, on the average, are more compassionate than men. Suppose also that there are two sets of roles, "female" and "male," and that because of the natural compassion of women, women are happier in female than in male roles. Now if females and males overlap with respect to compassion, some men have as much natural compassion as some women, so they too will be happier in female than in male roles. Thus, the first premise of the argument from well-being should read: Suppose that, because of natural psychological differences between the sexes, *most* women are happier in female roles and *most* men in male roles. The argument continues: If all roles are equally available to everyone, some of the women who would be happier in female roles will choose against their own well-being, and similarly for men.

Now if the conclusion that there should be sex roles is to be based on these premises, another assumption must be added— that the loss of the potential well-being resulting from societally produced adoption of unsuitable roles by individuals in the overlapping areas of the distribution is *less* than the loss that would result from "mistaken" free choices if there were no sex roles. With sex roles, some individuals who would be happier in roles assigned to the other sex perform roles assigned to their own sex, and so there is a loss of potential happiness. Without sex roles, some individuals, we assume, choose against their own well-being. But surely we are not now in a position to compare the two systems with respect to the number of mismatches produced. Hence, the additional premise required for the argument, that overall well-being is greater with sex roles than without them, is entirely unsupported.

Even if we grant, then, that because of innate psychological differences between the sexes members of each sex achieve greater well-being in some roles than in others, the argument from well-being does not support the conclusion that there should be sex roles. In our present state of knowledge, there is no reason to suppose that a sex role system which makes no discrimination within a sex would produce fewer mismatches between individuals and roles than a system in which all roles are open equally to both sexes.

III. EFFICIENCY

If there are natural differences between the sexes in the capacity to perform socially valuable tasks, then, it is sometimes argued, efficiency is served if these tasks are assigned to the sex with the greatest innate ability for them. Suppose, for example, that females are naturally better than males at learning foreign languages. This means that, if everything else is equal and females and males are given the same training in a foreign language, females, on the average, will achieve a higher level of skill than males. Now suppose that society needs interpreters and translators and that in order to have such a job one must complete a special training program whose only purpose is to provide persons for these roles. Clearly, efficiency is served if only individuals with a good deal of natural ability are selected for training, for the time and effort required to bring them to a given level of proficiency is less than that required for the less talented. But suppose that the innate ability in question is normally distributed within each sex and that the sexes overlap (see fig. 2). If we assume that a sufficient number of candidates can be recruited by considering only persons in the shaded area, they are the only ones who should be eligible. There are no men in this group. Hence, although screening is necessary in order to exclude nontalented women, it would be inefficient even to consider men, for it is known that no man is as talented as the talented women. In the interest of efficiency, then, the occupational roles of interpreter and translator should be sex roles; men should be denied access to these roles, but women who are interested in them, especially talented women, should be encouraged to pursue them.

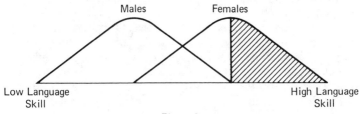

Figure 2

This argument is sound. That is, if we grant the factual assumptions and suppose also that efficiency for the society we are concerned with has some value, the argument from efficiency provides one reason for holding that some roles should be sex roles. This conclusion of course is only *prima facie*. In order to determine whether there should be sex roles, one would have to weigh efficiency, together with other reasons for such roles, against reasons for holding that there should not be sex roles. The reasons against sex roles are very strong. They are couched in terms of individual rights—in terms of liberty, justice, equality of opportunity. Efficiency by itself does not outweigh these moral values. Nevertheless, the appeal to nature, if true, combined with an appeal to the value of efficiency, does provide one reason for the view that there should be sex roles.

The arguments I have discussed here are not the only ones which appeal to natural psychological differences between the sexes in defense of sex roles, but these three arguments—from inevitability, well-being, and efficiency—are, I believe, the most common and the most plausible ones. The argument from efficiency alone, among them, provides a reason—albeit a rather weak reason—for thinking that there should be sex roles. I suggest, therefore, that the issue of natural psychological differences between women and men does not deserve the central place it is given, both traditionally and currently, in the literature on this topic.

It is frequently pointed out that the argument from nature functions as a cover, as a myth to make patriarchy palatable to both women and men. Insofar as this is so, it is surely worthwhile exploring and exposing the myth. But of course most of those who use the argument from nature take it seriously and literally, and this is the spirit in which I have dealt with it. Considering the argument in this way, I conclude that whether there should be sex roles does not depend primarily on whether there are innate psychological differences between the sexes. The question is, after all, not what women and men naturally are, but what kind of society is morally justifiable. In order to answer this question, we must appeal to the notions of justice, equality, and liberty. It is these moral concepts, not the empirical issue of sex differences, which should have pride of place in the philosophical discussion of sex roles.

NOTES

1. For support of sex roles, see, for example, Aristotle, *Politics,* Book I, Benjamin Jowett, trans. (Oxford: The Clarendon Press, 1885); and Erik Erikson, "Womanhood and the Inner Space," in *Identity: Youth and Crisis* (New York: W. W. Norton and Co., 1968). Arguments against sex roles may be found, for example, in J.S. Mill, *The Subjection of Women,* Reprint (Cambridge, Mass.: MIT Press, 1970) and Naomi Weisstein, "Psychology Constructs the Female," in *Sex Equality,* Jane English, ed. (Englewood Cliffs, N.J.: Prentice-Hall, Inc., pp. 205–215.

2. See John Money and Anke A. Ehrhardt, *Man and Woman, Boy and Girl* (Baltimore: Johns Hopkins Press, 1972); also Steven Goldberg, *The Inevitability of Patriarchy* (New York: William Morrow, 1973).

3. For Freud, see for example, "Some Psychological Consequences of the Anatomical Distinctions Between the Sexes," in *Sigmund Freud: Collected Papers,* James Strachey, ed. (New York: Basic Books, 1959), vol. 5, pp. 186–197. See also Karl Stern, *The Flight from Woman* (New York: Farrar, Straus and Ciroux, 1965), ch. 2; and Erickson, *op. cit.*

4. Mill, *op. cit.,* p. 27.

Jane Duran

Nurture Theories: A Critique

Sex difference theorists have generally moved in one of two directions in explaining those psychological trait differences they see between the sexes: either they have argued that "masculine" ("feminine") traits are innately linked to a person's sex (an essentialist, or "nature" view), or they have argued that they are linked to sex by virtue of environmental factors (a "nurture" view). I do not intend to examine the normative question of whether a society ought to have gender concepts such as those of "masculinity" and "femininity"; rather, I intend to examine critically the work of three nurture, or anti-essentialist, theorists. My leading thesis is that nurture theorists hold a number of tenets in common yet diverge upon a number of points.

We might think of the paradigm nurture theory as promulgating a group of related theses: (a) It is false that all men are "masculine," all women "feminine," where "are masculine" and "are feminine" mean "have those psychological traits which are taken *in our society* to be characteristic of males and females"; (b) We have some notion of what it means to apply the labels "masculine" and "feminine" to individuals, and it is true that all men are "masculine," all women "feminine," where "are

---

The author is indebted to Russel Kahl for many valuable conversations relevant to the material in this article.

masculine" and "are feminine" mean "have those traits which are thought to be characteristic of males and females *in the society in which each individual lives*"; (c) The causal factors involved in the formation of gender are, with some exceptions, mutable, and are environmental, not biological, in type.

Our task now is to examine the epistemological underpinnings of the nurture theories. This will involve the examination and exposition of the work of some relevant theorists both on an individual basis and collectively, insofar as each of the cited theories may be said to be representative, in some sense, of the nurture type.

I. AREAS OF CONVERGENCE

Various pieces of work by Margaret Mead, Robert Briffault, and Friedrich Engels seem to fit what we have described as the nurture theory. We want now to delve into the areas of similarity among these three theories. We will note initially that it seems trivially true that all the theorists deny the truth of such simply formulated statements "All men are by nature masculine, all women by nature feminine." But the further distinctions to be made are considerably more complex. Among the three theorists cited here, only Mead and Briffault actually hold thesis (a) as formulated above — we may refer to Marx and Engels (Engels, specifically, in "The Origin of Family, Private Property and State") as nonparadigmatic theorists since they do not hold (a) exactly as formulated.

But thesis (a) is clearly related to thesis (b), and it is the latter formulation which provides the basis for some of the most interesting work of the nurture theorists. Mead, for example, also holds (b) because of her anthropological model, constructed in *Sex and Temperament in Three Primitive Societies,* which matches the model of the average role training or social conditioning nurture theorist quite closely. The variations in social conditioning from society to society allow for variations in the gender forms produced. Mead's analyses of the Arapesh, Mundugamor, and Tschambuli tribes in New Guinea support the contention that there are no immutable masculine or feminine natures, and that such gender concepts as a society possesses are the result of forces functioning uniquely within that group.[1]

Robert Briffault may be said to agree to (b) for reasons somewhat similar to Mead's. In *The Mothers,* Briffault constructed a lengthy work the thesis of which is that sororal polygyny and fraternal polyandry were the norm in almost all early societies. In asserting (b), Briffault is relying on an account of the evolution and deviation of societies from their matriarchal origins as the primary causal factor in the assimilation of gender norms.

> ... human society ... must have had its origins in an association which represented female instincts only, and human culture must have been molded in the first instance not by the fierce passions of hunters battling for food and women, but by the instincts of the mothers.[2]

According to Briffault, societies will deviate from the early polyandrous standard in varying degrees, and hence it is unlikely that one standard would serve for even a small group of societies. He might be labeled a social evolution theorist — his argument is that had certain adaptive moves not been made on a grand scale, matriarchy, as the social norm, might persist and with it, differing concepts of the "masculine" and "feminine."

But Engels, whom we have characterized as nonparadigmatic, denies (a) insofar as the generalizations he makes are about all industrialized societies; he considers all men and all women in only these societies to conform to our society's standards of "masculinity" and "femininity." He would, however, be committed to (b), because he also thinks that the industrialized societies in question have the same notions of "masculinity" and "femininity" as ours. In other words, Engels holds that, for industrialized societies, it is true that all men or women have those psychological traits which are taken in our society to be characteristic of males and females. We may think of Engels' argument in this way: the classic Marxist account of sex role differentiation is at the same time our exemplar of the argument from division of labor or economic structure. From the standpoint of the nurture thesis, Engels is making the claim that the economic structure itself is the cause of our role assignments, and hence of our gender assignments. Since his position on sex roles is tied to his view of the part played by the modes and forces of production in the social superstructure, Engels would assert that one standard of gender assignment would hold for all industrialized countries.

A second thesis on which the theorists converge is (c). All nurture theorists make the appeal to environmental causes as the basis for the determinance of psychological traits or activities which are later labeled "masculine" or "feminine." Mead sees these factors as highly mutable. The surprising passivity of both sexes among the Arapesh — and the equally astonishing aggressiveness of both sexes among the Mundugamor — lead Mead to the conclusion that the post-Enlightenment Western view of gender roles has limited application, and that culture-to-culture variations based on and resulting from social plot and social constructs may be enormous. Here is Mead on the New Guinea tribes:

Each of these tribes had, as has every human society, the point of sex difference to use as one theme in the plot of social life, and each of these three peoples has developed that theme differently. In comparing the way in which they have dramatized sex difference, it is possible to gain greater insight into what elements are social constructs, originally irrelevant to the biological facts of sex gender. . . . And while every culture has in some way institutionalized the roles of men and women, it has not necessarily been in terms of the two sexes, nor in terms of dominance and submission.[3]

Briffault's environmental cause is, as we have noted, the evolutionary move away from matriarchy. Briffault offers a great deal of evidence, much of it drawn from previously published sources, to support his contention that fraternal polyandry was once the norm. The general line here is both that this type of social structure is the cause of certain notions of gender and that it can itself evolve into other structures — polygyny/polyandry, and gradually into patriarchy. In one crucial chapter, "The Matriarchal Phase in Civilized Societies," Briffault manages to cite almost all of the major known pre-Christian social organizations, attributing briefly to each some form of the matriarchy or polygyny/polyandry structure.[4] As a social evolution theorist, Briffault is a paradigmatic nurture theorist in much the same sense as Mead.

Engels sees the environmental cause of sex differences to be the economic structure of societies. Although we have not referred to his theory as paradigmatically nurture in type (on the grounds that it does not entail (a) as formulated), it is a paradigmatically nurture viewpoint with respect to (c). Engels, like Briffault, argues that at one time certain contemporary roles were either nonexistent or reversed due to the fact that economic conditions at that time were quite different from those of industrialized societies.[5] So for him, too, not only can the cause of sex differences change, it in fact does over a period of time.

II. AREAS OF DIVERGENCE

The points of divergence for nurture theorists are perhaps more interesting than the points of convergence, and we may again specify at least three points on which the theorists disagree.

(1) As was explicated in Part I, the theorists differ as to whether or not they adhere to thesis (a) as formulated. That is to say that some theorists—although not a predominant number among the small group to be examined here—hold that (a) as stated is itself false. (2) The theorists differ as to what they mean by the actual assignments of the labels "masculine" and "feminine." Some theorists regard such labels as primarily expressive of a cluster of personality traits; others seem to regard the stereotypes as having more to do with the fulfillment of certain societal roles. (3) Finally, they differ as to what the causal factors are in the formation of gender concepts. This area of disagreement is perhaps the most important. A crude delineation of the differences here would include at least three kinds of views: the view that social conditioning is the primary causal agent; the view that some sort of social evolution is the cause; the view that the economic structure of the given society itself is the cause.

When we inquire what is meant by the labels "masculine" and "feminine," we raise an interesting question which yields different answers for the three theorists cited. Mead's gender stereotyping seems to be largely in terms of a cluster of personality traits; she does not seem to have in mind someone's being masculine or feminine primarily on the basis of tasks performed. (Imagine, for example, a female homemaker in our own society who performs all the standard chores, but who is not passive, nurturant, compassionate and so forth.) As we shall see later, what Mead counts as evidence for the "feminization" of a culture is related directly to her interpretation of the gender terms as descriptive of personality constructs. But this type of evidence would not necessarily be compelling for another nurture theorist. Mead writes of the Arapesh:

It may be said that the role of men, like the role of women, is maternal. . . . Arapesh life is organized about this central plot of the way men and women, physiologically different and possessed of differing potencies, unite in a common adventure that is primarily maternal, cherishing, and oriented away from the self towards the needs of the next generation.[6]

It is difficult to assess whether Briffault sees some sort of psychological component in the application of gender terms, but his usage of the terms is not as straightforward, insofar as the personality trait/social role dichotomy is concerned, as one might wish. ("Many an Arab woman personally led the men into battle. . . . Yet these proud Amazons were not barbaric viragoes, but cultivated beauty, grace and elegance and all the accomplishments of their age."[7]) Briffault's greatest interest is the institution of the matriarchy, and it might be argued that a matriarchal social structure is identifiable more by virtue of the activities performed by the sexes than by virtue of their respective mental attributes. Since the overwhelming proportion of the evidence brought forward by Briffault has to do with activities engaged in, or social roles played, we can assert with some alacrity that Mead and Briffault disagree over the interpretations to be given to the relevant gender labels.[8]

By contrast, Engels seems to fall more clearly on the "activities" side of the dichotomy with regard to the application of the labels themselves. He defines a certain role by the tasks assigned to it. Such abstractions as "order of inheritance" are crucially important for Engels in characterizing the matriarchy, and the move from matriarchy to patriarchy is said by Engels to have begun with the loss of the mother as the primary figure for assignment of heritability. Throughout his analysis, Engels shows little or no interest in purely psychological characteristics as related to gender labeling.

[Descent according to mother right] . . . had, therefore, to be overthrown, and it was overthrown; and it was not so difficult to do this as it appears to us now. For this revolution—one of the most decisive ever experienced by mankind—need not have disturbed one single living member of a gens. All the members could remain what they were previously. . . . The reckoning of descent through the female line and the right of inheritance through the mother were hereby overthrown and the male lineage and right of inheritance from the father instituted. . . . The overthrow of mother right was the world-historic defeat of the female sex.[9]

Finally, the theorists diverge with regard to specifics on thesis (c). It is an unstated assertion of Mead's that the personality type of individuals in a society may be defined and/or described and that this personality type is largely the result of the type of childhood nurturance received (although Mead seems to recognize, in her description of the geographical factors involved in tribal behavior, that the social evolution of the group may be a factor as well). But if the causal factors involved in the ultimate assignment of gender for Mead are largely those of social conditioning/nurturance, any given assertion about the group becomes an easy target for counterexamples. More will be said later about the significance of Mead's vulnerability on this point.

Briffault's environmental cause is, as we have already seen, a certain social evolution. Again, we find Briffault and the two other theorists in agreement on a broadly-formulated thesis while disagreeing on its ramifications. Generously construed, Briffault's claim is that all or almost all known pre-Christian societies were matriarchal, or at least participated in the polygyny/polyandry structure. The general development of agriculture, the domestication of animals, and the rise of private property and civilization itself all influenced an evolutionary trend away from the matriarchy, according to Briffault, although he is not precise about how this occurred. Since Briffault does not rely, as does Mead, on a notion of gender as personality trait cluster, his thesis is not susceptible to the same sort of refuting evidence. However, although Briffault would agree that the environmental factors he views as causing sex differences are mutable (in the sense that societies do not remain stagnantly matriarchal or stagnantly patriarchal), they are so in a sense different from the sort of mutability Mead assigns to the causes she identifies. We can imagine various forms of nurturance, but given the factors which led to present-day society, we cannot imagine a strikingly different history for social structures.

Engels is concerned with economic structure as the environmental cause of gender differences. In the sense that the economic structure of a society might be thought of as the result of social evolution, Engels' line is similar to Briffault's. The smaller, specific claims made by Engels in "The Origin of the Family" are, at least in principle, susceptible to confirmation/disconfirmation and are on a par with most of Briffault's observations. But again, given Engels' version of social history, he would assign mutability to the causes he isolates in much the same way as does Briffault.

III. PROBLEMS WITH NURTURE THEORIES

The nurture theorists present us with a variety of causal explanations of the formation of gender concepts, as we have seen, but offer us relatively little in the way of criteria for deciding between competing explanations. This might be thought to constitute a problem for nurture theories, and there are other problematic areas as well.

A crucial area to which we now advert is related to thesis (b). When the theorists make the claim that we have some notion of what it means to apply the labels "masculine" and "feminine," they are relying on generalizations about the conduct of males and females in a given cultural milieu. But the very fact that the assertion is made presupposes some notion of gender.

Several conceptual difficulties arise here. What allows a researcher like Mead or Briffault to hold the related theses (a) and (b) is the obvious evidence provided by many technologically primitive and/or geographically remote societies which have notions of masculinity and femininity differing from our own. Yet some notion of gender is present from the outset. Furthermore, although Mead does not seem to be guilty of the kind of circularity which might be charged to the nature theorists ("All men have traits which reduce to attributes all men have"), it is not clear that what she has done is conceptually sound. Mead relativizes the notions of gender to a given society, and then seems to make a similar, but more modest, claim. We might say that Mead begs the question in some way, since, if we refer to the aforementioned phrase as a large-scale tautology, Mead presents us with a miniaturized version. To a question which is something like "Are all men (women) within a given society masculine (feminine)?", we receive an answer which resembles "All (or most) men (women) in the Arapesh society are masculine (feminine) by Arapesh standards—i.e., all (or most) men (women) in the Arapesh society have the traits that all (or most) men (women) in the Arapesh society have." The analytical nature of the response seems to stem at least partly from the fact that some notion of gender is at work from the very start. If Mead had tried to examine a society simply from the standpoint of traits possessed by its members (whatever the traits, and without regard to gender linkage), the air of circularity here might have been avoided. Given that some concept of gender is presupposed, however, the circularity seems inevitable.

The issue of evidence, insofar as each individual theory is concerned, has already been broached. We have noted that there are areas of overlap; Mead relies heavily on a notion of gender as psychological trait cluster, but these traits manifest themselves at least partially in activities. Briffault seems to be writing largely about activities and social roles, but some of the activities and roles described seem to be related in a pronounced fashion to what we might think of as certain psychological traits. Briffault and Engels both view the historical decline of the matriarchy as crucial to a latter-day view of gender, and both see it as the product of some sort of social evolution. But in the case of Briffault and Engels, what is to help us decide between competing explanations? The usual criteria of elegance, simplicity, and explanatory power are of little assistance here. Is it the economic structure of the society itself which gives rise to the superstructure, described as a mode of civilization, or is it the other way around? What difference, if any, does it make from the standpoint of the two competing theories? What sorts of evidence would help us to decide? Although neither theory is incoherent, neither one, as we have seen, is so explicitly stated as to be readily confirmable/deniable. And the problem of evidence and competing explanations is related to the problem of testability: Although the theorists retain testability-in-principle with regard to their explanation of the assignment of gender, different kinds of evidence would count as refuting each theory in question and some theories retain testability to a higher degree than others.

In a sense, Mead's theory is the most intellectually appealing precisely because it is the one of the three theories that looks as if it might be confirmable. That is to say that Mead specifies that certain types of nurturance — which might perhaps be quantified in some way by an enterprising psychologist — are responsible for certain sorts of personalities. Anthropologists could, in principle, visit a number of societies, note the types of nurturance provided, contrast results, and see whether or not Mead's hypothesis holds up. It is impossible to perform the same kind of experiment with Briffault's or Engels' competing explanations: even a thought experiment is likely to fail here because we cannot imagine what present-day society would be like if the decline of the matriarchy had not taken place, if the forces of production had not altered from those of antiquity, etc. In short, between Briffault's theory and Engels' there is little to choose. And between these two theories and Mead's, it is tempting to choose Mead's account, not because it seems more straightforwardly plausible, but simply because we would know what it meant to say that Mead's account is false.

However, Mead's thesis suffers from counterexamples. If it is a weakness in any sort of "nature" argument that there appear to be many people of both sexes who do not possess what is "naturally" given, it is also an oddity of Mead's hypothesis that each society has a fairly large number of deviants. With regard to the Arapesh, a deviant individual is one (of either sex) who is not passive, noninitiatory, nurturing, and so on. Mead depicts many such individuals in her delineation of the social structure, and also gives a careful description of the difficulties they may expect to encounter in their daily social functioning.[10] Each such individual is, of course, a counterexample to Mead's claim that it is the type of rearing or nurturance provided which determines the personality of the adult. The deviants presumably were reared in a manner similar to that of the other Arapesh; they, she tells us, are *naturally* aggressive.[11] In a relatively small society, such as any one of the New Guinea societies scrutinized by Mead, the number of deviants is itself small, and comparatively easy to assess. Her general line with regard to Arapesh childrearing—that both sexes are reared with a view toward nonaggressive, cooperative behavior, that individualistic, self-aggrandizing behavior is not promoted, and that overtly aggressive behavior is actively discouraged—seems to be the sort of thing that would be amenable to simple empirical confirmation, and certainly does not lack explanatory power. But as the number of deviants in a society such as the Arapesh grows larger (passing, one might suppose, a critical mass), some account of the origins of the deviance, in terms of the general type of nurturance, must be supplied for the general line to hold. To be fair, Mead makes no single claim with regard to nurturance and personality, and she might very well be satisfied with a claim along the lines of "*Most* of the personalities in a given society have been strongly shaped by social conditioning." Nevertheless, the problems of what constitutes a critical mass and how to identify it still remain.

Finally, suppose that the following were to happen. Suppose it were to be shown at some later point that some psychological trait x is inherently linked with all individuals of a given sex. Obviously, this would have to be a newly-defined or discovered trait, since nothing currently measurable indisputably meets these standards. In any case, we hypothesize for the sake of argument that such a discovery is made by some future generation of social scientists. Now if some measurable and discernible trait is always linked to sex (no falsifying counterexamples are found), this would tend to confirm the hypothesis of the nature theorists. It would, of course, also tend to show that the nurture theories are wrong, and that at least some of the causal factors involved in the production of psychological traits are not environmental. Unfortunately, this simplistic picture is of almost no help in deciding whether or not there is genuine merit to any given nurture theory. But it does give us a rough sketch of the kinds of circumstances which might be thought to countermand a nurture line in general.

Clearly, nurture theories can be formulated in such a way as to be susceptible to the results of relevant research in the social sciences and so as to conform to the desiderata of the philosophy of science in general. It is the grandiose claims of the essentialist view which would seem to be less confirmable. But the claims made by the nurture theorists must be clearly drawn, the causal relationships spelled out in an obvious manner, and the methodology at work visible and not itself reliant upon the hypothesis in some mysterious fashion. The nurture theorists would do well to look to some of the prescriptive statements of the philosophy of the social sciences when formulating such hypotheses.

NOTES

1. Peggy Reeves Sanday, "Margaret Mead's Views of Sex Role in Her Own and Other Societies," *American Anthropologist* 82 (June 1980): 340–49, argues that the later Mead modified this view to a great extent. In this article, I refer only to the work in Margaret Mead, *Sex and Temperament in Three Primitive Societies* (New York: William Morrow and Co., 1935).
2. Robert Briffault, *The Mothers* (New York: Universal Library, 1963), p. 28.
3. Mead, op. cit., pp. xvii–xix.
4. Briffault, op. cit., pp. 76–95.
5. Friedrich Engels, "The Origin of the Family, Private Property and State," in *Marx, Engels: Selected Works,* vol. II (Moscow: Foreign Languages Publishing House, 1962), pp. 216, 237 and 311.
6. Mead, op. cit., pp. 14–15.
7. Briffault, op. cit., p. 82.
8. Ibid., pp. 76–110.
9. Engels, op. cit., pp. 216–17.
10. Mead, op. cit., pp. 148–49.
11. Ibid; see specifically the passage about Wabe.

Owen J. Flanagan Jr.

Freud: Masculinity, Femininity, and the Philosophy of Mind

If you reject this idea as fantastic and regard my belief in the influence of lack of a penis on the configuration of femininity as an
idee fixe, I am of course defenceless.[1]

I. INTRODUCTION

My purpose in this essay is to discuss critically Sigmund Freud's
(1856–1939) views on the nature and causes of "masculine" and
"feminine" personality and behavioral traits. The essay is divided into three sections. In the first section I describe three different models of the mind which Freud deployed, at different
times, in analyzing human personality. The proper interpretation of Freud's position on masculinity and femininity rests to a
large extent on the answer to the question of which philosophy
of mind, or which mixture of philosophies of mind, he embraced
when writing on sex differences. In the second section I isolate
two distinct Freudian positions on the nature and causes of
masculine and feminine personality traits, the first from 1905,
the second from 1925. These two positions are based on dif-

My thanks go to the National Endowment for the Humanities for a generous
grant which supported this research and to Joyce Knowlton Walworth for her
valuable criticisms.

ferent philosophies of mind. In the final section I provide criticisms of Freud's later and favored position on sex differences.

II. THREE MODELS OF THE MIND

There are still, among Freud scholars, three candidates for Freud's favored mental model, for his preferred philosophy of mind. The three models are called "mechanism," "evolutionism," and "mentalism." Each model places different emphases on nature and nurture, on heredity and social forces, and thus the different models, to a certain extent, explain sex differences in incompatible ways. My own interpretation is that Freud was a philosophical "mechanist" when he wrote "Three Essays on Sexuality" in 1905 but that he had fully converted to an idiosyncratic "evolutionistic-mentalism" by the time he wrote "Some Psychical Consequences of the Anatomical Distinction Between the Sexes" in 1925.

a. Mechanism.

The mechanistic model of the mind was the favored model during the last quarter of the nineteenth century when Freud received his training as a neurologist.[2] Proponents of "mechanism," inspired by a belief in strict causal determinism and the model of reflexes, sought to explain behavior in terms of "reflex arcs." Environmental events caused sensory stimulation of the organism which caused physiochemical changes in the organism's nervous system resulting eventually in overt action.

The model was thought to be adequate both for reflexes (for example, shining light is an environmental event which stimulates the eye, which in turn undergoes physiochemical changes ultimately resulting in pupil contraction) and for complex human action (for example, early childhood punishment of masturbation is encoded in the brain as a traumatic memory resulting in [physiochemical] guilt feelings and odd sexual behavior in adulthood).

Since Freud was trained as a neurologist, his primary focus, to the extent that he espoused this model, was on the middle portions of the arcs, on the portions where the physiochemically-encoded psychic changes take place. Nevertheless, the model itself commits a theoretician who embraces the model to the

belief that the *ultimate causes* of psychic changes, the true ini-
tiators of the arcs, lie in the *environment*. Therefore to the extent that Freud was a mechanist, he can be read as viewing male-
female differences as primarily caused by relations within the
family, by socialization, and by acculturation. His early (i.e.,
1905) view on sex differences is, in my interpretation,
mechanistically inspired.

b. Evolutionism

The inspiration for "evolutionism" was evolutionary theory.[3]
This explanatory model assumed, in accordance with Darwin,
that most morphological traits (e.g., size and eye color) and
many behavioral traits (e.g., mating "strategies") had evolved
because they had contributed to the survival, and therefore to
the reproductive success, of ancestral members of the species.
Because these ancestors had survived, traits which they possessed were passed on and found with higher frequency in their
descendents than the traits of less successful or unsuccessful
members of the species.

Some scientists, apparently including Freud, appended to
their Darwinism a tenet of Lamarck's older theory of evolution
which allowed for a very rapid acquisition of traits. They believed in the hereditary acquisition of learned traits.[4] If an
organism's ancestors learned a skill or developed a behavioral
trait, this skill or trait would be biologically encoded and could
be passed on to descendents within a generation. This premise
therefore allowed for the biological inheritance of cultural
habits, of social skills, and even of historical memories.[5] To the
extent that Freud espoused "evolutionism," he favored explaining male-female differences in terms of biology, heredity, and
anatomical destiny.[6]

c. Mentalism

This philosophy of mind is less a model than a style of explanation.[7] A "mentalist" analyzes mental events in causal chains with
other mental events and sets aside, without denying, the
mechanistic claim that mental events are actually neural events
kicked off by the environment, or the biologistic claim that mental traits are caused by heredity.

By the end of World War I Freud was dissatisfied with

"mechanism." He said of the search for biological correlates of neurotic thoughts that "there are either *no* observable changes in the anatomical organ of the mind to correspond to them, or there are changes which throw no light upon them."[8] Because of this Freud resolved in 1917 that

psychoanalysis must keep itself free from any hypothesis that is alien to it, whether of an anatomical, chemical, or physiological kind, and must operate with purely psychological auxiliary ideas.[9]

In actuality "mentalism" is compatible with both the environmentalism of "mechanism" and the nativism of "evolutionism," since Freud did not deny that there might be either (or both) environmental or biological catalysts for the chains of mental events. This is why I refer to it as a style, rather than as a model, of explanation. Nonetheless, the style involves focusing on the causal relations between purely mental phenomena like "feelings," "beliefs," "unconscious and conscious wishes," "repressed memories," "anxieties," "complexes" and the like and on examining the relations between these phenomena as if they constituted a closed, self-contained system.

This focus makes it difficult to tell whether or not Freud saw nature or nurture, or both, as the ultimate cause of masculine and feminine personality traits since he is, when he employs this style of explanation, primarily concerned with the machinations of the "black box," the human mind, and somewhat unconcerned with what initiates these machinations or with their outcomes.[10] Nevertheless, on my reading, Freud typically supported his favored, i.e., post-1925, analyses of sex differences by allying "mentalism" and "evolutionism."

III. FREUD'S VIEWS ON MASCULINE AND FEMININE TRAITS

Freud's position on masculine and feminine traits developed in two stages. His early position was more mechanistic and environmentalistic than his "mature" view which combined features of evolutionism and mentalism.

a. The Early View: The Symmetry Thesis

In both stages of Freud's thinking about masculinity and femininity there are two important variables to keep in mind. These are:

    (i)   The child's sense of its own body.

    (ii)   The child's relationship with its parents.

If we organize our analysis around these two variables, we can describe Freud's early view on masculinity and femininity in the following way: Boys and girls naturally explore their own bodies. Freud described the sexuality of children as "polymorphously perverse." In approximately the fourth year, the many-sidedness of the child's explorations begins to diminish and the child focuses play on the genitals; the child begins to masturbate. Freud thought that the masturbation of boys and girls was strictly analogous; boys play with their penises; girls with their clitorises. He says, "the auto-erotic activity of the erotogenic zones is, however, the same in both sexes, and owing to this uniformity there is no possibility of a distinction between the two sexes such as arises after puberty."[11]

Freud described the sexuality of female children as "of a wholly masculine character."[12] But he insisted in a footnote—which was added ten years after this passage—that he meant "masculine" neither in a "biological," i.e., anatomical, sense nor in a "sociological," i.e., social role, sense but in the sense which "is the essential one and the most serviceable in psychoanalysis," namely, "'masculine' and 'feminine' . . . in the sense of activity and passivity."[13] Freud pointed out that actual men and women show a combination of "masculine" and "feminine" traits in this unusual psychoanalytic sense of the terms.

So given that boys and girls both are sexually very active, engage in virtually identical sex play and thus have very similar body sense, how do sex differences develop? Relations with the parents, the second variable, are decisive in Freud's early view. Freud believed that boys and girls develop a strong attraction to their opposite sex parent and a powerful jealousy toward their same sex parent at about the time they begin to masturbate. He referred to this attraction-jealousy constellation as the Oedipus Complex. Freud believed that the development and characteristics of the Oedipus Complex were perfectly symmetrical in boys and girls, so that the girl was attracted to the father, the boy to the mother.

The male and female child, in seeking the affection of their opposite sex parent, begin to take on the characteristics of the same sex parent of whom they are jealous. This happens because the child actually wants to be like the same sex parent; it is precisely (for all the child knows) by being like the same sex parent that the child can win the affection of the opposite sex parent.[14]

The important thing to notice is that the latter analysis is perfectly compatible with "mechanism," with an environmental account of sex differences. Biology is necessary to set the sexual attraction to the opposite sex parent into play, but after that the child *learns* how to be a "man" or a "woman" through modelling, identification with, and observation of, his or her same sex parent. But the child, on this account, is not learning how to be *the* prototypical male or female; nor is the child just "becoming" *the* prototypical male or female thanks to some blueprint contained in the biological wiring; he or she is actively learning to be like his or her *particular* mother or father. Given the vast range of individual differences in parents, the child could be learning any of a large number of different personality traits. One could assume, however, that there would be some traits which a given culture would assign more frequently to men than to women and vice versa and that, therefore, boys and girls would, on the average, be socialized in the ways the particular culture characteristically makes available to members of their sex. Nevertheless, assuming that Freud is correct in his belief that the Oedipus Complex is the crucial episode in the development of sex differences, in his early account he provides no reason for thinking that the actual traits a child develops on the way to becoming a "man" or a "woman" are anything other than *learned* once the child's biological sex sets the attraction to the opposite sex parent into motion.

b. The Later View: Penis Envy and the Assymetry Thesis

In 1925 Freud attempted to solve two theoretical problems facing his 1905 symmetry thesis. First, the mother is the original love object for the child of both sexes. This means that the female child has to shift her initial affiliation away from her mother in order to enter the Oedipal phase in a way the male child does not. Second, the female child has to discover her vagina (which during the genital masturbation stage "is still undiscovered").[15] Freud claimed to bring "forward nothing but observed facts" in pointing out that adult female sexuality is largely vaginal. Since the masturbation of the female child is exclusively clitoral, this means that in "the change to femininity the clitoris should wholly or in part hand over its sensitivity, and at the same time its importance, to the vagina."[16]

If Freud was right, the female child has to change both her body sense *and* her relationship with her parents in a way the male child does not. Freud tried to solve the riddle of how this happens, i.e., how it is that a girl passes "from her mother to an attachment to her father," or how she passes from "her masculine phase to the feminine one to which she is biologically destined" by the "penis envy" hypothesis."[17]

Freud claimed that girls were bound to make a "momentous discovery":

They notice the penis of a brother or playmate, strikingly visible and of large proportions, at once recognize it as the superior counterpart to their own small and inconspicuous organ, and from that time forward fall a victim to envy for the penis.[18]

The "penis envy" hypothesis solved both the problem of the shift from clitoral to vaginal primacy and the problem of the shift from the primacy of mother love to father love. The little girl, according to Freud, discovers "that she is castrated."[19] This is a "wound to her narcissism." This injury to the girl's ego causes her to express disappointment and dissatisfaction with "her inferior clitoris" by abandoning her efforts to gain "satisfaction from it."[20] The shift of the female child's "love" from the mother to the father is then explained by the fact that "girls hold their mother responsible for their lack of a penis and do not forgive her for being thus put at a disadvantage."[21] The father takes the mother's place in the girl's eyes because the father has precisely what the girl wants, precisely what she needs to assuage her ego: a penis.

Meanwhile the male child, according to Freud, has also noticed the differences in male and female genitalia. But what the girl experiences as envy, the boy experiences as fear. The male child realizes that he could be castrated, that his more powerful father, who is his rival for his mother's affections, could cut off his penis. The shock of this discovery delivers the boy from the Oedipus Complex. He gives up the hope that he will win his mother from his father and replaces his mother with more appropriate love objects. Freud says that "in boys . . . the complex is not simply repressed, it is simply smashed to pieces by the shock of threatened castration."[22]

Unlike Freud's 1905 position, the latter view combines evolutionism with mentalism. The early view explained male and female differences in terms of the child's identification with its same sex parent, from whom the child learned the traits which that particular parent possessed. The post-1925 view is evolutionistic because it sees "nature" as the central causal force. It is the child's inevitable observation of the biologically-detemined genitals (not the attraction to his or her particular and unique opposite sex parent) which is *the* decisive factor in all subsequent psychosexual development.

The later view is mentalistic as well as evolutionistic because the primary focus of the analysis, once the biological catalyst sets off the process, is on the inner dynamic of mental processes like "fear," "envy," "love," "hate," and "feelings of wounded narcissism." Freud gives little attention to "nurture," and makes virtually no mention of any unique environmental *input* that might occur in any particular child's life, e.g., the child might lack a same or opposite sex parent or might never see the genitalia of the opposite sex. Nor is there mention of idiosyncratic behavioral *outputs* or atypical personality configurations, e.g., female children who remain obviously attached to their mother, or boys who display envy toward girls. Freud theorizes as if the Oedipal drama operates in a closed system, and in an inevitable and universally repetitive fashion, immune from outside influences once put in motion by the child's biological sex. All boys fear, all girls envy; all boys love their mother, all girls love their father; all girls feel wounded, all boys feel superior.

Freud obviously believed in individual differences caused by environmental (and perhaps constitutional) factors; otherwise he would have been unable to offer explanations for individual pathology.Nevertheless his discussions of sex differences show virtually no sensitivity to individual differences and contain hardly a mention of what factors in the family or in a culture might lead to such differences. This unfortunately is the toll of the philosophical alliance of "evolutionism" and "mentalism."

In any case Freud believed that his post-1925 view on child development could account for a wide array of masculine and feminine traits commonly found in adults. I describe five of these in the following paragraphs. It should be noted at the start that Freud, probably to his detriment, made no distinction between behavioral and personality traits, not that it is an easy distinction to draw. In the examples, I have tried to make it clear whether the trait in question is best construed as a behavioral or personality trait.

a. Activity-passivity

Although Freud thought that boys and girls were about equally active pre-Oedipally, he thought that because girls give up active masturbation in a way that boys do not, females become more passive in terms of overt behavior than males. "Along with the abandonment of clitoral masturbation a certain amount of activity is renounced. Passivity now has the upper hand. . . ."[23]

b. Degree of Narcissism

Freud believed that the wound to the female's ego from the discovery that she does not have a penis results in a greater amount of narcissism and a greater amount of self-centeredness (both behaviorally and psychologically) in females than in males. "Her self love is mortified by the comparison with the boy's far superior equipment."[24] This psychic injury leads to self-doubt in females "so that to be loved is a stronger need for them than to love."[25] It also results in greater vanity in females than in males as a "compensation for their original sexual inferiority."[26]

c. Degree of Jealousy

Freud believed that the envy females feel—and males do not—upon discovering the differences in their genitals, accounted in part for the fact that females behaved in adulthood, on the average, more enviously than males. He says "envy and jealousy play an even greater part in the mental life of women than of men. It is not that I think these characteristics are absent in men or that I think they have no other roots in women than envy for the penis; but I am inclined to attribute their greater amount in women to this latter influence."[27]

d. Moral Sense

The superego, an individual's moral and social sense, is rooted in fear. For this reason males develop a more powerful superego than females. Freud states that the fear of losing the penis destroys the Oedipus Complex for the boy and "a severe superego is set up as its heir."[28] The overwhelming castration fear the male child experiences makes it impossible for him to forget (at least unconsciously) the possible horrendous implications of not obeying moral and social law, of not relinquishing his incestuous desires. The male personality, but not necessarily male behavior, is therefore more likely to be rule-governed and guilty than the female personality.

The male's moral development is also aided by the fact that once the Oedipus Complex is "smashed to pieces," the boy looks less toward his family, less to his mother and father as love object and role model, respectively, and more to people outside the family. This prepares the way for the male child to find role models in his peer group, in the school and in the culture at large. Freud thought that a mature, "impersonal," moral sense required precisely such a widening of perspective beyond the narrow boundaries of one's own family.[29]

Freud argued, however, that because females do not fear castration they do not have the same motivation as boys to give up their Oedipus Complex, develop a strong superego, and find "interests" and "models" outside the family. Furthermore, he believed that the greater "enviousness" of females militated against their developing a strong "sense of justice."[30]

e. Cultural Achievement

Great artistic and scientific achievements do not come naturally to humans. They require work, and humans would rather play, especially sexually, than work. Artistic and scientific achievements are possible when sexual impulses are rechannelled (sublimated) from impossible objects and fantasies to appropriate objects (e.g., from parent to intellectual endeavors) in compliance with the demands of the "Reality Principle." For the same reasons that males have stronger superegos than females, they are led to sublimation earlier and more easily than females. When the Oedipus Complex is "smashed to pieces" the male child is forced to look away from his mother as a source of pleasure and to things and people outside the family. But since girls do not fear castration, and thus lack the main motive for overcoming the Oedipus Complex, their chance of developing skills based on sublimation suffers:

Girls remain in it (the Oedipus Complex) for an indeterminate length of time; they demolish it and, even so, incompletely. In these circumstances the formation of the superego must suffer; it cannot attain the strength and independence which gives it its cultural significance. . . .[31]

IV. A CRITIQUE OF FREUD'S VIEWS
ON MASCULINE AND FEMININE TRAITS

My critical comments are devoted primarily to Freud's post-1925 view first, because this is the view he himself ultimately settled on and second, because the earlier view, thanks to the mechanistic philosophy which supports it, can be interpreted as a fairly traditional socialization model in which the parents, especially the same sex parents, serve as the primary role models (thanks to their own parents and, therefore, thanks ultimately to the culture) for masculine and feminine behavior.

There is one common philosophical objection which might be thought to undermine the entire Freudian enterprise and, therefore, to defeat his views on sex differences by implication. The objection is that the theory postulates unobservable entities, e.g., "unconscious wishes," "superego" and the like, and that this is objectionable.

It is impossible to see how the claim that Freud's theory postulates unobservables, which is correct, is a criticism, however, since every mature scientific theory engages in postulation of unobservables. Electromagnetic fields and energy quanta are just as unobservable as unconscious wishes. It may be that Freud introduces unobservables without sufficient care, but that is a different question which can only be discussed by analyzing each unobservable in turn. The following three criticisms, however, weigh more heavily and specifically against Freud's views on sex differences.

a. Unfalsifiability

This is the claim that given the way Freudian theory is formulated there are no empirical results which could possibly count against it.[32] A theory is logically unfalsifiable if it allows every logically possible outcome, and therefore automatically counts everything that happens as a verification.

There is reason to think that some portions of Freudian theory are constructed in this way. An example would be the portion having to do with the sexual content of dreams; here Freud lists virtually every possible everyday symbol as a sexual one and he therefore makes it close to logically impossible to have a nonsexual dream.[33] Freud's dream theory precludes the possibility of nonsexual dreams because he defines the vocabulary of dreams as exclusively sexual from the start.

With respect to the question of the falsifiability of Freud's views on sex differences, however, one must say in fairness to Freud that the theory is *logically* falsifiable. For example, the theory does imply that females, at least on the average, can not turn out to have stronger superegos than males; and that females must not (at least initially) find penises laughable and not worth having; and that males must not find their fathers unthreatening.

Nevertheless, although the theory is not logically un- falsifiable, it may be unfalsifiable in practice, in the sense that Freud, or your average Freudian, would not give it up under any circumstances. For example, suppose I say that I have always found my father threatening. This would count, if you are a Freudian, as verification of my castration fear. Suppose instead I say that I have always found my father completely unthreaten- ing. You might, if you are a Freudian, claim that I am resisting admitting the unconscious terror I have of my father, in which case you have taken my denial of threatening feelings as verifica- tion of my castration fear. But given that I only have two logically possible responses at my disposal and given that you are counting either my admission of fear or my denial of fear as proof of my castration anxiety, you are, in effect, precluding the falsification of the theory.

Since the Oedipal episode is the central factor in subsequent psychosexual development according to Freud, and since it in- volves the most upsetting of memories, psychoanalytic theory would predict that most people either would not remember or they would deny their memories of the episode. Since the entire episode is carried out intra-psychically with virtually no behavioral manifestations in the first place (e.g., children don't actually have sex with their parents, they just "fantasize" about it) and since most everyone will deny the episode, a Freudian can in practice preclude any possible falsification by counting all the "remembered" Oedipal events and all the denied ("forgotten" in the theory's terms) Oedipal events as verifications of the theory. But in lieu of overt behavioral evidence of the complex in the first place, these affirmations and denials are all the evidence there is for the Oedipus Complex!

b. The Evidence for the Oedipus Complex

Freud claimed to have discovered the Oedipus Complex, not in observation of children, but during his own self-analysis. He writes in a letter to Fleiss,

. . . libido towards *matram* was aroused; the occasion must have been the journey with her from Leipzig to Vienna, during which we spent a night together and I must have had the opportunity of seeing her *nudam*. . . .[34]

The means by which a hypothesis is generated has no bearing on the strength of that hypothesis; the hypothesis is as strong as the subsequent tests show it to be. Freud claimed to have tested his theory in clinical settings with his patients and to have found that his patients had memories (the symbolic significance of which they either admitted *or* denied) similar to his own. Freud's "evolutionism" then led him to postulate a universal Oedipus Complex which affects *all* members of the species regardless of the cultural or individual peculiarities of their family structure.

But according to Erich Fromm, himself an analyst,[35] anthropological evidence shows that something like an Oedipus Complex *in boys* is found to a degree which is directly proportional to the degree to which a particular family is patriarchal (in which childrearing is the mother's task, breadwinning is the father's task, and especially in societies in which there is labor competition among males). In such families, which are more common in some cultures than in others, males tend to be greatly attached to their mothers and in competition with their fathers. This, of course, could easily be explained without evolutionistic assumptions. To the extent that the mother is the primary person with whom the male child has a relationship, he will naturally be attached to her; to the extent that the society functions on competition between males, father and son will have mixed feelings toward each other. But since there is nothing necessary about the patriarchal family, there is nothing necessary about the Oedipus Complex. Furthermore, according to Fromm, evidence for Oedipal Complexes in females, even in patriarchal cultures, is insubstantial.[36]

c. The Evidence for Penis Envy

The penis envy hypothesis is where Freud's "evolutionism" really gets in the way. Notice that in order for this envy to get under way, Freudian theory requires (1) that the female child actually observes the genitals of a male and (2) that a penis is the sort of thing which a little girl is "wired" to be envious of. Given, however, that there must be some, if not many, children who lack siblings or playmates of the opposite sex, or who live in cultures where nudity is inappropriate and thus where there are few chances to see the genitals of the opposite sex, there must be some children who never make the actual observation required to set-off the envy. Secondly, one has to wonder why a penis would necessarily be the sort of thing which automatically makes a female child envious. After all, female children must have encounters with all sorts of things shaped like penises without experiencing envy.

Freud anticipated both these objections and tried to protect his theory by deploying the Lamarckian portion of his "evolutionism." Freud thought that if any female failed to actually observe male genitals, she would "remember," thanks to her inherited species memory, what male genitals were like. Then she would feel envious because she would also "remember," thanks to the same species memory, just how important and valuable a penis is. Freud says that

. . . the penis (to follow Ferenczi [1925]) owes its extraordinary high narcissistic cathexes to its organic significance for the propagation of the species. . . .[37]

Of course, the idea that there is such a species memory and that it attaches such importance to the penis is evolutionistic nonsense. In fact when one thinks about it, *if* "organic significance for the propagation of the species" is a reason for envy, then one would predict, given the actual observations that most children make, that children of both sexes would feel "womb envy."[38] Babies obviously come from mothers; the causal role of the father, and especially the causal role of the father's penis, is, I assume, a very late discovery in the average child's life.

V. CONCLUSION

Juliet Mitchell, a British feminist, has defended Freud on the grounds that he provided an analysis of patriarchal society.[39] Although this may be true, it is true by accident. Freud certainly did not see his theory that way. "Evolutionism" led Freud to analyze characteristic sex differences as if they were largely uninfluenced by familial, social, and cultural factors. Species membership and inherited sex are the crucial variables in Freud's post-1925 account. The developmental drama of male and female children is universal *and* sex specific.

If, however, we free Freudian theory from the weight of his

"evolutionism" and therefore eliminate the tenuous suite of claims of Oedipal universality, penis envy and castration fear, there is much to be said for what remains. Children do develop powerful affection toward, and identification with, their parents. A child's sense of its biological sex and a sense that its sex is not shared by half the species affects the child's choice of role models. To the extent that the chosen role models have traits which the culture assigns to members of the child's sex, personality differences between men and women, for better or for worse, will be perpetuated. The theory so framed is compatible with classical social learning models, and brings the discussion back to square one, i.e., to the question of whether any of the traits we teach, or let the children of either sex learn, are worth having in the first place.

NOTES

1. Sigmund Freud, Lecture XXXIII, "Femininity," *New Introductory Lectures on Psychoanalysis* (New York: W.W. Norton, 1933), p. 117. This lecture, Freud insists, is mainly a rewrite of his 1925 work "Some Psychical Consequences of the Anatomical Distinction Between the Sexes." I employ it throughout as such.
2. Erich Fromm, *Greatness and Limitations of Freud's Thought* (New York: Harper and Row, 1980) considers this model, sometimes called the Helmholtz model, to be Freud's main and most important mental model.
3. Frank Sulloway in *Freud: Biologist of the Mind* (New York: Basic Books, 1979) argues that Darwinism plus a good amount of Lamarckianism was Freud's favored model, especially after 1905, when Sulloway thinks Freud abandoned "mechanism" for "evolutionism." Sulloway says that around this time Freud moved from "*proximate*-causal theory to *ultimate*-causal theory" (p. 365). This is important for our purposes since all Freud's important work on masculinity and femininity is post-1905.
4. This hypothesis was fostered, it seems, by "mechanism" and its tenet that learning was actually encoded in the physiology of the organism.
5. C.G. Jung, Freud's renegade student, took this Lamarckian tenet so seriously that he made his own theory turn on the thesis that all humans share, from the start, certain species memories, which he referred to as the "collective unconscious."
6. "Evolutionism," however, does not necessarily lead to hereditary determinism; it only usually does. One can, for example, use the

tactic some modern "sociobiologists" have and claim that humans have evolved to possess the trait of being "plastic," of being terrific learners.

7. Ernest Jones in his famous biography, *The Life and Work of Sigmund Freud* (New York: Basic Books, 1961) reads Freud as espousing this model.
8. Sigmund Freud, Lecture I, "Introduction," *Introductory Lectures on Psychoanalysis* (New York: W.W. Norton, 1917), pp. 20–21.
9. Ibid., p. 21.
10. See B.F. Skinner, "A Critique of Psychoanalytic Concepts and Theories," in *Cumulative Record,* ed. B.F. Skinner, 3d ed. (New York: Appleton-Century Crofts, 1973) where he criticizes Freud's "mentalism" for "stealing the show" from both environmental causes and the behavioral outcomes.
11. Sigmund Freud, "Three Essays on Sexuality," 1905, vol. VII, *The Complete Psychological Works,* ed. J. Strachey (London: Hogarth, 1953), p. 219.
12. Ibid.
13. Ibid.
14. Oedipus ended up marrying his mother precisely because he was so successful at being just like his father, so successful that he dethroned his father, the King.
15. Freud, Lecture XXXIII, "Femininity," op. cit., p. 104.
16. Ibid.
17. Ibid., p. 105; Freud in both his 1905 view and his post-1925 view claims that there are small but noticeable differences in male and female children and that these differences are instinctual. He says, "A little girl is as a rule less aggressive, defiant and self sufficient; she seems to have a greater need for being shown affection and on that account to be more dependent and pliant." Ibid., p. 103.
18. Freud, "Some Psychical Consequences of the Anatomical Distinction Between the Sexes," 1925, vol. XIX, *The Complete Psychological Works,* op. cit., p. 252.
19. Freud, Lecture XXXIII, "Femininity," op. cit., p. 111.
20. Ibid., p. 113.
21. Ibid., p. 110.
22. Freud, "Some Psychical Consequences of the Anatomical Distinction Between the Sexes," op. cit., p. 257.
23. Freud, Lecture XXXIII, "Femininity," op. cit., p. 113.
24. Ibid., p. 112.
25. Ibid., p. 117.
26. Ibid.
27. Ibid., p. 111.
28. Ibid., p. 114.
29. Freud, Lecture XXXI, "Dissection of the Psychical Personality," in *New Introductory Lectures on Psychoanalysis,* op. cit., p. 57.

30. Freud, Lecture XXXIII, "Femininity," op. cit., p. 119.
31. Ibid., p. 114.
32. Karl R. Popper, *Conjectures and Refutations: The Growth of Scientific Knowledge* (New York: Harper, 1963) makes this charge against Freud and Marx.
33. Freud, Lecture X, "Symbolism in Dreams," in *Introductory Lectures on Psychoanalysis,* op. cit., pp. 149–69.
34. Freud, *The Origins of Psychoanalysis* (New York: Basic Books, 1954), Letter of 3.10.97.
35. Fromm, *Greatness and Limitations of Freud's Thought,* op. cit., pp. 30–34.
36. Ibid., p. 27.
37. Freud, "Some Psychical Consequences of the Anatomical Distinction Between the Sexes," op. cit., p. 257.
38. See Karen Horney, *Feminine Psychology* (New York: W.W. Norton, 1967) for a critique of Freud's views on sex differences by a great woman psychoanalyst. It was Horney who developed the notion of "womb envy."
39. Juliet Mitchell, *Psychoanalysis and Feminism* (New York: Vintage Books, 1974), p. xi.

Part III
. . . Or Neither?:
Is the Debate Resolvable?

Introduction

Not until comparatively recently have some philosophers asked whether the psychological sex difference debate is a potentially resolvable one. Suspicions that it might not be resolvable have centered around two questions raised by psychological sex difference theories. Can it be shown, without bias, that there are any psychological trait differences between the sexes to begin with? And even if it can be, is it likely that biological factors, environmental factors, or some combination of such factors will ever definitively be shown to be the causes of such differences?

As was pointed out earlier, the paradigm nature theorist begins with the thesis that all men are "masculine" and all women are "feminine" where the words in quotes are defined in terms of words referring to the sorts of psychological traits listed previously (Introduction, Part I) in Groups Y and X, respectively. Even the weakest of paradigm nurture theories concedes that for our society there is a statistically significant correlation between being female (male) and being "feminine" ("masculine") so defined. Both types of theorist agree that the question as to why there are such differences in gender is in need of an answer.

The research done in the past decade or so[1] has the surface appearance of supporting the claim that there is a statistically significant correlation (though not a universal one) between being a male (female) in our society and having the sorts of psychological traits from Group Y (X). The exception is that none of this research even vaguely supports the view that intellectual ability is more highly correlated with being male than with being female.[2] A few statistical correlations show up in such research fairly regularly. Tests typically seem to show males to be aggressive, active, self-confident, impulsive, and the like.[3] Being female is often correlated with having a low self-concept, being fearful of success, and having verbal acumen, empathy, and the like.[4]

But two different kinds of arguments have been advanced in support of the claim that we should be suspicious of such "confirmations" of psychological sex difference theses. One kind of argument is to the effect that they are *in fact* based on biased data. Naomi Weisstein,[5] for example, has suggested that in general, whatever beliefs researchers have had about the psychology of women have later been confirmed by the data they obtained, which she argues is strong evidence of research bias. Some more specific types of bias that might be found in past data collection and categorization are explicated by HOAGLAND, SOBLE, and GRIM in what follows. For instance, some researchers have construed certain behaviors as revealing aggression, say, only when that behavior is exhibited by males, not by females. Some researchers have construed behaviors as "nurturant" only when exhibited by females. It therefore comes as no surprise to find that only males are considered "aggressive" and only females are considered "nurturant" in the resultant data.

The type of bias noted above, however, is, at least in principle, avoidable if researchers select a clear-cut set of behaviors as revealing aggression or nurturance in *any* person whatever their sex.[6] A second kind of argument makes the stronger claim that no psychological sex difference thesis formulated in terms of the "masculine" and "feminine" as we have defined them *could be* confirmed without bias. A case for this point of view is made by SARAH HOAGLAND in what follows.

Hoagland says that the very concepts of femininity and masculinity construed in terms of lists like X and Y are "not empirical" ones by which she apparently means that claims containing the terms "masculine" and "feminine" so defined are not subject to objective empirical testing. If she is right, it would follow that no psychological sex difference thesis formulated in these terms could ever "really" be confirmed (or disconfirmed, for that matter) and thus there could be no scientific justification[7] for holding that such a thesis is true, much less for trying to explain why it is true. Her justification for the view is, at least in part, that a number of sex difference theorists use the terms "feminine" and "masculine" prescriptively which, as was spelled out in the Introduction to Part I, results in their failing to allow actual counterexamples to their theses as bona fide ones.

ALAN SOBLE disagrees. He admits the terms are often used prescriptively with the result described by Hoagland; but researchers need not use them in this way. They might instead use them purely descriptively. Granted, a number of evaluative decisions have to be made in the attempt to determine just how many of the traits from Groups X and Y have to be present, and to what degree they must be present, in order to apply the terms descriptively. But having to make such decisions in order to ascribe "masculinity" and "femininity" to a person would not distinguish the ascription from that of many other terms in the social sciences, and it therefore does not rule out claims containing such terms from the realm of the "empirical."

Hoagland hints at a response to this type of argument by way of her example of the resistant housewife. Even in the purely descriptive usages of "masculine" and "feminine," in which the terms are mere shorthand notations for some combination of terms referring to the sorts of traits in Groups X and Y, the sort of "empirical" testing to which claims containing them are subject is necessarily biased in favor of one sex over the other. So although such claims are "empirical" if by that we mean only that they can be tested, they are not "empirical" in the sense that they can be tested with *objectivity*. To understand this point of view, consider the following. We attribute psychological traits (which are construed as unobservable mental entities) to persons on the basis of observing the overt behavior of those persons. But in order to attribute the psychological trait in question to a person, the researcher has to have some notion of what behaviors reveal the trait in question. Some behaviors will be classified as aggression-revealing or nurturance-revealing, and others will be ruled out. But what if, as a matter of fact, women who are aggressive and men who are nurturant do not exhibit those selected behaviors? In that case it appears that many aggressive women and many nurturant men will unjustifiably be ruled out from the class of "aggressive" or "nurturant" persons in the resultant data.

The argument is analogous to that offered by some in charging that IQ tests are racially biased. If minority group members

who are intelligent do not characteristically exhibit their intelligence by giving the "right" answers to IQ test questions, but
whites who are intelligent do, there is reason to believe that there
is an implicit race bias in the attribution of the term "intelligent"
only to those who perform well on those tests.

But what if we attempted to eliminate sex bias by expanding
the list of selected behaviors to allow for women behaving in
ways other than the ones previously selected and still being aggressive, or for men behaving in ways other than the ones
previously selected and still being nurturant? Here a number of
points should be noted. We should first of all be wary of changing theoretical claims — or their accepted test conditions — in
midstream. With different lists of "aggression-revealing"
behaviors, for example, we will have significantly different tests
and, in a sense, different claims to be tested. Secondly, once the
new behaviors are ruled-in, far more women would be considered "aggressive," far more men "nurturant." This would tend
to disconfirm, not confirm, a psychological sex *difference* claim.
Thirdly, since no behavior is logically inconsistent with the
presence of any psychological trait, it might be suspected that
the list of ruled-in behaviors would have to be expanded to in-
finity (an impossible task) to avoid the very possibility of bias.

But it might be argued that the charge that bias is necessarily
involved is too strong. Perhaps women who are aggressive
behave in the same ways as aggressive men and perhaps men
who are nurturant behave in the same ways that women who are
nurturant behave. Whether our tests are biased or not depends
on whether this claim is true. And if it is true the tests are not
biased as charged.[8]

The trouble is that we can no more "objectively" test this
thesis than we can the ones at issue — and for the same reasons.
In the absence of a reliable way to test this thesis, we should have
to conclude that it is unlikely that the bias question (and thus the
question of whether any given confirmation is a "real" one) will
ever be resolved.

Two approaches to sex difference theory would avoid this
problem altogether by shifting the locus of attention from
psychological differences between the sexes to behavioral ones.
One approach would be for those psychologists interested in the
subject of sex differences to commit themselves to some form of
operationism, thereby avoiding the ontological commitment to
unobservable mental entities. But it has been argued that serious

methodological difficulties for the social sciences result from a commitment to operationism.[9] A second approach would be to maintain an ontological commitment to mental traits in persons, but to construe these traits as held by everyone at one time or another and to hold that there is no set or given way in which persons "act out" such traits behaviorally. This approach, suggested elsewhere by Mary Anne Warren,[10] would entail construing all psychological traits as essentially *human* ones while allowing for the possibility of purely overt behavioral sex differences.

Suppose that some way is found to avoid the methodological problems discussed above without resorting to a theory which shifts the locus of attention to behavioral sex differences. And suppose further that at some point in the future, Group X and Y psychological sex differences are objectively confirmed. Would any evidence definitively decide between competing explanations of such differences? PATRICK GRIM argues convincingly that it would not.[11] But in the absence of a definitive answer to the question, he adds, there are compelling ethical grounds for acting on the assumption that nurture, not nature, explanations are correct.

NOTES

1. Serious research into the question of whether there are psychological sex differences was begun only some fifteen years ago. Up until then, there was apparently no doubt in anyone's mind but that there are.

2. It would be a mistake to construe Maccoby and Jacklin's *The Psychology of Sex Differences* (Stanford: Stanford University Press, 1974) as taking exception to this claim. In her *The Nature of Woman* (Point Reyes, Calif.: Edgepress, 1980) Mary Anne Warren points out that "In their important review of the research in this area, Maccoby and Jacklin find evidence of statistical differences between the intellectual talents of males and females, but not such as to justify any attribution of overall mental superiority to either. Thus, females consistently excel in a range of skills labeled 'verbal,' while males excel in visual-spatial perception and analysis" (p. 379).

3. See, for example, Bardwick, Maccoby and Jacklin, Williams, Hutt and the Nova Transcript cited in the "Further References" section to Part III of this volume.

4. See, for example, Horner, Maccoby and Jacklin, and the Nova

Transcript in the "Further References" section to Part III of this volume.

5. Naomi Weisstein, "Psychology Constructs the Female," in *Woman in Sexist Society,* ed. Vivian Gornick and Barbara K. Moran (New York: Signet, 1971), pp. 207–24.

6. Further criticisms of the standard psychological tests for "masculinity' and "femininity" can be found in Hilary M. Lips and Nina Lee Colwill, *The Psychology of Sex Differences* (Englewood Cliffs, N.J.: Prentice-Hall, 1978) and in *Beyond Sex-Role Stereotypes: Readings Toward a Psychology of Androgyny,* ed. Alexandra G. Kaplan and Joan P. Bean (Boston: Little, Brown and Co., 1976).

7. This is, of course, not to deny that there may be overriding ethical grounds for assuming the thesis to be false in the absence of convincing scientific evidence for its truth or falsehood. I am indebted to Patrick Grim for this point.

8. By analogy, if minority group members who are intelligent behave in the same ways as do whites who are, IQ tests would be similarly rescued from the same charge.

9. A convincing defense of this viewpoint can be found in Michael Martin's "An Examination of the Operationist's Critique of Psychoanalysis," *Soc. Sci. Inf.* 8, no. 4, pp. 65–85.

10. This alternative is suggested in a different but related context for a different purpose. See Warren's "Androgyny" in her *The Nature of Woman,* op. cit., p. 17.

11. See also John Stuart Mill, *The Subjection of Women* (Cambridge, Mass.: MIT Press, 1970), pp. 22–27 and Janice Raymond, *The Transsexual Empire* (Boston: Beacon Press, 1979), p. 114. for articulations of the same view.

Sarah Lucia Hoagland

"Femininity," Resistance and Sabotage

Scientists and other male elite named wimmin "feminine," the most pervasive label infecting our lives. Yet "femininity" is not an empirical concept. It did not arise as a result of, nor is it susceptible to, empirical investigation. It is not based on fact. Instead it is akin to a metaphysical category, and those in power use it to determine perception of fact, to define the social perception of wimmin. Using the feminine stereotype, scientists[1] and conservatives who are not scientists[2] portray female behavior as submissive, and in the process legitimate male domination. I will argue that behaviors typically labeled feminine indicate not submission, but rather *resistance,* to male domination; we will see that the concept "femininity" has been used to obscure and bury female resistance, as well as female autonomy and female bonding.

I have argued elsewhere that "femininity" is not an empirical

This article is a significantly revised version of "On the Status of the Concepts of Masculinity and Femininity" which appeared in Volume 4 of the *Transactions* of the Nebraska Academy of Sciences, printed by the Nebraska Department of Education, Lincoln, 1977. The sabotage thesis was first mentioned in an article which appeared in *Sinister Wisdom,* Vol. 6 (Fall, 1980): 70–2. Printed by permission of *Transactions* and the author.

I wish to express thanks and love to Kate Burke whose sparking and sparkling mind constantly a-mazes me and whose comments have been very helpful in completing this paper.

concept.[3] In the first place particular character traits alleged to fall under the feminine or masculine categories are valued differently depending on whether they apply to wimmin or men. Aggression is regarded as a flaw in wimmin and an asset in men while dependence is regarded as an asset in wimmin but not men. Such valuation indicates at the very least that use of the label "feminine" is prescriptive, not descriptive: when aggression is found among wimmin it is punished. Society attempts to control and limit aggression through social sanctions against those labeled feminine in a way not attempted among those labeled masculine.

More importantly, such traits are not only valued differently, they are *perceived* differently, an indication of the metaphysical nature of femininity. An aggressive man is seen as normal, and a middle class aggressive man is seen as healthy, confident, and ambitious. An aggressive womon, on the other hand, is seen as frustrated if not neurotic, and heterosexual coercion is embedded in the stereotype because such a womon is seen as in need of a "good" (i.e., more aggressive) man.

The metaphysical nature of the feminine stereotype is apparent in the "humorous" characterization of the differences between businessmen and business wimmin who behave in identical ways:[4]

A businessman is aggressive.
A business woman is pushy.
A well dressed businessman is fashionable.
A well dressed business woman is a clothes horse.
He's careful about detail.
She's picky.
He loses his temper because he's involved in his job.
She's bitchy.
He gets depressed from work pressures.
She has menstrual tension.
He's a man of the world.
She's been around.
He's confident.
She's conceited.
He's enthusiastic.
She's emotional.
He isn't afraid to say what he thinks.
She's opinionated.
He's a stern task maker.
She's difficult to work for.

He follows through.
She doesn't know when to quit.
He's firm.
She's stubborn.
He's an authority.
She's a tyrant.

Yet another example is Dory Previn's song, "When a Man Wants A Woman":

When a man wants a woman
He says it's a compliment
He says he's only trying to capture her
To claim her; to tame her
When he wants ev'rything ev'rything of her
Her soul, her love, her life forever and more.
He says he's persuading her
He says he's pursuing her
But when a woman wants a man
He says she's threatening him
He says she's only trying to trap him
To train him, to chain him
When she wants anything anything of him
A look, a touch, a moment of his time
He says she's demanding
He swears she's destroying him
Why is it
When a man wants a woman
He's called a hunter
But when a woman wants a man
She's called a predator

These two examples indicate that identical behavior is perceived to be different depending on whether it is attributed to wimmin or men. In both cases when a womon steps outside the limits of the feminine stereotype she is subject to derision, attack, and denial. To suggest the behavior is qualitatively different begs the question; it presupposes that wimmin and men have different natures prior to investigating the hypothesis. More significantly, such a suggestion fails to consider the context of these perceptions—a society based on the rule of the fathers. Femininity exists to limit wimmin; in these cases we are unable to *perceive* certain behavior outside the feminine stereotype.

In other cases, the behavior is detectable as challenging femininity, but it is denied to be either normal or female. If femininity were an empirical concept then female behavior would provide endless counterexamples to the feminine labeling of wimmin's characters.[5] Empirical concepts are subject to challenge and their applications to refutation. Yet wimmin who act in ways which do not fit the feminine model are not treated by scientists as counterexamples to scientific hypotheses (prejudices, pre-judgments) about wimmin and wimmin's characters. Instead, scientists and others label wimmin whose behavior is clearly not limited by the feminine model "abnormal." Recently an even more insidious move is underfoot in science. Wimmin who will not remain confined to the feminine stereotype are denied our womonhood. For example, pursuing his hypothesis that hormones pass on specific behavioral traits in conformity with sex-role stereotypes, John Money is developing an ideology that masculine minds appear in female bodies. Such a move whitens out, obliterates the concept of a strong, autonomous womon; she is now a male trapped in a female body.[6] In this view, a strong, autonomous womon must really be a man.

In general, scientists and other men in power discredit and attempt to render invisible counterexamples to the feminine stereotype, using "femininity" as a standard of womonhood, femaleness, even though they may differ on a few of the minor particulars as to what exactly constitutes femininity. Measures or standards determine fact, no amount of research into wimmin's "true natures," no appeal to fact, will either confirm or challenge the concept, the label, "femininity." The importance of realizing the coerciveness of "femininity" lies not in the tired male question of whether we can ever "discover" wimmin's "true nature." The importance lies in realizing how "femininity" determines the social perception of wimmin, and how it is used to enforce male domination and heterosexuality.

Characterizations which ordinarily pass under the label "feminine" include: passive, emotional, irrational or even nonrational, unassuming, cooperative (with whom?), unthreatening (to whom?), behind the scenes (whose scenes?), weak, gullible (when?), childlike, infantile. These characterizations present a significant picture of male fantasy. In 1946 Viola Klein documented the fanciful and contradictory nature of the scientific collection of feminine characteristics. For example, she points to a general paradox while discussing Otto Weininger's work: How can one talk about positive male and female characteristics such that each person has a few from both categories while at the same time depicting one set of those characteristics in negative terms, as voids?[7]

More than being contradictory or simply negative, however, the feminine stereotype as applied to wimmin maintains existing lines of power and promotes heterosexual bias by defining wimmin in relation to men and characterizing as normal the womon who remains totally accessible to male authority. A "normal" womon, under the male-identification of wimmin, does not bond with wimmin and she does not remain autonomous. Caroline Whitbeck has isolated three prevailing theories composing the foundation of the feminine characteristics, all of which define wimmin in relation to men: womon as partial man, womon as opposite man, and womon as helpmate to man.[8]

Following this, one of the most pervasive effects of the male naming of wimmin feminine is the obliteration of any conceptual hint of female resistance to male domination, resistance to attempts to limit or control a womon's integrity. One searches in vain for portraits and historical depictions of female autonomy, female resistance, female bonding. Patrihistorians claim that wimmin have remained content with our lot and have accepted male domination throughout time with the exception of a few suffragists and now a few "aberrant" feminists. Yet upon examination it becomes clear that within the confines of the feminine stereotype, no behavior, no set of actions *count* as resistance. Any behavior that cannot be squeezed into the confines of the feminine, passive stereotype has been discounted as an aberration or it has been buried.[9]

If nothing one can point to or even imagine counts as proof against the claim that all (normal) wimmin are feminine and accept male domination, then the claim is not empirical, it is not based on examination of fact. And we are attempting to work with a closed, coercive conceptual system. We have been unable to re-cognize resistance to male domination among wimmin because under the male-identified feminine stereotype, resistance is considered abnormal, an indication of insanity, or incredibly, proof of submission.

For example, acts which the namers use to support the feminine stereotype of white middle-class wimmin, the current paradigm of all womonhood, indicate resistance. Alix Kates Shulman in *Memoirs Of An Ex-Prom Queen,* portrays a "fluffyheaded" housewife who regularly burns the dinner when her husband brings his boss home unexpectedly.[10] And she periodically packs raw eggs in his lunchbox. Such acts are used as "proof" of wimmin's "lesser rational ability" by those in power, but in fact they indicate resistance — sabotage. Such acts may or may not be openly called sabotage by the saboteurs. But wimmin engage in them as an affirmation of existence in a society which denies us recognition independently of a man. When we are isolated, one from another, through heterosexual coercion, these are rational alternatives to untenable situations, to traps, within a patriarchal context.

Donna Deitch's documentary, "Woman to Woman," offers a classic example of sabotage.[11] Four wimmin, two housewives, a daughter, and the interviewer, sit around a kitchen table. One housewife protests that she is not a housewife, that she is not married to the house. The interviewer asks her to say what she does all day. The womon relates that she starts by getting up, feeding her husband, feeding her children, driving them to the school bus, driving her husband to work, returning to do the dishes, make the beds, going out to do the shopping, returning to do a wash. She continues relating her activities for a normal Monday and half of a Tuesday before she stops, shocked, and says: "Wait a minute, I AM married to the house." She complains of difficulty in getting her husband to give her money for the household, of frustration because he nevertheless holds her responsible for running the house, and of degradation because she must go to him, apologetically, at the end of each week to ask for extra money when he could have provided her with sufficient funds at the beginning of each week. Suddenly she gets a gleam in her eye, lowers her voice and leans forward, saying: "Have you ever bought something you didn't need?" Excitement brews and they all lean closer as she states: "You have to know you're alive, you have to make sure you exist." She has separated herself from her husband's perceptions of her; she is not simply an extension of his purposes, of his will, she is reclaiming (some) agency — sabotage.[12] Yet under the feminine stereotype, we are barred from claiming her as a sister re-sister.

Significantly, femininity is used to characterize any group men in power wish to justify dominating. Ten years ago Kate Millett pointed out that femininity characterizes traits that those in power cherish in subordinates.[13] Ten years ago also Naomi Weisstein noted that feminine characteristics add up to typical minority group characteristics.[14] An investigation of the literature shows that Nazis characterized Jews as feminine and used the ideology in the justification of their massacre. Men accused at the Salem witch trials were characterized as feminine.[15] And an investigation of white British anthropological writing reveals that Black South Africans were labeled feminine. The model for oppression in Anglo-European thinking is the male conception of femininity. A feminine being is one who is by nature relatively passive and dependent. It follows that those to whom the label is applied must be seeking protection (domination) by nature and should be subjected to authority "for their own good." "Femininity" portrays those not in power as wanting and needing control. It is a matter of logic, then, that those who refuse control are abnormal.

Consider the fact that white history depicts Black slaves (though not white indentured servants) as lazy, docile, and clumsy on such grounds as that slaves frequently broke tools. Yet a rational womon under slavery, comprehending that her situation is less than human, that she functions as an extension of the will of her master, will not run to pick up tools. She acts instead to differentiate herself from the will of her master, she breaks tools, carries on subversive activities—sabotage. Her master, in turn, perceiving her as subhuman and subrational, names her clumsy, childlike, foolish, perhaps, but not a saboteur.

If officially slaves were subhuman and content with their lot and masters were only acting in slaves' best interest, then any resistance to the system would be depicted by those in power as an abnormality or an indication of madness. Indeed, in recollecting the stories of her grandmother's slave days, Annie Mae Hunt tells us that "If you run off, you was considered sick."[16] That is to say, slaves existed in a Weltanschauung where running away from slavery was perceived as an indication not of (healthy) resistance but of mental imbalance. Such was the extent of control the masters exercised through the power of naming—*nothing* one did could be perceived as resistance. In fact the behaviors of slaves out of which the masters constructed and fed the slave stereotypes provide evidence of resistance and sabotage.[17]

During the Holocaust and, more significantly, after it, in the telling of the stories, Nazis as well as liberal historians have depicted Jews under Hitler's reign of terror as cooperative and willing victims. This stereotype, as is true of the slave stereotype, is still alive today. Yet again, one must ask, what would *count* as resistance? For example, Jews at Auschwitz committing suicide by hurling themselves against an electric fence would be depicted as "willing victims," and such behavior has been used to portray Jews as failing to resist Nazi aggression. In fact, Jews in concentration camps committing suicide were not willing victims. In determining the time of their own deaths they were resisting, interfering with the plans of the masters, exercising choice, and so establishing a self, differentiating themselves from the will of the masters. Holocaust literature is full of indications of Jewish resistance, of sabotage, yet the stereotype of the willing (i.e., feminine) Jewish victim persists today.[18] Again, "femininity" is used to obscure resistance.

Consider one paradigm of femininity, the white, upper-class Victorian lady. In *The Yellow Wallpaper,* Charlotte Perkins Gilman portrayed conditions faced by such wimmin in the 1880s.[19] These conditions included a prescription of total female passivity by mind gynecologists such as S. Weir Mitchell, prescriptions arising as a result of male scientists' sudden interest in wimmin as the first wave of feminism attracted their attention, prescriptions enforced by those in control. The heroine is taken by her husband to a summer home for rest. He locks her in a nursery with bars on the windows, a bed bolted to the floor, and hideous wallpaper, shredded in spots. He rebuts her despair with the rhetoric of protection, refusing to indulge her "whims" when she protests the room's atrocity. He also stifles all other attempts at creativity, flying into a rage when he discovers her writing in her diary. In the end, she manages to crawl behind the wallpaper and escape into "madness." Charlotte Perkins Gilman shows us a womon with every avenue of creativity, of integrity, patronizingly and paternalistically cut off for "her own good," to "protect" her, and we watch her slowly construct her resistance. Not surprisingly, male scientists and doctors of the day saw nothing more in the story than a testament to "feminine" insanity.[20]

Resistance, in other words, may even take the form of insanity when one is isolated within the confines of male domination and all means of maintaining integrity have been systematically cut off. Under such conditions insanity becomes a more viable alternative than submission. Mary's long descent into oblivion on morphine in *A Long Day's Journey Into Night* is another example of resistance to domination. But the coerciveness of "femininity" dictates that such behavior be perceived as part of the "mysterious" and "intricate" nature of womon rather than recognized as resistance.

Significantly, one and the same word governs insanity and anger: madness. As Phyllis Chesler has documented, mind gynecologists call wimmin mad whose behavior they can no longer understand as functioning in relation to men.[21] On the other hand, the *Oxford English Dictionary* defines "mad" as it relates to anger as "ungovernable rage or fury." One must ask, "ungovernable" by whom? Madness in anger and madness in "insanity" indicate that men have lost control.[22] When wimmin are labeled mad, it is often because we have become useless to men or a threat to male supremacy.

Thus, to maintain the feminine stereotype men will characterize more obvious forms of resistance as insanity when wimmin engage in them. Thus insanity becomes a part of the "feminine" nature and resistance is rendered institutionally invisible. Just as slaves who ran off were perceived as insane, so are wimmin who fight back against battering husbands. Wimmin who kill long-term battering husbands are, for the most part, forced to use the plea of insanity rather than that of self-defense. The most famous case is that of Francine Hughes who killed her husband after fourteen years of beatings and psychological abuse.[23]

However, institutionally characterizing wimmin who fight back as insane was still not enough. Perceiving the plea of insanity as a license to kill even though it means incarceration for an unspecified amount of time, media men began a campaign against battered wimmin who fight back, depicting them as getting away with murder.[24] Funds for battered wives shelters are now being withdrawn on the grounds that the shelters break up the family. And agencies working on "domestic violence" focus on preserving the family intact, burying the slave conditions of wimmin within the nuclear family by obliterating the distinction between aggressor and victim.[25] Once again, the conceptual framework that renders female resistance invisible comes full circle. The concept of femininity not only blocks any social perception of female resistance, it lays the groundwork for denying the problem of male domination when female resistance threatens to break through the stereotype and become visible.

I have stressed the fact that feminine behaviors indicate resistance to point to the phenomenal reversals those in power have perpetuated. To dominate a people one must first use force, but eventually one must find other means.[26] One effective means of maintaining power is to rob the oppressed of any positive self concept and so prevent us from identifying with each other. Then one can portray us as accepting, indeed desiring our lot, and each individual sees herself as alone and abnormal when she resists. The feminine stereotype is the most effective tool that exists for this purpose, and scientists who "investigate" femininity under the guise of establishing social fact perpetuate and legislate patriarchal value, both male domination and compulsory heterosexuality.[27]

This is true to such an extent that scientists *condemn* female competence and autonomy as threatening to males and subversive to the patriarchal family, hence as socially undesirable. Thus Daniel P. Moynihan popularized the theory of the Black matriarch who castrates Black men, and implied that for Black men to claim their manhood, Black wimmin must step behind them and become submissive.[28]

Female bonding is so threatening that it is altogether erased. For example, one will find the term "maiden aunt" employed in sociobiology in a lesbian context, burying the idea of a female rejecting a male and promoting the idea that a female is unable to attract one. The latter feeds an unsupported theory of male dominance while the former does not.[29] Among humans, Lesbians are either depicted as men or are rendered invisible.

As a final note, I wish to merely indicate an additional consequence of the heterosexual coerciveness of "femininity." The feminine stereotype provides a basis for the ideology of special protection for wimmin, thus enforcing heterosexuality. For men to maintain the conceptual framework in which they can see themselves as protectors, they must establish and maintain an atmosphere in which wimmin are in danger; they must create our victim (feminine) status. To maintain the ideology of special protection of wimmin, men have portrayed us as helpless, defenseless, innocent — victims, and thereby, targets to be attacked. If we act in self-defense and thus step out of the feminine role, becoming on their terms active and "guilty," men step up overt physical violence against us to reaffirm our victim status. When they cannot control us through protection, the safety valve they fall back on is overt violence, predation (pornography, rape, "domestic violence" [wifebeating], "incest" [daughter rape]). In short, the ideology of special protection of wimmin emerging from femininity sets us up as targets which in turn compels us to turn to men for protection and enforces heterosexuality.[30]

The patriarchal naming of wimmin feminine goes even further. The separate valuation of aggression in men and wimmin affects what is tolerated in society in terms of violence. Male violence against wimmin is an integral part of society, it is expected that men will rape, batter, maim, torture, mutilate, and murder wimmin. Rape, wifebeating and "incest" are at best ignored. But, as noted above, wimmin who fight back face the full brutality of the system.

"Femininity," I have argued, is a label whereby one group of people are defined in relation to another in such a way that domination and submission are portrayed as part of the biological essence of those involved. Under the feminine stereotype, a portrait of naive contentment with being controlled is painted such that resistance is rendered invisible or perceived as abnormal, mad, or of no consequence. Men of minority groups such as Blacks and Jews are slowly and painfully emerging from under the domination of femininity.[31] Unfortunately they often do so by laying claim to "masculinity" which does not challenge the dualism that justifies oppression. Heterosexist ideology and the failure to examine the coercive conceptual framework of "femininity" keeps wimmin locked in an ideology of male domination. Be we Black, Jewish, WASP, Iranian, Hispanic, Native American, Asian American, or a member of any of the many other cultures in which wimmin survive, be we working class, middle class, or upper class,[32] within our various situations we remain saddled with the label "femininity." Female resistance, female autonomy and Lesbian bonding do not exist within patriarchal ontology. Instead scientists and other male elite have limited the boundaries of female behavior and set us up for attack, control, and domination.

NOTES

1. See, for example, E.O. Wilson, *Sociobiology: The New Synthesis* (Cambridge, Mass.: Harvard University Press, 1975).

2. See, for example, Marabel Morgan, *The Total Woman,* and *Total Joy* (Old Tappan, N.J.: Flemming H. Revell Co., 1972 and 1976.)

3. Sarah L. Hoagland, "On the Status of the Concepts of Masculinity and Femininity," *Transactions of the Nebraska Academy of Sciences* 4 (August 1977): 169–72. The argument that follows is an extension of the arguments I developed in this paper.

4. Loosely adapted from "The Executive Woman," *Family Circle,* May 1976.

5. See footnote 4.

6. See the discussion of Money's thesis in Janice G. Raymond, *The Transsexual Empire: The Making Of The She-Male* (Boston: Beacon Press, 1979), Chapter II.

7. Viola Klein, *The Feminine Character* (Chicago: University of Illinois Press, 1971), p. 60.

8. Caroline Whitbeck, "Theories of Sex Difference," in *Women and Philosophy: Toward A Theory Of Liberation,* ed. Carol C. Gould and Marx W. Wartofsky (New York: G.P. Putnam's Sons, 1976), pp. 54–81.

9. For example, the Amazons are repeatedly depicted as mythical creatures (with attendant male fantasies such as the alleged removing of one breast) even though there is proof of their existence both in Africa and Asia. For example, in the Fall of 1979, Soviet archaeologists uncovered the remains of a tribe of Amazons that lived 1200 years ago in Balabany in the Soviet Republic of Moldavia (*Chicago Sun-Times,* September 9, 1979). I have yet to see further information on this anywhere.

10. Alix Kates Shulman, *Memoirs Of An Ex-Prom Queen* (New York: Bantam, 1973).

11. Copies of the film can be obtained from Donna Deitch, 3644 Carnation Avenue, Los Angeles, CA 90026.

12. This material is taken from a paper I presented at the AAAS, January 1979, in which I argue that there is patriarchal deception in science at all three levels: naming, describing, and explaining. I also argue that the problem emanates not simply from observer bias but lies at the heart of scientific methodology. That paper, "Naming, Describing, Explaining: Deception and Science," is available through the Eric Clearing House (Information Analysis Center for Science, Mathematics, and Environmental Education, The Ohio State University, 1700 Chambers Road, 3rd floor, Columbus, Ohio, 43212).

13. Kate Millett, *Sexual Politics* (New York: Avon, 1971), p. 47.

14. Naomi Weisstein, "Psychology Constructs the Female, or: The Fantasy Life of the Male Psychologist," reprint (Boston: New England Free Press, 1968).

15. Research of Betty Carpenter, personal communication, Spring 1978, Lincoln, Nebraska.

16. Ruth Winegarten, "I Am Annie Mae: The Personal Story of a Black Texas Woman," *Chrysalis* 10 (Spring 1980): 15.
17. Since formulating the thesis, I have come across documented evidence of it. See, *Puttin' On Ole Massa,* ed. Gilbert Osofsky (New York: Harper and Row, 1969); *Great Slave Narratives,* ed. Arna Bontemps (Boston: Beacon Press, 1969); and *A Documentary History Of Slavery In North America,* ed. Willie Lee Rose (New York: Oxford University Press, 1976).
18. See Simone Wallace, Ellen Ledley, Paula Tobin, letter to *Off Our Backs* (December 1979): 28.
19. Charlotte Perkins Gilman, *The Yellow Wallpaper* (New York: The Feminist Press, 1973).
20. Elaine R. Hedges, "Afterword," Charlotte Perkins Gilman, op. cit.
21. Phyllis Chesler, *Women And Madness* (Garden City, N.Y.: Doubleday and Co., 1972).
22. When reading between the lines, when claiming wimmin from the past, we must examine alternatives available and in that context understand the behavior. Thus insanity itself can be a form of resistance. In addition, other behavior is depicted as insanity. As a result, there is a fine line that fades between insanity and behavior of the resister who is able to maintain the confidence of her perceptions. If everyone around you perceives your behavior in a light other than your intention, your perceptions struggle in a very different world.
23. Ann Jones, *Women Who Kill* (New York: Holt, Rinehart and Winston, 1980), pp. 285–91.
24. Ibid., p. 291.
25. Kathleen Barry, *Female Sexual Slavery* (Englewood Cliffs, N.J.: Prentice-Hall, 1979), p. 142.
26. Pat Robinson (et al.), "A Historical and Critical Essay for Black Women in the Cities," *The Black Woman,* ed. Toni Cade (New York: New American Library, 1970), pp. 198–210.
27. See Adrienne Rich, "Compulsory Heterosexuality and Lesbian Existence," *Signs* 5 (Summer 1980): 631–60. Of interest also is Marilyn Frye, "Assignment: NWSA-Bloomington-1980, Speak on 'Lesbian Perspectives on Women's Studies,'" *Sinister Wisdom* 14 (Summer 1980): 3–7.
28. See Jean Carey Bond and Pat Peery, "Is the Black Male Castrated?" *The Black Woman,* ed. Toni Cade (New York: New American Library, 1970), pp. 113–19.
29. See Sarah Lucia Hoagland, "Androcentric Rhetoric in Sociobiology," *Women's Studies International Quarterly* 3, nos. 2/3 (1980): 285–93.
30. See Sarah Lucia Hoagland, "Violence, Victimization, Violation," *Sinister Wisdom* 15, forthcoming.
31. This is not to say, of course, that the *experience* of Black men or

Jewish men has been identical to that of white wimmin or Black wimmin or Jewish wimmin. It is not to say, for example, that Black male slaves and white wimmin who were wives of Southern plantation owners had the same experiences. Black slaves were perceived as beasts. If wives of Southern plantation owners were perceived as animals (pets), still there were significant differences. Even poor white Southern wimmin and upper class Southern white wimmin did not have the same experiences. My point here is simply that the concept of femininity was used in the justification of the Weltanschauung of dominance and submission in such a way that resistance, in all its various forms, becomes invisible.

32. See Kathleen Barry, *Female Sexual Slavery* (Englewood Cliffs, N.J.: Prentice-Hall, 1979), Chapter 7.

Alan Soble

The Political Epistemology of "Masculine" and "Feminine"

> Depressed woman to her lover: "If we're in love,
> then why are we so unhappy?"
> Man: "Wait. I have a better idea. Maybe we're
> not unhappy."
> Hample,
> *Inside Woody Allen*

This paper is both an essay in the philosophy of the social sciences and an essay in political philosophy. This combination is necessary because the former depends on the latter, or so I shall argue. Hence the expression in the title: *political* epistemology; there is not, and can not be, any other kind. There is no such thing, practically or theoretically, as "neutral" research. But it does not follow from the normative basis of the social sciences that they are also "nonempirical" and "unscientific." This conclusion is not new, but it does bear repeating, and I offer here more reasons for asserting it.

My discussion is dialectical. I consider, in Section I, a number of reasons for holding that the social sciences are "nonempirical" and/or "unscientific." I deny the power of these reasons to

Copyright © 1980 by Alan Soble. Printed by permission of the author.

I thank Shirley Laska (Sociology, The University of New Orleans), Alison Jaggar (Philosophy, The University of Cincinnati) and the editor, Mary Vetterling-Braggin, for their assistance. My views should not be attributed to them.

establish the desired conclusion, primarily by relying on Ernest Nagel's distinction between characterization and appraisal. But I argue that the "essential contestability" of social scientific concepts (an idea due to W. B. Gallie and Alasdair MacIntyre) undermines the usefulness of Nagel's distinction for preserving the empirical basis of the social sciences. Indeed, the essential contestability of social scientific concepts raises the central question about the relation between the normative dimension of the social sciences and their scientific credentials. I answer this latter question, in Section II, by elucidating the logical relations among characterization, essential contestability, and the logic of scientific research (in particular, the logic of falsification). My conclusions are that (1) in both the social and the natural sciences, political decisions are *unavoidably* the epistemological groundwork of empirical research, and that, therefore, (2) the empirical nature of social science is not undermined by the essential contestability of its concepts. I briefly discuss this political epistemology in Section III and I show how it provides an interesting reading of Marx's declaration—the point is not to interpret the world, but to change it.[1] Finally, I draw out some implications of this political epistemology for the value of social scientific research conducted by women or carried out according to "the feminist perspective."

A word about the other half of my title, "masculine" and "feminine." Consider the claims that all (or most) men are masculine, that all (or most) women are feminine, and that all masculine persons are aggressive. Are these claims true, are they false, or is their truth-value indeterminate? Are these claims empirical and testable, or are they thoroughly evaluative? These are not idle questions. The way in which they are answered is a symbol, if not a symptom, of the sort of society we live in; at the same time, how we answer them will depend on epistemological considerations which are, if I am right, political.

I. CHALLENGING AND DEFENDING SOCIAL SCIENCE

(A) *Suppose* that "masculine" is shorthand for "analytic, self-reliant, aggressive, and assertive," and that "feminine" similarly stands for a list of property terms which, for the most part, are either incompatible or incommensurable with those properties constitutive of masculinity.[2] Now, to call a male person "masculine" or "aggressive" is commonly, in our society, to point to an asset, to praise, or to flatter him. But when "masculine" and "aggressive" are used to speak about a female person, they usually serve to point to a flaw, to criticize, or to raise suspicions about her.[3] Similarly, to call a male person "feminine" or "emotional" is commonly to criticize him, while using these same words to describe a female person is to approve. "Masculine," "feminine," and their component terms, then, are strongly evaluative because a value judgment is embodied in any claim using them. Thus the terms could never be used in truly empirical research. (Here we have an often-heard challenge to the credentials of the social sciences.)

We could defend research which uses these terms by arguing that even though "masculine" and "aggressive" are thoroughly evaluative, the values embodied in their use are objectively verifiable. On many cognitivist accounts of the meaning of normative terms, sentences employing "masculine" or "aggresive" are either true or false, and verifiable, even though these sentences state normative views. I do not think, however, that this defense is a very helpful one, because it must demonstrate that some cognitivist account (say, naturalism or neo-descriptivism) is correct. I doubt that such a demonstration will soon (or ever) be forthcoming.

The response which I wish to make relies on a distinction proposed by the positivist philosopher of science Ernest Nagel. Nagel distinguishes between two kinds of judgments, *characterizing* judgments and *appraising* judgments.[4] To make a characterizing judgment is to decide whether or not to classify something as an object or act of a certain kind. Should we call this wooden object a chair or a stool? Because the criteria for identifying chairs and stools are somewhat fuzzy, for some objects a judgment is involved in placing items in one category or the other. (Clearly, similar judgments are required to set up the identifying criteria initially. For this reason, in this paper I will speak interchangeably of problems of characterization and problems of setting up identifying criteria.) Is this act an aggressive act, or is it something quite different — mock or play aggression, satire, a defensive move, even deceptively passive? In making an appraising judgment, in contrast, one is claiming that the object or act is good or bad, objectionable or welcome, favorable or unfavorable. Thus, given a piece of behavior, we can ask two questions about it: first, should this act be categorized, for example, as an act of aggression (or is it something else?), and second, is this act commendable or repugnant (either in spite of, or on account of, its aggressiveness, and perhaps even regard-

less of how it is characterized)? With the first question we are inquiring about the proper identification of the act; with the second
we are inquiring about its worth, value, morality, aesthetics.

Nagel's point is that it does not follow from the fact that a
term is often used to make appraising judgments (as in the uses
of "masculine" and "aggressive" which embody value
judgments), that the term cannot be employed in purely
characterizing judgments. Therefore we can admit that to call a
male person "aggressive" is commonly to praise him, without being compelled to admit that the term is so value-laden that it is
futile to employ it in social science research. Indeed, the very act
of condemning a female person by calling her "aggressive"
presupposes that we have a criterion for the identification of aggressive acts or persons, a criterion used in a characterization of
her behavior and one which is both temporally and logically
prior to the appraising judgment that *her* aggression is a flaw.
"Aggressive" can be used in purely characterizing contexts,
without *entailing* any particular appraising judgment[5] (and
without committing the user to a view as to how such appraisals
might be grounded meta-ethically).

(B) What is the nature of the judgments made in characterization (or, equivalently, in setting up identifying criteria)? Does
Nagel's distinction between characterizing a person as masculine
and appraising him or her as masculine succeed in eliminating
bothersome value judgments? There are a number of arguments
which can be offered on behalf of a "no" answer. I want to
discuss these arguments, even though they do not demonstrate
their intended conclusion, because we can learn something important about the social sciences from them. Let us consider the
problems of constructing identifying criteria for "masculine"
and "feminine" and of deciding whether any person is masculine
or feminine.

(1) Immediately there will be some uncertainty as to whether a
person is masculine if (and only if) he or she exhibits *all* or only
most of the properties listed (e.g., aggressiveness, self-reliance).
A judgment is needed for the application of the term: should the
identifying criterion be "all" or "most," and if the latter, exactly
how many? Second, even if a person exhibits all the properties
on the list, it is possible that he or she does not exhibit some of
them to a high enough degree. Thus, for both quantitative and
qualitative reasons—how many properties must be exhibited,
and to what extent do they have to be exhibited, in order that
"masculine" be applicable?—some judgments are required. Note

that the same point can be made about the component terms themselves, which fact shows that the semantic phenomena we are dealing with are not restricted to "masculine" but extend to all the important terms in the social sciences. "Aggressive," for example, is itself shorthand for a list of properties, dispositions, and behaviors. And judgments are involved in deciding how many of these items must be exhibited, and how frequently and to what extent, in order to apply the term.

There is also the task of deciding what particular properties are components of "masculine" and "feminine." There are no brute facts which dictate that certain sets of property terms, rather than other sets, are the components. There is no guarantee that any cluster of component properties selected will be found in enough people (or in enough stages of the lives of persons) in order that "masculine" can usefully stand for a set of property terms.[6] But if these sorts of qualitative and quantitative problems are the only judgmental weakness in characterization, we have not found a very powerful reason to condemn the social sciences. For example, it will not do to complain that "the differential designation of behaviors and personality characteristics as masculine or feminine" is a piece of fallacious "stereotypy" *simply* on the grounds that none of the component properties are "exclusively in the repertoire of one sex and not the other."[7] Whether such differential designation—the construction of lists of component properties for "masculine" and "feminine"—is objectionable (and "mere stereotypy") cannot be decided only by showing what is obvious, that the categories are not perfect. In addition, it must be argued that the imperfections are (or are not) greater than a specific "acceptable level" of tolerance. The scientific community uses established standards of tolerance for cases such as this.[8]

(2) Another argument is that various biases infect the selection of identifying criteria. Consider this typical claim from the social sciences:

The term *aggression* is used to apply loosely to a collection of behaviors whose general intent is to threaten or hurt another individual. In animal studies it usually covers acts of physical threat or attack, while in human studies it can mean these as well as negativistic, hostile acts, quarreling, and verbal abuse. . . . The evidence is very persuasive that males are more aggressive than females are.[9]

The objection that could be raised here is that *if* aggression has been defined in male terms, *if* the identifying criteria of "aggressive acts" or "aggressive persons" have been constructed under the influence of paradigmatic male aggression, then the claim that men are more aggressive than women is a trivial tautology masquerading as an empirical truth.[10]

This objection is very important in alerting social scientists to the dangers involved in selecting and applying identifying criteria which are too narrow or which are simply reproductions of their prior beliefs about persons and their properties. Whether and to what extent female persons are seen as aggressive depends crucially on the identifying criterion of "aggression," and a prior belief in the nonaggressiveness of female persons can lead to lopsided criteria.[11] But it does not follow that characterization judgments are by their nature necessarily infected with unavoidable mistakes or blindnesses. The very fact that some persons are able to discover the biases in identifying criteria selected by other persons shows that we are not dealing with concepts which are necessarily suspicious. What the objection might succeed in showing is that social science must be receptive to the points of view of persons who either have different beliefs or who are not prone to the same biases. (I discuss the value of alternative viewpoints in Section III (B).) But the objection does not show that the distinction between characterization and appraisal is unhelpful. Indeed, it apparently presupposes that distinction in allowing that characterization judgments are amenable to correction and improvement.

(3) By pointing out that aggression in male persons is commonly considered an asset and that aggression in female persons a flaw, it might further be argued that such double standards in *appraisal* undermine the adequacy of characterization or in other ways weaken the credentials of the social sciences. For example, if social scientists believe that aggression in female persons is a fault, they might construct identifying criteria which leave no room for it, or they might, even when using adequate identifying criteria, fail to see that aggression.[12] Or if female subjects know that their aggression is commonly perceived as a fault, and if male subjects know that their aggression is a virtue, and if these subjects behave in experiments as they think they *ought* to, then social science will not accurately record the distribution of aggression.[13] But these problems with research, while very important and occasionally insidious, do not prove that adequate characterization cannot be done, or that deficient characterizations are not correctible. Indeed, one way to prevent these errors is to insist on a more self-conscious appreciation of

the distinction between characterization and appraisal. Furthermore, without this distinction we probably could not make sense of why these errors are errors at all.[14]

(C) *Nevertheless,* all is not well with the distinction between characterization and appraisal. Nagel's major example of a concept which can be involved in both characterization and appraisal indicates that he did not fully appreciate his own suggestion that characterizations, especially in the social sciences, might rely on value judgments. His example is the medical notion of "anemia."[15] Some uses of "anemic" are appraisals: a person who is anemic is in an undesirable state, is ill, or abnormal, or unhealthy, and perhaps even unreliable, a burden, unfortunate, or pitiable. But "anemic" can also be used without committing the user to this excess baggage, when the user means simply that the person's red blood cell count is below a certain level. On Nagel's view a characterizing judgment is involved in the decision about how low this count must be before the term "anemic" can be applied. But this is such a weak sense in which a term depends on judgments that it could never be used in an argument attempting to show that value judgments or evaluations in the social sciences undermine their empirical nature. Nagel's example of anemia conceals the problems arising when we consider the characterization of items dealt with in the social sciences, like aggression and masculinity.

The notion of concepts which are "essentially contestable" can be seen as correcting Nagel's understatement of the case that value judgments are involved in characterizations and in setting up identifying criteria. A concept is essentially contestable when in principle there is no single correct answer to these questions: (1) is this item to be characterized as a thing of *this* kind (i.e., as instantiating this concept), or as a thing of this *other* kind (i.e., as not instantiating the concept in question)? and (2) — which is equivalent — is *this* the analysis of the concept, or is *this* the identifying criterion, which should be used to decide which objects instantiate the concept?[16]

Consider the terms "art," "science," and "educational institution." All can be used in characterizations and appraisals. But the characterization of "science" is not as clear-cut as the characterization of "anemia." Suppose we were thinking about astrology. We could ask at least these two questions: first, does astrology count as a science? and, second, is astrology worthwhile, laudable, and so forth (because it is a science, or despite the fact that it is not)? The first question is the important one. Deciding whether astrology is a science is not like the decision as to how low the red blood cell count has to be in order to apply "anemic." The criteria which divide the sciences from the non-sciences are qualitatively different from the kind of criterion used to divide anemic from nonanemic states. In the latter case we settle on a number, or a range, not arbitrarily, but still a simple number representing years of experience diagnosing and treating patients. In the former case, a standard of performance or of excellence is involved; something counts as a science only if it measures up to this standard. At a certain point we cease to say that an item is bad science or science done badly and say, instead, that it is not science at all. Really bad art no longer counts as art. An educational institution which fails to satisfy certain standards of performance is not merely an inefficient or poor educational institution, but cannot be categorized as an educational institution at all. Thus the characterization of the items studied in the social sciences are very substantially value-laden. Consider "art." Suppose we wanted to formulate generalizations about women's contribution to art throughout history. If we were to count as art objects only, say, painting and sculpture, then men turn out to be more artistic than women. On the other hand, if we were to include as art objects "domestic artifacts: quilts, letters, diaries, lullabyes, gardens,"[17] then women turn out to be massive contributors to art through history. It is essentially contestable whether to include these items as art objects. (This example is very close to one of Gallie's: are "egalitarian" societies democracies? are "self-ruled" societies democracies? or are only "majoritarian" societies democracies?) Furthermore, it will not do to include letters *simpliciter*. Even if letters (and so forth) were the kinds of things which were candidates for being art objects, surely not all letters *are* art objects. Only "good" letters, letters which satisfied some standard of artistic excellence, would actually be art objects. The selection of this standard is fully a normative enterprise. This is why characterization depends on full-blown value judgments and why these and other concepts in the social sciences are essentially contestable. There is no decision procedure for uniquely establishing the standards of performance of excellence presupposed in characterization.

Note that even when taking essential contestability into account, we can still maintain the general distinction between the use of a term in characterization and its use in an appraisal. The kind of value judgment involved in setting up identifying criteria or in characterization is a very specific and peculiar value judgment: which standard of excellence should be employed; does this item X meet the standards of performance which characterize things of type Y? One can supply answers to these questions without being committed to using the term in any of its (other) appraising senses. But that characterization depends on normative judgments seems to provide more than enough reason to conclude that social science is ultimately "nonempirical." If "masculine" and "aggressive" are essentially contestable, should they not be eliminated from the social sciences in order to protect what remains? In Section II (C) I will argue that such plausible line of thought is wrong.

II. CHARACTERIZATION, ESSENTIAL CONTESTABILITY, AND THE LOGIC OF SCIENCE

(A) Consider the generalization $(x)(Ax \rightarrow Bx)$,[18] which means that anything which is A (or has property A) is also B (or has property B). In order to discover the truth-value of this generalization, one must at least examine something one knows is A (or has A). If this particular something is also B (or has B), then the generalization has been confirmed; if it is not B (or does not have B), then the generalization has been falsified. "Has been falsified," however, is ambiguous. In one sense, when a particular has been found which is A but not B, the generalization has been *logically* falsified. But "has been falsified" can also mean that persons have accepted the counterexample as bona fide and have rejected the generalization. In this sense falsification is a practice, an action, or a decision, rather than, as in the first sense, a logical relationship between the hypothesis (a sentence) and evidence.[19] Many of the interesting questions in the philosophy of science arise because in the face of a logical falsification a practical falsification need not follow. This is a claim not only about the logical relationship between practical and logical falsification, but also about the history and sociology of science as a human enterprise.

It is no overstatement to say that violent debates have occurred (and still do) over whether a particular logical falsification should or should not be followed by a practical falsification. Defenders of a generalization who refuse to reject it in practice when confronted with logical falsification are accused of special pleading, dogmatism, and intellectual dishonesty. Alternatively they can be praised for having the courage of their convictions or for not giving up the ball game until the last batter has been retired. On the other side, those who want to reject the generalization in practice can be seen either as the real proponents of truth and clarity or as witless followers of fads who abandon theories prematurely and whimsically.

The difficulty of deciding when a practical falsification should follow a logical falsification can be seen by considering one possible position about the relationship between them: *purism*.[20] On the purist thesis *all* logical falsifications must be followed by practical falsification. But logical falsification cannot be taken as a sufficient condition for practical falsification, for on that criterion very few generalizations and none of the interesting theories we have in the various sciences would survive or would even have been proposed and investigated in the first place. Every theory "suffers" from some discrepancies between its predictions and what is observed to be the case—to insist on a perfect match (purism) would be to jettison all science, both natural and social. There have been many theories which when first proposed were already faced with logical falsifications, but which eventually became the predominant beliefs of society and of scientists even though some logical falsifications and "anomalies" *persisted*.[21] To insist on the purist relationship would effectively halt the introduction of new (and *possibly* better) theories,[22] and would force us to abandon all current theories. Logical falsification is ubiquitous.[23]

It is therefore a weak critique of social scientific studies of masculinity and femininity to say *only* that "the presence of counterexamples has not stopped florid and overarching theories of the natural or biological basis of male privilege from proliferating,"[24] for the existence of counterexamples (logical falsifications) cannot be sufficient for rejecting a theory or for refusing to create a new one. Sarah Hoagland similarly relies on the purist thesis to criticize social science when she argues that "masculine" and "feminine" are not empirical because counterexamples to claims about masculinity and femininity are not accepted, in practice, as real counterexamples. She writes:

. . . the easiest way to detect the status of a concept is to form a generalization and test it by counterexamples. If a concept is empirical in nature, that is, susceptible to research, the generalization will be susceptible to refutation.[25]

But Hoagland does realize that this criterion is inadequate when she continues: "there are limits to discarding counterexamples, beyond which they become significant. In the case of investigations of differences between men and women. . . , the discarding of counterexamples . . . is carried to extremes."[26] Hoagland does not, however, spell out when such discarding does and does not go beyond "acceptable limits." To complain that in the social science of masculinity and femininity the discarding of counterexamples is too "extreme" is only to recognize the problem and not to provide an answer.[27]

(B) In order to test the generalization $(x)(Ax \rightarrow Bx)$, we need to *know* that the particular under examination is A or has A. We need to be able to identify cases of that which is referred to by the antecedent of the conditional.[28] The testing procedure, then, is only as reliable as the procedure for identifying the item in question; a logical falsification is only as reliable as the identification it presupposes. These identifications, or characterizations, are both temporally and logically prior to the testing procedure. It is useless to test the claim that all grass is green unless one already knows what counts as a case of grass (or of green). Furthermore, one must be able to identify grass independently of the suspicion that all grass is green; one must look for properties of grass other than its suspected greenness to identify it. The basis of the testing procedure, then, is identification and characterization. That which permits us to test generalizations — and that which thereby allows us to treat the generalizations as empirical — is the identifying criterion. A decision about how to characterize the items being studied provides the required groundwork for carrying out empirical research. The fact that the credibility of empirical investigation depends on the adequacy of characterization (indeed: that the very possibility of empirical investigation depends on formulating identifying criteria) is the reason that the "essential contestabiliy" of social science concepts is such an important issue.

In the face of a logical falsification one is not compelled to falsify the generalization in practice. One *could* simply ignore the logical falsification; one could argue that the logical falsification is trivial because the generalization has already been logically confirmed innumerable times; one might hope that the logical falsification will "disappear," and so forth. This type of response to a logical falsification looks very suspicious, and were it not for the fact that occasionally in the history of science such tactics have been vindicated in retrospect, we could safely reject them. But never mind; this type of response to a logical falsification — this strategy for refusing to follow a logical falsification with a practical falsification — is hardly as interesting as the strategy suggested by the logical dependence of empirical investigation upon characterization. Because a logical falsification is only as reliable as the adequacy of the characterization it presupposes, one can refuse to turn a logical falsification into a practical falsification if one has reasons for doubting that the item studied has been characterized correctly,[29] or, even if *it* has been characterized correctly, if one has reasons for supposing that some other identifying criterion should have been employed or should now be developed and employed.

Consider, as an example, this claim:

We cannot argue that biological aggressiveness in human males prevents nurturance, since boys in many societies, and men in our own and elsewhere, can provide anything from occasional to extensive care of young children.[30]

The author is disputing the generalization that human males, because (or when) they are naturally aggressive, do not have nurturing capabilities; she does so by exhibiting counterexamples, by pointing out the existence of human males who provide "occasional to extensive care" of children. But one who wanted to defend the generalization could do so, or one could prevent the movement from logical to practical falsification by saying that the *care* provided by these male persons is not precisely *nurturance,* that their care is *not good enough* to qualify as nurturance (perhaps it is only "tending to" or "looking after"), or that even though behaviorally their care is apparently nurturance, it is not accompanied by the psychological dispositions or attitudes which are necessary for "true" nurturing capability.[31]

The generalization, therefore, can be protected from logical falsification by insisting on a narrow analysis of nurturance, i.e., by adjusting the concepts used in the generalization.[32] Whether the generalization emerges as true or as false will depend on the criteria by which nurturance is identified. This means that the *truth-value* of the generalization will depend on the outcome of a *normative* debate (is the care "good" enough to count as nurturance?). Finally, this means that the truth-value of the generalization will depend on a characterization which is essentially contestable. Is this not sufficient to show that the social sciences, to the extent that they employ concepts like these, are nonempirical and unscientific? Does this not mean that we are better off saying that many claims in the social sciences have no determinate truth-value at all? If "acceptable limits" to counterexamples can only be decided by normative debate—if at all!—does this not mean that the challenge to the social sciences has been successful? We have arrived at the same plausible conclusion we arrived at in Section I.

(C) MacIntyre agrees that the essential contestability of social science concepts *presents* a challenge to their scientific credentials: ". . . we do not know how to decide whether a given alleged instance of a phenomenon is to be treated as a counterexample to a proposed generalization or as not an example of the phenomenon at all, because debate remains open about which the central, standard, and paradigmatic instances of the phenomenon are."[33] MacIntyre then throws up his hands in despair and *concedes* the success of the challenge. But this is much too hasty. Many of the concepts in the natural sciences are just as essentially contestable as the concepts in the social sciences, although not for the same reason. And if it is the bare fact of essential contestability which presents the challenge, natural science is no more immune from criticism than is social science. Even though some of the concepts of the natural sciences are essentially contestable, and even though there is no unique procedure for setting "acceptable limits" to counterexamples, progress has been made in the natural sciences because, as a matter of historical fact, various political considerations have worked to *make* logically contestable concepts uncontested, to establish more-or-less by fiat "acceptable limits" to counterexamples, and to dictate when logical falsification must be followed by practical falsification. The concepts of the natural sciences which are essentially contestable are contestable *not* because (like the concepts in the social sciences) they depend on normative judgments about standards of excellence.[34] Nevertheless, because in the natural sciences political considerations play a necessary role in *forcing* a solution to the problem of setting "acceptable limits" to counterexamples, these considerations are essential in allowing empirical research to get going upon a foundation of uncontested—but still logically contestable—characterizations.

Another example from the social sciences will indicate the

epistemological role that characterization plays in empirical research:

> . . . the fact that women who are not lesbians greatly enjoy sex with other women was plainly evident at every party we went to.[35]

"Some women who are not lesbians enjoy sex with women" will be true or false depending on what criteria are used for identifying lesbians (or for identifying cases of "great enjoyment"). If a lesbian is a woman who enjoys sex with women, then the generalization is false; if a lesbian is a woman who considers herself a lesbian, then it is true; if a lesbian is a woman who never has or enjoys sex with men, then its truth-value is unclear; and if a lesbian is a woman with a certain political perspective and life-style, then it *might* be true. The criteria for deciding which persons are gay are notoriously difficult to formulate without any analytic problems or philosophical puzzles whatsoever. But if we are to make *any* significant generalizations about gay persons, sooner or later we must settle on a characterization.[36] The characterization is the basis of any empirical research, and this applies equally to the social and the natural sciences. If natural science has seemed to avoid this problem because of its "internal logic," that is an illusion. For various reasons, political considerations have been more successful in forcing decisions at the foundation of the natural sciences than they have been in the social sciences.

For MacIntyre, debate about characterization in the natural sciences comes to an end, but in the social sciences essential contestability prevents such a happy outcome. In MacIntyre's view, then, a large part of social science, in which the foundation continues to crumble, cannot be said to be empirical research. But (as Kuhn has shown well enough) this view captures neither the logical difficulties in overcoming the contestability of identifying criteria in the natural sciences,[37] nor the social and political considerations which play such an important role in encouraging and forcing natural scientists to embrace some and reject other identifying criteria. For example, at one time the power of the Church was great enough to direct science to pursue and develop certain theories and not others (despite, of course, discrepancies between *all* the theories—even the favored ones—and observations).[38] In modern society the decision as to when a logical falsification does or does not demand a practical falsification is made largely by those agencies which fund research. A decision by a federal agency to continue to support research on "standard" cancer chemotherapy and pharmacology and to refuse to support research on laetrile (or even on an investigation of environmental causes and prevention rather than therapy), is ipso facto a decision as to when logical falsification is turned into practical falsification (*all* approaches to the treatment of cancer are beset with counterexamples and anomalies). The same decision — a funding decision — could also effectively determine (and sometimes does) for the social sciences which theories or approaches are to be pursued and, by implication, which identifying criteria are to be upheld as the foundation of research. A funding agency could effectively settle the disputes about the characterization of "nurturance" and "lesbian," not by finding a philosophical solution to the puzzles or a correct and unique answer, but simply by allocating funds in response to political pressures.[39]

It is of course widely recognized that the personal interests and values of scientists play a role in the selection of problems pursued and theories advanced and investigated. Nagel says that "this fact . . . represents no obstacle to the successful pursuit of objectively controlled inquiry in any branch of study."[40] This misses the point entirely. First, funding (and publication) decisions influence what is pursued and what theories are advanced as much as the values and interests of scientists influence them; and it is not implausible to claim that the possibility of funding and the opportunity for publication influence, if not determine, the interests and personal values of scientists. Second, the effect of a funding decision is not simply on what problems are attacked, but also on the translation of logical into practical falsification and on the fate of essentially contestable concepts.[41] Funding decisions affect the epistemological foundation, and not merely the surface (the utilitarian or pragmatic "priorities"), of scientific research.[42] The normative issues which make the concepts of the social sciences essentially contestable can be "resolved" (not "solved") by the National Endowment for the Humanities, the National Institutes of Mental Health, various foundations, and the publication policies of academic journals. That the direction of the natural sciences is determined in that way shows that one cannot so quickly deny the empirical status of the social sciences without also calling into question the paradigm of empirical research, the natural sciences. Political considerations *preserve* rather than undermine the empirical nature of both.[43] Political considerations shut the gap between logical and practical falsification, a gap which cannot be closed in any other way and which must be closed to permit even the possibility of empirical research.

(D) What should be said, then, about claims like "all (or most) males are masculine," "all men are masculine," "all women are feminine," and "all masculine persons are aggressive?" These claims contain essentially contestable concepts. I have argued that the truth-value of such claims is underdetermined by the facts or by observations, and is a function of the identifying criteria employed and the prevailing "acceptable limit" to counterexamples. I would not object to the idea that such a politically-based epistemology is a form of conventionalism. Thus I would claim that the truth-value of these claims is *not* indeterminate even though the claims contain essentially contestable concepts and even though their truth-value depends on a normative judgment. The claims *are* true or *are* false at the time they are asserted, and this truth-value is determined consistently with the current "resolution" of contestability, that resolution produced by the exertion of effective political power.

A whole set of claims about persons and their properties (even the claim that all males are precisely men) is thereby arguably true, or at least true given the background in which they are commonly asserted. They cannot be disproven simply by pointing out that there are male persons, for example, who do not engage in fighting behavior, or that there are female persons who batter and abuse their children. It takes a combination of exhibiting such persons *and* a modification of the resolution of contestable concepts to change the truth-value of the claims. This means that a prior change in the political power exerted in and over the sciences is required, and *this* in turn probably requires a radical redistribution of political power in society in general. Having said that, I am now in a position to offer an interpretation of Marx's declaration: the point is to change the world.

III. RESEARCH AND POLITICAL ACTIVITY

(A) My epistemological thesis does not reject foundationalism, although it does assert that foundations are to be sought and found in an unusual place: political power. This is to claim primacy of the sociology of knowledge over the "logic" of scientific research. But the thesis of the political groundwork of empirical research is not a Kantian thesis to the effect that a transcendental (political) a priori is the precondition of the possibility of knowledge. When I say that identifying criteria are sustained politically, and that the gap between logical and practical falsification is closed politically (and could only be closed politically), I mean that, at most, a pragmatic a priori provides the required foundation. This non-Kantian foundation is, nevertheless, quite able to do the job asked of it.

This epistemology is incompatible with a correspondence theory of truth,[44] because the truth-value of a proposition is determined, ultimately, by the political considerations which force a logically contestable concept to be uncontested in fact. The truth-value of a proposition is underdetermined by the facts. It might therefore be illuminating to think of this epistemology as connecting up with Jürgen Habermas's consensus theory of truth.[45] Understood within such a theory of truth, my epistemological thesis would be that the only sense [apart from the conventionalist sense admitted in Section II (D)] that could be given to the claim that *this* is the correct analysis of an essentially contestable concept is that *this* is the analysis which *would* prevail under ideal political conditions—say, when a political consensus about the concept is reached democratically among persons who are perfectly free and rational. The exertion of political power in our nonideal world provides the groundwork for empirical research primarily by encouraging or forcing an effective (even if not a democratic) consensus among practitioners of a science or an area of science. In the natural sciences, political power has succeeded in generating consensus when it was required; this has been less true in the social sciences. This fact does not, however, mark a logical distinction between them, but rather historical and sociological differences. It is not even accurate to say that consensus has been lacking in the social sciences; it seems more to the point to say that there has been one-sided consensus, that "acceptable limits" to counterexamples to claims about men and women and their properties have been set, and thereby knowledge created, by a particular group or exclusive club which has enjoyed a good deal of political power. It would be silly to object to this sexist social science by clamoring for stricter adherence to the logical canons of scientific research. What, then, is the remedy?

The answer, briefly, is for women—with an important qualification to be added in the next subsection—to gain political influence over, if not to seize outright, the mechanisms which direct research, and to counteract, if not replace, the power exercised in those mechanisms. But this requires that the major institutions of this society be changed dramatically, and be changed *first*. Changes in knowledge *follow*. Marx's Eleventh Thesis calls for political action, not more research. G.A. Cohen reads the Eleventh Thesis as saying that the point is to change the world "so that interpretation of it is no longer necessary."[46] I am reading it as saying that the point is to change the world so that sexist interpretations of it become politically impossible and new knowledge is created. My reading of Marx has him denying the common idea that an understanding of the world and its sexism comes first and social change second, with the former leading to the latter only if such understanding can be and is rationally justified.[47] The historical materialist account of knowledge is entirely compatible with a political epistemology.

(B) It is often suggested that the major evils of sexist social science — the invisibility of women in history, the ignoring of women's experiences, observer bias, and the various double standards[48] — can be corrected only by increasing the number of social scientists who are women. Because "an exclusively male study of a society is usually incomplete,"[49] the "necessary first step [is] . . . to establish and promote women in their professional scientific disciplines, for only then will a more thorough examination of omissions and a better distribution of knowledge . . . be possible."[50] *If* male social scientists and female social scientists, as male persons and as female persons, interpret the facts differently,[51] *if* they are able to discover different facts, offer different explanations and "complete" the viewpoints of each other, then (on this view) there is good reason — for the sake of achieving a better approximation to the truth itself — to insist on and establish equality between the sexes in the social sciences. (Note that an argument for equality based on its necessity in securing truth cannot settle for equality of opportunity to become a social scientist, but must rather strive for equality of result.)

Now, I do agree that there ought to be more, even an equal number of, women scientists, but I would not offer the argument under discussion. The view that the perspective of women should be brought to bear on the social sciences to make them more complete, more truthful, and less one-sided, is nothing but the idea (which has pernicious and sexist implications) that males and females are natural sexual complements (or that masculinity and femininity are yin-yang counterparts) writ large to encompass the practice of science.[52] Of course, to bring more women into the social sciences is a better remedy than other suggestions, for example, that all that is required is greater perseverance, sincerity, and open-mindedness on the part of male scientists, that women's issues be made the object of a concerted research effort, and that nonsexist social science be attained by a more rigorous application of the principles of scientific rationality and objectivity.[53] But increasing the number of women scientists is a better remedy not because doing so allows science to get closer to the truth, but rather because doing so gives women the opportunity to exert power over the resolution of contestable concepts and over the translation of logical into practical falsification. It gives women the power to *create* truth, not *discover* it.

This remedy of "bringing" women into the social sciences cannot be the whole solution. First, it leaves open the question of how women are to be given the opportunity to exert power over contestable concepts. If they have lacked *this* power, it is likely because they have lacked, and still do lack, other powers. Power must be exerted someplace in order to bring women into the sciences in the first place. It is not unreasonable to say that those who currently have the power in and over the sciences to determine the course of research and the fate of contestable concepts will not quietly move aside and make room for women who would contest that fate. Furthermore, equality between the sexes in the social sciences would not guarantee a "better distribution of knowledge" because many women scientists would (and do) determine the fate of contestable concepts and set acceptable limits to counterexamples in exactly the same way these are done currently by male scientists. (Think about Reagan's promise—to appoint a woman to the U.S. Supreme Court.) Relying on "the perspective of women" or "the feminist perspective" (as so many writers do) is inadequate. There is no single, monolithic, comprehensive "perspective of women" or "feminist perspective." There are no insights, viewpoints, and interests which all women (or all feminists) have in common in a pluralistic society. To insist on promoting the perspective of women, therefore, is to reify women's experiences and interests in exactly the same way that sexist social science reifies women with its claims about stereotypical femininity.[54]

Attempts have been made, of course, to define the core of the "feminist perspective" or to find the common denominator of women's experiences and interests which ought to guide the scientific practice of women in research. It has been said that women scientists can "inform our understandings of the world with a commitment to overcoming the subordination and devaluation of women."[55] Here, then, is what is common to all women's experience, their subordination and devaluation. This is, however, unsatisfactory. Not only do women disagree (sometimes violently) about what is to count as a case of subordination or devaluation, but also many women fail to recognize any substantial subordination and devaluation at all. And among those who do recognize institutional sexism, it is characterized in widely divergent ways and incompatible tactics are proposed to deal with it.[56] "Subordination," "devaluation," "feminist," and "sexist" are all essentially contestable concepts.[57] The widespread existence of "false consciousness" among women[58] and the disputes among the different varieties of feminism undercut any epistemological benefit to be gained by increasing the number of social scientists who are women. The required feminist political consensus and power is not available, and will not be forthcoming as long as our major institutions are controlled as they are today. Until a dramatic change in the balance of social power occurs, some women scientists will continue to employ the "acceptable limits" to counterexamples established for them by mainstream social science. This is why praxis (Marx's change in the world) must come first, and why more empirical research is irrelevant, whether it is done by women or by men.

NOTES

1. See the Eleventh of his "Theses on Feuerbach," in, for example, *Karl Marx. Selected Writings,* ed. David McLellan (Oxford: Oxford University Press, 1977), p. 158.

2. The Bem Sex Roles Inventory lists twenty properties each for masculinity and femininity. The latter includes "cheerful," "gentle," "shy," "understanding," and "yielding."

3. Sarah Hoagland points out that the component properties of "masculine" and "feminine" are evaluative in the strong sense, and she concludes, for this reason, that "'masculinity' and 'femininity'

are not based on empirical findings" ("On the Status of the Concepts of Masculinity and Femininity," *Transactions of the
Nebraska Academy of Sciences* 4 [1977]: 169–72), at p. 170.
Hoagland is actually more concerned with the fact that "aggressive"
as an evaluation is applied according to a double standard, rather
than with the fact that it is evaluative. See my discussion in Section
I (B, 3).

4. *The Structure of Science* (New York: Harcourt, Brace, and World,
1961), Chapter 13, especially pp. 490–95. Nagel's terminology is
"characterizing value judgment" and "appraising value judgment";
I prefer simply "characterizing judgment" and "appraising judgment." On his definition, an appraisal is already an evaluation, so
his term is redundant. And "characterizing value judgment" concedes exactly the question which needs investigation: what is the
nature of the judgments in characterization? (Thanks to Alison
Jaggar for bringing this to my attention.)

5. When Juanita Williams writes that "the differential designation of
behaviors . . . as masculine or feminine . . . implies that males . . .
ought to exhibit the masculine ones and females the feminine
ones," she overlooks the distinction between characterization and
appraisal. She apparently realizes this later when she writes that the
differential designation is guilty of "setting the stage" (a weaker
claim than "implies") for differential appraisals. See her
Psychology of Women: Behavior in a Biosocial Context (New
York: W.W. Norton, 1977), p. 341.

6. I could add: *and* in order that masculinity be usefully considered an
ontological category. Margrit Eichler has written about the terms
"masculine" and "feminine" (in *The Double Standard: A Feminist
Critique of Feminist Social Science* [New York: St. Martin's Press,
1980], p. 120) that they "should be used only as labels for empirically established configurations of variables which are differentiated
by sex, never as generally valid descriptors. The reason is that
masculinity and femininity are not generated by innate factors, but
are the result of social factors." But her argument is faulty. First, if
(as she is willing to grant for discussion) "masculine" did stand for a
cluster of empirical variables, then the term would be an excellent
candidate for a "valid descriptor" (here the logic of "masculine"
does not differ from the logic of any of its components). Second,
there would be prima facie reason to treat masculinity as an ontological category. That is, whether masculinity is generated (when
it is generated) by innate or social factors (or by a combination) is
irrelevant to whether it is a valid descriptor or an ontological
category.

7. Williams, op. cit., p. 341. Compare with Eleanor Maccoby and
Carol Jacklin's *The Psychology of Sex Differences* (Stanford: Stanford University Press, 1974), p. 12.

8. In Section II it is argued that it is exactly this fact — that standards of tolerance are set by the scientific community — which demonstrates the political groundwork of knowledge. My objection at this point is that one cannot criticize social scientific concepts merely by showing that the concepts are imperfect, for *all* concepts are imperfect.

9. Williams, op. cit., p. 150.

10. Hoagland, op. cit., p. 169.

11. If social scientists did not expect to find much aggression in female persons, if they have a prior belief that not much of it exists, it is possible they will not perceive it when *faced* with it, even if their identifying criteria are adequate to the task. Furthermore, if they do not expect to find much aggression in female persons, this expectation itself might cause it to be absent in their subjects. See Robert Rosenthal, "On the Social Psychology of the Psychology Experiment: The Experimenter's Hypothesis as Unintended Determinant of Experimental Results," *American Scientist* 51, no. 2 (1963): 268–83. For discussion, see Naomi Weisstein, "Psychology Constructs the Female," in *Woman in Sexist Society,* ed. V. Gornick and B.K. Moran (New York: Basic Books, 1971), pp. 133–46, at pp. 138–39.

12. This objection is different from the one considered in B(2), which said that prior belief in the nonexistence of the aggression of female persons infected the selection of identifying criteria and/or the observation of that aggression. Here the point is that prior belief in the existence of noncommendable aggression infects the selection of criteria and/or its observation.

13. See Liz Horwitt (quoting Clara Mayo) in "The Draft," *Bostonia* 54, no. 3 (1980): 29.

14. Hoagland (op. cit., p. 170) argues that differential appraisal generates falsehoods in the social sciences. If aggression in male persons is explained by reference to (commendable) confidence, and if aggression in female persons is explained by reference to (uncommendable) frustration, then social scientists are "bound" (her word) to conclude that male persons and female persons are *different* — even though they are the *same* (both can be aggressive). Now, were astronomers to explain the orbital motion of the Moon around Earth differently from the orbital motion of Phobos around Mars, by using concepts as disparate as confidence and frustration (say, gravitation in one case and love/hate in the other), we should have good reason to complain. But it does not follow from this explanatory absurdity that the characterization of orbital motion is inadequate. When Hoagland writes that scientists who employ "masculinity" and "femininity" are *bound* to conclude that men and women are essentially different, she is trading on an equivocation. One sense of *bound* is "logically required"; in this

sense, were it true that scientists who employ "masculine" were bound to conclude that the aggression of men and women is to be explained differently, then Hoagland would have shown something important about the logical status of that concept. The other sense of "bound" is "likely" (as in the claim that Karim Abdul-Jabbar is bound to score an average of twenty points a game this season). But only in this sense is her claim plausible; and this psychological observation does not establish a stronger thesis that the concepts are logically fallacious in some way.

15. Nagel, op. cit., p. 492.
16. The notion of "essentially contestable" concepts has been developed by Alasdair MacIntyre ("The Essential Contestability of Some Social Concepts," *Ethics* 84 [1973]: 1–9) who follows W.B. Gallie ("Essentially Contested Concepts," *Proceedings of the Aristotelian Society* 56 [1955–56]: 168–98). The notion of essential contestability I employ supplements Gallie's analysis (in emphasizing "standards of excellence") by drawing on some insights of Leo Strauss (see his "What is Political Philosophy?" in *What is Political Philosophy? And Other Studies* [Glencoe, Ill.: The Free Press, 1959], pp. 9–55, especially pp. 21ff). My discussions of "art-objects" (pp. 10–11) and "nurturance" (p. 16) combine Strauss and Gallie, while the discussion of "lesbian" (p. 18) is purely Galliean. Nagel does discuss Strauss (op. cit., pp. 490–91), but he misses the point that the distinction between characterization and appraisal does not capture Strauss's distinction between the sociology of art and the sociology of trash. The distinction between art and trash must be made within the domain of characterization itself. Also note that when I say that the only value judgments in characterization are about standards of excellence, I do not go whole hog with Strauss.
17. Catharine R. Stimpson, "Neither Dominant nor Subordinate," *Dissent* 27, no. 3 (1980): 304.
18. Unless I specifically indicate otherwise, when I speak about this generalization, $(x)(Ax \rightarrow Bx)$, or about "the generalization," I mean *any* generalization. Do not insert terms (like "masculine" or "aggressive") unless the context is appropriate. I intend to make some *general* points about characterization and the logic of research.
19. "Has been confirmed" is ambiguous in the same way; it can refer either to a logical relationship among sentences or to a practice. Examining only one thing which is A and finding that it is also B counts as a logical confirmation, but in practice the generalization would not be *considered* confirmed until more items had been examined.
20. The purist thesis is Popperian in flavor, although it is doubtful that Popper would insist on it. Purism is similar to "dogmatic" or

"naive" falsificationism; see Imre Lakatos, "Falsification and the Methodology of Scientific Research Programmes," in *Criticism and the Growth of Knowledge,* ed. I. Lakatos and A. Musgrave (Cambridge: Cambridge University Press, 1971), pp. 91–195.

21. Thomas S. Kuhn, *The Copernican Revolution* (Cambridge, Mass.: Harvard University Press, 1957), and *The Structure of Scientific Revolutions,* 2d ed. (Chicago: University of Chicago Press, 1970).

22. Paul K. Feyerabend, *Against Method* (London: NLB, 1975), especially Chapter 3.

23. The ubiquitousness of falsification undermines Lewis Coser's neat Popperian defense of Marxist social science. See his "In Praise of Marx," *Dissent* 27, no. 3 (1980): 335–40. A defense of Marxist social science which recognizes the advantages of a Kuhnian view over a Popperian view is provided by Paul Sweezy, "A Crisis in Marxian Theory," *Monthly Review* 31, no. 2 (1979): 20–24.

24. Weisstein, op. cit. (fn. 11), p. 142.

25. Hoagland, op. cit., p. 170.

26. Ibid., p. 171. Read her expression "discarding counterexamples" as "refusing to turn a logical falsification into a practical falsification."

27. But it is clear what kind of answer Hoagland would like to provide: one within standard philosophy of science such that logical criteria of "acceptable limits" can be set out. This kind of solution is suggested by a misunderstanding of the depth of the problem. As I will argue, there is no logical epistemology which stands on its own two feet apart from political considerations.

28. What I say about the antecedent applies as well to the consequent.

29. Much of what I say here and later is close to, and derives from, what is known as the "Duhem-Quine" thesis. See *Can Theories Be Refuted?,* ed. Sandra Harding (Dordrecht: D. Reidel, 1976).

30. Nancy Chodorow, *The Reproduction of Mothering* (Berkeley: University of California Press, 1978), p. 30.

31. Let me symbolize the dispute. The generalization under discussion is, say, $(x)(Mx \rightarrow -Nx)$, which means (for the domain of persons) that if a person is a male, that person will not be nurturant. (The *explanation* for the generalization is that those who are aggressive for biological reasons cannot also be nurturant.) The logically falsifying counterexample is, then, Ma & Na, i.e., a male person who *is* nurturant. The defender of the generalization responds by asserting that because the concept of "nurturance" has been misapplied, the appropriate description is really Ma & $-$ Na (which logically confirms, or at least fails to logically falsify, the generalization). The defender of the generalization has yet another possible response if we understand that generalization in a different way. Suppose it were $(x)(Mx \& Ax \rightarrow -Nx)$, which says that if a person is male *and* is aggressive, that person will not be nurturant. The logically falsi-

fying counterexample, then, is Ma & Aa & Na, i.e., a male person who is both nurturant and aggressive. A male person who is simply nurturant (Ma & Na) does *not* count in this case as a counterexample. Therefore a defender of the generalization could say that even though it might be correct to characterize *this* male person's behavior as nurturance, *this* male does not happen to be an aggressive person. (Note that the dispute does not get off the ground at all if the parties have not settled the qualitative and quantitative problems in characterization I discussed in Section I (B, 1).)

32. See Kuhn's discussion (*The Structure,* op. cit., pp. 131-35) of the early days of Dalton's atomic theory. Proponents of this new and already logically falsified theory had to make some radical readjustments in their concepts of substances ("solution" and "compound," in particular), in order to advance the law of fixed proportions. For a superb analysis of the different strategies which can be used to handle counterexamples, see Imre Lakatos, *Proofs and Refutations* (New York: Cambridge University Press, 1976).

33. MacIntyre, op. cit., p. 2. Here MacIntyre parts company with Gallie. On the latter's view, there is an "exemplar" for contestable concepts. What parties contest is that aspect or property of the exemplar which is most important for its identifying criterion. If there were no exemplar, the parties would be employing different concepts, and would not be contesting the same concept.

34. Gallie claims (op. cit., p. 174) that *naturalistic* concepts are not contestable because they yield predictions. (Or because their use can be predicted?) But here he seems to overlook the kind of point made by Nelson Goodman in *Fact, Fiction, and Forecast* (Cambridge, Mass.: Harvard University Press, 1955). I would claim that naturalistic concepts are contestable precisely because the predictions based on them are contestable. "*Exactly what* in this set of facts is projectible?" is a question without a unique correct answer.

35. Donald Symons, *The Evolution of Human Sexuality* (New York: Oxford University Press, 1979), p. 249.

36. We could try, perhaps, to operationalize "lesbian." It has been suggested by Mayra Buvinić that operationalism ought to be carried out more frequently in research on women in order to avoid value-biased results; see her "A Critical Review of Some Research Concepts and Concerns," in *Women and World Development,* ed. Mayra Buvinić (Overseas Development Council, 1976), pp. 1-20, especially pp. 4-5. But as MacIntyre points out, "To operationalize would be to participate in the debate, not to escape it" (op. cit., p. 8). An operational definition of "lesbian" represents only one possible "acceptable limit" on counterexamples to claims about lesbians.

37. The same phenomenon is found also in legal reasoning about "hard cases"; see the two essays by Thomas D. Perry, "Judicial Method and the Concept of Reasoning," *Ethics* 80, no. 1 (1969): 1-20 (esp.

pp. 5–6), and "Contestable Concepts and Hard Cases," *Ethics* 88, no. 1 (1977): 20–35.

38. If our society were still under the control of the Church, we would take seriously this passage from the encyclical *Humanae Vitae:*

> It is supremely desirable . . . that medical science should be the study of natural rhythm to succeed in determining a sufficiently secure basis for the chaste limitation of offspring. In this way scientists . . . will by their research *establish the truth* of the Church's claim that 'there can be no contradiction between two divine laws—that which governs the transmitting of life and that which governs the fostering of married love.'

> (The Pope Speaks: The Church Documents Quarterly 13, no. 4 (1969): 329–46, at p. 342; italics added.

39. I should say a few words about how my view differs from Norman S. Care's critique of MacIntyre, "On Fixing Social Concepts," *Ethics,* 84, no. 1 (1973): 10–21. Care argues that a practical resolution ("closure") of contestable concepts can be achieved politically (p. 14), and clearly I agree. But Care fails to see the epistemological significance of practical closure. Because he ignores the dependence of the testing of generalizations on the resolution of contestability, and because he does not recognize contestability in the natural sciences, it never occurs to Care that practical closure is epistemologically *the whole story.* Thus his thesis is substantially weaker than my own. Furthermore, Care implicitly relies on the characterization-appraisal distinction (p. 15) in arguing that contestability is not as troublesome for social science as MacIntyre claims; on Care's view, contestability affects only appraisal. But as I have been arguing, the characterization-appraisal distinction does not help as much as Nagel thinks it does, because contestability affects characterization and identifying criteria independently of its affects on appraisal (see fn. 16).

40. Nagel, op. cit., pp. 486–87.

41. The epistemological significance of funding decisions is also overlooked by Arlene Kaplan Daniels in her essay "Feminist Perspectives in Sociological Research," in *Another Voice: Feminist Perspectives on Social Life and Social Science,* ed. Marcia Millman and R. M. Kanter (Garden City, New York: Anchor Books, 1975), pp. 369–70.

42. Harvey Brooks' essay on the "priorities" is especially insensitive, in its emphasis on the issue of "truth v. utility," to the epistemological effect of funding decisions: "The Problems of Research Priorities," *Daedalus* 107, no. 2 (1978): 171–90, especially p. 173 and pp. 177–83.

43. The political *preservation* of the possibility of empirical research in both the natural and the social sciences is the reason that one cannot respond to my "equivalent-to-the-natural-sciences-defense" of

the social sciences by saying "so much the worse for the natural sciences." My claim is that all knowledge depends on but is also made possible by political considerations. Only the most extreme skeptic would jump for joy over an "equivalence" defense.

44. Even though Dorothy Smith (in "Some Implications of a Sociology for Women," in *Woman in a Man-Made World,* ed. N. Glazer and H.Y. Waehrer [Chicago: Rand McNally, 1977], pp. 15–29) emphasizes, as I do, the sociology of knowledge ("Knowledge is fundamentally a socially organized relation," p. 16), she still implies that a politically correct social science would reveal "the world's actual mode of organization" (p. 27).

45. This type of approach is employed by Perry in his analysis of judicial reasoning in hard cases (see fn. 37). He argues that only a consensus theory can explicate the claim that hard cases have a unique, correct solution; "we can only mean the one [solution] in which all, or the bulk, of competent and distinterested lawyers in the field or fields of law concerned would concur" ("Judicial Method," p. 5). Here, too, the "correct" legal decision is underdetermined by the facts of the case.

46. *Karl Marx's Theory of History: A Defence* (Princeton, N.J.: Princeton University Press, 1978), Appendix 1, p. 339.

47. "In terms of scholarship, feminist efforts are geared towards the exploration . . . of sex roles . . . in order to be able to understand and ultimately to overcome them" (Eichler, op. cit. [fn. 6], p. 9). This view, I am arguing, puts the cart before the horse.

48. See Eichler (fn. 6), Weisstein (fn. 11), Williams (fn. 5), and the good summaries provided by Maccoby and Jacklin (fn. 7), pp. 3–13, and by Marcia Westkott, "Feminist Criticism of the Social Sciences," *Harvard Educational Review* 49 (1979): 422–30.

49. Ruby Rohrlich-Leavitt, Barbara Sykes, and Elizabeth Weatherford, "Aboriginal Woman: Male and Female Anthropological Perspectives," in *Toward an Anthropology of Women,* ed. Ranya Reiter (New York: Monthly Review Press, 1975), pp. 110–26, at p. 110. The word "usually" in the quoted passage is curious; it entails that there are no theoretical objections to the claim that any study done exclusively by men could be "complete."

50. Daniels, op. cit. (fn. 40), p. 370.

51. "*Scientific American* reports that French investigators . . . refer to the postcopulatory songs of the male cricket as 'triumphal songs.' A rather different view of supposed postcoital merrymaking appears in *Science* magazine's account of the 'ultrasonic postejaculatory songs' of the male rat, perhaps because one of the investigators was a woman. It turns out that vocalizations are less those of 'triumph' than fatigue-'desist-contact' signals . . ." (Elaine Baruch, "The Politics of Courtship," *Dissent* 27, no. 1 [1980]: 56–63, at p. 56). Note that there is a dispute here about characterization, not precisely "interpretation."

52. At the very least, the view seems to *endorse* a kind of double standard which it otherwise would find to be objectionable. See Section I (B, 2,3). The natural complement theory of male and female persons has usually been employed to argue that scientists ought only to be males and that the abilities of females make them suitable for other activities. I doubt that the trick of using the natural complement theory against itself, to justify equality in the sciences in general between the sexes, can avoid concluding that a sexual division of labor *within* the social sciences is also justified (e.g., that women scientists are better able to pursue some problems, or that women scientists are to be given the "mopping up" operations to "complete" the studies begun by men, etc.).

53. These views have much in common with the naive belief that significant social change can be achieved in a liberal capitalist democracy by making appeals to the good intentions, benevolence, and legal responsibility of government officials and business leaders. For discussion, see my "Philosophical Justifications, Political Activity, and Adequate Health Care," *Georgia Law Review* 11 (1977): 525–38.

54. Some analytic work needs to be done to clarify the concepts of "feminist perspective," "women's perspective," and "female perspective" (and their analogues, "male perspective" and "men's perspective"). An otherwise eye-opening and excellent critique of contemporary sociology (Marcia Millman, "She Did It All For Love: A Feminist View of the Sociology of Deviance," in *Another Voice,* op. cit. [fn. 40], pp. 251–79) is flawed because these distinctions are not recognized. For example, Millman claims that belief in stereotypical femininity "renders the *male* sociologist blind" to women's experiences (pp. 260–61), and she proposes "a *feminist* perspective" (p. 265), *women's* research (p. 272), *and* research done by females (p. 274) as correctives to a "*male*-biased orientation" (p. 265; not "men's biases"). Yet she also suggests that Erving Goffman (as a male? as a man? as a feminist?) has established and utilized a methodology which ought to be embraced as *the* corrective (by females doing research? by feminists?).

55. Westkott, op. cit. (fn. 47), p. 430. Hilda Smith writes that "a feminist viewpoint" is not constituted by "complaints about the position of women. . . . Unless the writer asks the question 'why' about the actions she considers detrimental to women, she is no feminist. And further, if . . . her answer does not include an understanding of women as a sociological group (as opposed to merely a sex or biological entity), then again she is no feminist," ["Feminism and the Methodology of Women's History," in *Liberating Women's History,* ed. Berenice A. Carroll (Urbana: University of Illinois Press, 1976), pp. 368–84, at pp. 370–71]. Smith's criterion of feminism excludes Shulamith Firestone's *The Dialectic of Sex* (New York: Bantam, 1971), a groundbreaking work in the current feminist revolution.

56. See *Feminist Frameworks,* eds. Alison Jaggar and Paula Struhl (New York: McGraw-Hill, 1978). Jaggar apparently forgets the fact that "feminism" is not monolithic when she argues (in "Male Instructors, Feminism, and Women's Studies," *Teaching Philosophy* 2, nos. 3–4 [1979]: 247–56) that only women should teach feminist philosophy. One version of feminism—liberal feminism—would surely reject her conclusion that "sex *is* a characteristic relevant to one's ability to teach courses on the philosophical issues of feminism" (p. 247).

57. To say that *enough* women are subordinated, and that they are subordinated to a *sufficient* degree (in order to defend the claim that our society is institutionally sexist) is to take a stand on "acceptable limits" to counterexamples. And to say that a particular treatment of women does count as a case of subordination is to assert a characterization which presupposes a standard of (negative) excellence (this treatment is "bad" enough to count as subordination).

58. Appeals to the phenomenon of "false consciousness" among women is a common tactic employed to defend (to save from logical falsification) the claim that eliminating sexist institutions is in the interest of all women. From the point of view of *mainstream* social science this maneuver has always smacked of going well beyond "acceptable limits" to counterexamples. Thus I find it ironic (in addition to philosophically misconceived) when feminist or Marxist philosophers or social scientists object to mainstream social science by invoking purism (see pp. 13–14).

Patrick Grim

Sex and Social Roles: How to Deal with the Data

Women consistently score higher on verbal aptitude tests than do men, whereas males generally do better on tests involving "visual-spatial" skills: that is, depth perception, mazes, picture completion, map reading, and the like.[1] On questionnaires women rate moving, marriage, and loss of a job as more stressful than do men.[2] Women appear to be more sensitive to sound volume and higher frequencies than men, are better at fine coordination and rapid decisions,[3] and it has been proposed that women are able to "read" facial expressions more readily.[4] Men consistently test out as more aggressive.[5]

What are we to do with data of this sort? One way it is often used is as a justification for social practices involving a division of labor on sexual lines. If women are more sensitive to stress and less aggressive than men, it is argued, we should leave those tasks calling for aggression and tolerance of stress to men. If women are "communicative" animals and men are "manipulative" animals, we should leave the "communicative" tasks of childrearing to women.[6] If men excel at mathematical tasks and women have superior verbal skills, our engineers should be male and our telephone operators should be female.

I am grateful to Mary Vetterling-Braggin, David Pomerantz, and Kriste Taylor for their help with revisions on an earlier draft.

Fine coordination and rapid decision making qualify women as excellent typists, whereas better spatial perception indicates that jet pilots should be male.

The form of this argument should be familiar: our data shows that men and women differ in certain ways, and those differences (so the story goes) justify a differentiation of social roles along sexual lines. The argument is quite clearly public property and appears with tedious regularity in common conversation. But it also appears in one guise or another throughout much of the literature on sex differences.[7] It is this form of argument I wish to attack.

My attack is in three parts. In the first section I hope to raise briefly some embarrassing questions concerning the data itself. The data on which arguments of this form rely may not always be as objective, nor as clearly indicative of fundamental differences, as is often made out. In the second section I hope to address a general practical problem regarding sexual differences and our own ignorance. In the final section I will argue that the inferences often drawn from data regarding sexual differences are neither as direct nor as tight as is commonly assumed. Even if we have appropriately hard data demonstrating clearly fundamental sexual differences, the data may not support the conclusions regarding social roles which it appears to support.

I. QUESTIONING THE DATA

Without an authoritative appeal to scientific data regarding sexual differences, an argument of this type would not even get off the ground. The argument as a whole, in fact, might be seen as an attempt to transfer to its social conclusions the scientific respectability of the data on which it relies. In a later section we will consider whether the argument succeeds; whether the data, however good, supports the social conclusions it appears to. But for now let us consider the data itself. Is it always as tight as it appears to be?

In order for the data to supply appropriate support for the argument at issue, it must be something more than merely a record of how men and women raised in our society have happened to turn out. That alone would not tell us whether observed characteristics are fundamental characteristics, independent of social influence, and would not show that people might not turn out quite differently in some other social context. Thus it wouldn't show, as the argument is designed to show, that social roles should quite generally be distinguished along sexual lines. If the differences at issue are merely a reflection of our own social order, they are part of what can be changed, rather than invariables which dictate the form that social change can or should take. So any data relied on in arguing for general social role differentiation along sexual lines must give some indication that observed differences are more than mere social epiphenomena. Only data which in some way goes beyond a simple record of differences between women and men in the context of a particular status quo can do this.

It is because of this basic requirement that our data must in several ways be free of social influence. To the extent that our data reflects a given social situation rather than indicating sexual differences independent of social influence, it will be of little help in deciding, however indirectly, how society ought to be.

There are at least two ways in which data regarding sexual differences may be a reflection of our society rather than of something more. The data may not, first of all, be appropriately *hard* data; the apparent differences such data show may in fact be the result of social influences on or inherent in the ways in which the data are collected, counted, and represented. The data of a sexist observer might not be hard in this sense; the differences observed are in fact merely in the eye of the observer. But even if our data are appropriately hard — even if the ways in which it is accumulated are free from illegitimate social influence — the differences for which we then have evidence may themselves be the result of social influences. Given the systematically different ways in which children of different sexes are brought up in our society, it would be surprising indeed if no psychological differences showed up on our tests.[8] But this is not the data we need. Somehow we must have an indication that our data are not to be explained in social terms; that the differences objectively recorded are genuinely *fundamental* differences.[9]

Though in principle distinct, the requirement that our data be hard data and the requirement that recorded differences be genuinely fundamental differences tend to blur in practice. The concern I want to raise here tends toward worries regarding the hardness of some of our data, though questions of fundamentality are clearly at issue as well. My objections are not intended to impugn all data we have or might collect. But they are intended as a warning by example of how easily the implicit operation of social factors may be overlooked.

Consider first the question of aggression. Is one sex more aggressive than the other? Perhaps no other question in the history of testing for sex differences has had so long a history involving such a variety of test procedures. But despite the apparent simplicity of the question, a bit of reflection shows that any attempt to put it to the test involves a number of pitfalls. That in turn is good reason to think that much of the testing already done has been subject to those pitfalls, and thus good reason to be generally suspicious of the data regarding sexual differences with regard to aggression.

One difficulty is what gets counted as aggression. In a sexist society such as ours it would not be surprising to find that male and female behavior is interpreted differently as aggressive. A guffawing, hand-clamping, back-slapping female is more likely to be considered aggressive than is her male counterpart, who is merely considered outgoing or friendly. A rumor-spreading male, on the other hand, may more readily be considered aggressive than his female counterpart, who is merely "catty." It may also be that whether or not an individual's behavior is perceived as aggressive depends on the sex (and social conditioning) of the perceiver; a female observer is more likely to see Joe's constant sexual overtures to women as aggressive than is another male. If "aggression" is socially loaded in these ways, it is hardly a proper tool for collecting or representing objective data; any tests we try to perform concerning the relative aggressiveness of the sexes will be shot through with social prejudices from the start. Another way of putting the point is this: "aggressive" may be a term which in subtle ways is applied differently to men than to women. If so, it is not a neutral characteristic which we can compare in the two cases. Asking whether one sex is more aggressive than the other is more like asking whether one sex is more attractive than the other than like asking whether one is generally taller; neither "aggressive" nor "attractive" is applied to each group with the objective impartiality of a yardstick.

Consider another piece of data mentioned earlier; the fact that women generally rate moving, marriage, or loss of a job as more stressful than men. This has been taken as an indication that women are more sensitive to, and less tolerant of, stress.[10] But we might draw other conclusions instead. In a job market in which women are consistently discriminated against, the loss of a job is a greater disaster for a woman than for a man. Women may be more stressful about losing jobs, not because they are

such delicate creatures, but because, things being as they are, the
loss of a job is in fact as more serious matter for women than for
men. Consider also marriage, the second item on the list. Given
our social situation, the social burdens of marriage fall harder
on the shoulders of women than men; a man often takes a wife
on the side whereas a woman tends to enter married life like a
career change. Small wonder that women find the prospect of
marriage more stressful than do men. The statistics on sex,
stress, and moving fit a similar pattern. Ozzie doesn't have to
worry much about moving because moving, in its excruciating
organizational detail, isn't his job; Harriet does it. Thus the fact
that women rate particular tasks and situations as more stressful
than do men may tell us more about those tasks and situations
than about women and men; it may indicate simply that those
tasks and situations are already distinguished along sexual lines.
The problem noted above with testing for aggression was that "aggression" may not be a term applied sufficiently sex-neutrally to
allow for legitimate comparison. The difficulty here is that job
loss, marriage, and moving may not, as things stand, be sex-
neutral tasks, and thus may not be suitable as neutral gauges
of any fundamental difference between the sexes with regard to
stress.

These cases are presented only as warnings of how our testing
can go wrong in subtle ways and how as a result our data may in
some cases be neither as hard nor as fundamental as it appears to
be. It is easy to imagine similar difficulties in other tests, and
perhaps pervasive difficulties with standard modes of testing in
general. Because of social differences in upbringing, the environment of a laboratory or the phenomenon of being observed
may not themselves be appropriately sex-neutral.

Does this indicate that all our data on sex differences in
something less than hard data, or that there are insurmountable
problems in testing the types of claims with which we began?
Not at all. All that is indicated is that some data which might
pass for hard data is not hard at all, that differences may appear
fundamental when they are not, and that there are often deep
and pervasive difficulties to be wary of in testing for sexual differences. This does, I think, justify a bit of skepticism in review-
ing the accumulated research on sexual differences and calls for
more than a bit of caution in trying to assemble better data.
But it does not constitute a blanket objection to all such investigation, and I doubt that any a priori considerations alone could
do so.

II. WHAT TO ASSUME WHEN YOU DON'T KNOW WHAT TO ASSUME

The arguments of the previous sections can be understood as arguments that our ignorance is greater than our research might lead us to believe. Not all our data regarding sexual differences are genuinely hard data revealing genuinely fundamental differences. In this section I want to address the question of how we should act and what we should assume when we are to some extent ignorant as to how we should act and what we should assume.

Consider a case which appears quite frequently. We have, we think, objectively established a genuine difference between men and women in our test sample; men score higher on characteristic f_1, whereas women score higher on characteristic f_2. But we aren't sure how the difference is to be explained; whether as a fundamental and socially independent characteristic of men and women in general, or as merely a result of differences in the upbringing of men and women in our sample. In such cases we often have theorists at loggerheads; one group insists on explaining the differences as fundamental, whereas the other attempts to present plausible suggestions as to how the data might be explained as the result of social conditioning.

There are two questions we might raise concerning such cases: how the dispute is to be resolved, if it is to be resolved,[11] and how we should act and what we should assume in cases in which the dispute remains unresolved.

There is no easy answer to the first question. In order to establish whether or not an observed difference is a fundamental difference we might employ cross-cultural testing (on the theory that fundamental differences will be universal in ways in which socially inculcated differences will not), testing of newborns (if possible, given the characteristics at issue), or testing for developmental patterns at different ages (on the somewhat shaky assumption that social factors will show a more pervasive influence with time). We might also rely on links to other data. If we find that certain observed differences correlate very well with certain hormonal balances, and if we have independent evidence that hormonal balances of the right type are largely independent of social influences, we will have evidence that the difference at issue is a genuinely fundamental difference.

Thus in some cases we can expect the dispute to be resolvable in one way or another. But this point can easily be overstated as a conviction that all such disputes are in all cases easily resolvable by appeal to some decisive form of additional testing. They are not. Few of the phenomena to which appeal is made in order to settle such disputes are unambiguously decisive. Cross-cultural testing has pitfalls of its own, and there are various explanations for cultural universality short of innatist hypotheses. Some social influences may be constant in a way which does not show variation over time, and we know of many strictly physical characteristics which vary with age. The differential characteristics at issue are generally complex enough to make testing of newborns impossible, and the physical data to which we attempt to establish correlations cannot always be shown to be itself independent of social influences. Only in exceptional instances does some crucial experiment decide the case. Such disputes are resolved, to the extent that they are resolved at all, by a subtle accumulation of plausibility—none of it clearly decisive—on one side or the other. Often even this does not occur; the additional tests appealed to are themselves ambiguous enough to allow for either interpretation. A gray area remains and for the sake of unanimity each side may blur the dispute by speaking of what various data suggest rather than of what they show and by speaking of differential tendencies which may involve both social and fundamental factors, rather than of differential characteristics of solely one kind or the other.

To some extent we are presently ignorant of whether certain differences between men and women reveal fundamental differences or are to be attributed to social causes. To some extent, we will always be ignorant. Does this matter? If whether certain differences are fundamental or social in origin may be of moral relevance in shaping a society—an issue more fully considered in the following section—then our ignorance does matter. What we don't know may hurt us in the attempt to make our society what it ought to be.

This in effect saddles us with a quandary as to how to act in ignorance. There are differences between men and women which may be genuinely fundamental or which may be social in origin. How we ought to treat men and women may depend on which explanation is correct, but we cannot claim to *know* which explanation is correct. In that case which ought we assume; should we treat the differences at issue as fundamental until proven otherwise, or as social in origin until and unless the evidence indicates otherwise? The dilemma is both of practical importance and as unavoidable as our own ignorance.

It might be thought that in such a situation the decision we face is genuinely arbitrary; since the available evidence cannot tell us which alternative to choose, nothing can, and we might lose either way. I am not sure, however, that this is quite our predicament. Allow me to sketch in broad outlines a form of argument which would suggest that there are ethical reasons for treating men and women as if one explanation were correct even if we don't know which explanation is correct. Because of a number of fairly obvious complications the argument here is merely a sketch, and all I would claim for it at present is that it is suggestive. But it is, I think, an argument worthy of further development, and for that reason, although "merely suggestive," is not to be despised.[12]

The argument can be presented conveniently in the form of a gain-loss grid, similar to simple models of economic decision making. We might assume a fundamental explanation for differences at issue, and might be either right or wrong. We might assume a social explanation for the differences, and once again might be either right or wrong. My strategy will be to propose that the risks we run are less significant and the prospective gains greater on the assumption of a social explanation, and thus that to the extent that we are ignorant we should assume that observed sex differences are to be explained in social terms.

Theory True

	Fundamental	Social
Fundamental	1	2
Social	3	4

Theory Assumed

Figure 3

There is one class of prospective gains and losses which appear to balance out between our alternatives: the promise of social efficiency and the threat of social disutility. If we assume either explanation for observed differences, and if we're right, other things being equal, we can expect the social programs we introduce or the social structures we build on the basis of our theories to work more smoothly overall. If our assumed theory is wrong, we can expect to suffer on the same score.[13]

But consider also the matter of social injustice. The treatment of differences which are in fact merely social as if they were fundamental — the outcome represented by (2) — seems to be a clear instance of socially unjust treatment. Standard paradigms of racism and sexism involve precisely this feature; that differences between individuals or groups, real or imagined, are taken to be inherent and fundamental which are not. The stereotypical black is thought to be *inherently* lazy and stupid, not merely socially handicapped, and racism would be quite a different matter were this not the case. The true sexist holds not just that some particular group of women are by force of circumstance scatter-brained and fragile, but that women are so by nature. Part of the injustice of racism and sexism is simply that the stereotypes don't fit. But even if they did, sexist and racist treatment would be unjust because the characteristics involved are not the *fundamental* characteristics they are assumed to be.

On this model, I think, we must envisage social injustice of an all-too-familiar sort as one of the potential losses to be entered against the assumption of a fundamental explanation for observed differences.[14] Is there a comparable threat of injustice on the other side?

It must be admitted that the outcome envisaged in (3) includes losses above and beyond mere social disutility. Two of the ethically most significant losses are the following. If we attempt to correct for differences which are not of social origin by social means, we can expect a disproportionate distribution of social goods. If we pour our social resources into attempts at social remedy for low scores on some characteristic among some particular group, and if the original low scores are in fact of social origin, we can in a sense see ourselves as distributing social goods with some form of equity. The low-scoring individuals were presumably short-changed or handicapped at some point, and our attempts to correct the situation are both compensationally and distributively just. But if we end up "compensating" in this way for "social ills" which are not social ills at all, we will be allotting a greater share of our social energies to a particular group, those with low scores on the characteristic at issue.

By the same token, in such an outcome we may be doing more to develop the lower potential of some than we are doing to develop the higher potential of others. That individual with a greater fundamental potential will have his or her potential developed to a lesser degree (though not to a lower level) than will those with a less handsome fundamental endowment.

Both of these, I think, are indeed social and ethical losses. We do, all things being equal, regard equal treatment as a requirement of distributive justice. And we do hold as an ideal the full development of each individual's potential. But it should be noted that these losses can be entered against outcome (2) as well as against outcome (3). If we treat social differences as if they were fundamental we can expect a disproportionate distribution of social goods, simply because we will be dealing with differences here as well. Nor would it be at all surprising to find that the treatment of social differences as if they were fundamental results in the differential development of various potentials; the crippling and neglect of individual potential have been a constant feature of this form of treatment in the past. Thus the losses envisaged in (3) are also losses to be entered against (2), in addition to the quite basic injustice of (2) discussed above. The risks of (3) don't balance out those of (2) simply because those same risks, and more, appear in (2).[15]

A closely related point can be put in terms of the prospective gains, above and beyond social utility, to be entered in boxes (1) and (4). To the extent that observed differences are social in origin rather than fundamental, they can in principle be socially avoided; society might be constructed such that those differences did not appear at all. To the extent that differences are genuinely fundamental, as in (1), this is not possible. But there is another and more glowing way of expressing this difference. One of our standard social ideals is that of a truly egalitarian society, a society of equals. When that ideal is criticized, it is generally criticized as utopian or unrealistic. But it is not criticized, other than in corrupted forms, as ethically undesirable. This is important because, to the extent that differences at issue are merely social, an approximation of the ideal of egalitarianism is a real possibility. To the extent that differences are fundamental, we will always fall short of that goal. Thus in a sense the prospective gains of box (4) are greater than those of box (1); (4) allows a prospect of egalitarianism which (1) does not, and thus a closer approximation of a deeply seated ethical ideal.

If this argument is correct, there are ethical reasons to prefer a social explanation of observed differences over a fundamental explanation to the extent that we remain in ignorance. The prospect of social injustice is less on such an assumption, and the prospective gain in terms of approximating an egalitarian ideal is greater. Ethically, we have more to gain and less to lose.

The argument is, I think, a suggestive one. But I must admit that the presentation above is incomplete in a number of respects. Some of the intuitions regarding justice on which it relies call for a more complete examination than I am able to offer here, and there may be ethically relevant matters which have been neglected. So at present all I would claim for the argument is that it is a suggestive sketch. But what it suggests is of importance; that even our treatment of the data regarding sex differences, and of our own ignorance, is an ethical matter which calls for more than mere data.

III. WHAT IF IT'S ALL TRUE?

In the previous sections we have raised some doubts concerning the data on which the arguments at issue rest and have suggested that there may be ethical reasons for treating differences as social rather than fundamental in cases in which we can not claim to know which they are. But let us suppose that in some case we do have firm and unambiguous empirical evidence of differences between the sexes; let us suppose that we can *prove* that men are characteristically more aggressive, that women are generally more "communicative," and the like. What follows from suitably hard data revealing suitably fundamental differences even if we have it? Not as much, I think, as is often assumed.

Let us assume some fundamental characteristic of men f_1 and some fundamental characteristic of women f_2. Let us also suppose a set of tasks $t_1, t_2, \ldots t_n$ for which characteristic f_1 is a prime qualification, and a different set of tasks $t'_1, t'_2, \ldots t'_n$ for which f_2 is a prime qualification. Does it follow, as the argument at issue has it, that social roles ought to be distinguished along sexual lines such that men are assigned tasks $t_1, t_2, \ldots t_n$ and women are assigned tasks $t'_1, t'_2, \ldots t'_n$? It at least does not follow as night the day; allow me to catalog a number of major qualifications required in any such inference.

There are very few tasks indeed which call for one and only

one simple qualification. Brain surgery demands dexterity, but not dexterity alone, and plumbing demands physical strength and a degree of limberness, but not these alone. The most dexterous of brain surgeons and the strongest and most limber of plumbers might nonetheless be a very bad brain surgeon and a very bad plumber; each might lack foresight, experience, spatial perception, and appropriate forms of mechanical imagination. The general lesson here is that qualification for most tasks is a complicated matter of a balance of different abilities, some of which may be tied to fundamental characteristics and many of which may not be. Thus no single simple characteristic, and no small group of characteristics, however fundamental, can alone be expected to decide the question of who should be assigned which tasks; some other capacity or group of capacities, fundamental or social in origin, might always outweigh the significance of any inherent difference. Thus even given fundamental sexual differences, and even given that some of those differences involve characerics which are qualifications for different sets of tasks, we cannot conclude that those tasks ought to be divided on sexual lines without considering *all* qualifications relevant to those tasks, including qualifications which are not tied to fundamental differences.

Consider also a second difficulty. There are precious few fundamental differences in the data which are not at best merely statistical differences, often very slight, which show up in testing large groups of men and women. A statistical difference of this type may not alone indicate very much. That women score higher on average in a characteristic f_1 is perfectly consistent with each of the following; that those who score most highly on f_1 are men, and that a finite number of occupational slots calling for only characteristic f_1 will best be filled entirely by men.[16] A statistical difference of this type is even consistent with the claim that your chances of selecting an individual satisfying a specific requirement for a high f_1 score are greater if you draw from a pool exclusively of men than from either a pool exclusively of women or from a randomly mixed pool.[17] A higher average score on f_1 among women does not entail that any woman scores above all men, that most women score above all men, that the highest score is a woman's or that the lowest is a man's, or that the majority of women score more highly than the majority of men.[18] Nonetheless the statistical difference in such a case is quite standardly represented by saying that "women score more highly with regard to f_1 than do men," and this latter phrase has a peculiar tendency to be misread (and misused in argument) as if it were the quite different claim that all women score more highly with regard to f_1 than all men. This subtle shift can, of course, make all the difference between truth and falsity.[19]

The importance here of this elementary error is that a *clear* justification of universally applied sex-role differentiation would require the stronger universal claim: that all women score more highly with regard to f_1 than do all men. From the mere fact that the average score for women with regard to f_1 is higher than the average score for men it simply does not follow that tasks calling for f_1 ought to be assigned to any particular group at all, unless we nominate those with high f_1 scores as such a group. Consistent with the truth of the statistical claim, and depending on the circumstances, that group might be composed exclusively of women, might be composed exclusively of men, or might be composed of any proportion of the two.

We are assuming, for the moment, that the data regarding sexual differences on which arguments of the type at issue rely are beyond reproach, i.e., genuinely hard data revealing genuinely fundamental sexual differences. But this is not the only data which is required if the argument is to go through. Given different characteristics f_1 and f_2, and sets of tasks t_1, t_2, . . . t_n and t'_1, t'_2, . . . t'_n, we must also have firm and objective data concerning the importance of those characteristics for those tasks. Oddly enough, those who present arguments for social role differentiation on the basis of sexual differences generally neglect to supply this second batch of data, substituting instead a form of armchair speculation which they would rightly reject in other contexts. From the fact (if it is a fact) that women have greater fine coordination and are better at rapid decisions, it is too often concluded that they would make good typists.[20] But why not brain surgeons or astronauts?; these too call for the characteristics in question. The fact (if it is a fact) that men are more aggressive is similarly taken to justify a role-assignment as soldiers and businessmen. But is not aggression also a qualification for the protective role of babysitters? In order for the link from fundamental traits to social roles to be a properly logical link, free from the corrupting influence of social prejudice, we would need independent demonstration of a correlation between certain traits and certain tasks or occupations. That data would have to be as hard as the data regarding the fundamental differences itself. At this point the argument for social role differentiation characteristically takes the form of armchair speculation as to what makes a good typist, a good businessman, and the like. But if we allow armchair speculation at this point, we might as well have allowed armchair speculation as to basic sexual differences to begin with.

Another group of major assumptions lies hidden in the argument as well. Let us assume that a particular characteristic — aggression, for example — is a salient characteristic of contemporary businesspeople and is perhaps even essential to the current structure of business itself. Let us also assume that men are more aggressive than women, and here we might even assume that men are *universally* more aggressive. Does it follow that businesspeople ought to be male? Only if we add an additional ethical premise: that contemporary businesspeople are as businesspeople ought to be, and that the current social structure of business is as it ought to be. What this shows is that no form of the argument at issue can be a pure extrapolation from data, however good; it must always involve a premise as to how society *ought* to be as well. In actual use, I think, the hidden assumption is always that our society is at least by and large as it ought to be. So it shouldn't be too surprising that the argument is generally used as a defense of the status quo; it relies on an assumption in favor of the status quo. But with different assumptions as to how society ought to be we would get different results. If aggression in business is a social handicap rather than a social strength — if, for example, it is that aggression which generates the ills of corporate capitalism — then we ought not encourage aggression in business, and perhaps quite generally ought not encourage aggression in positions of power. If males were universally more aggressive than females, we should do all we can to deny them a role in business and to keep them from occupying positions of power.

Consider finally the question of whether certain differences ought to be exploited or compensated. The fact (if it is a fact) that men and women differ in particular ways does not alone dictate how we ought to deal with those differences. Some differences between people are differences we rely on in constructing a social order — differences as to interests, needs, and desires, for example. But some differences are ones we attempt to correct or compensate for rather than to exploit. We don't give the curably ill different jobs simply because they are ill; we try to cure them. We don't simply arrange work for amputees which is better done without certain limbs; we at least attempt to supply mechanical replacements. If there are differences which *cannot* be corrected or compensated for, of course, we learn to live with them. But nothing has been said to indicate, and as far as I know none of the data shows, that any of the supposed differences between men and women are differences for which correction or compensatory treatment is impossible. The statistics on aggression do not show that males could not be trained to be less aggressive, or females to be more so. Superior verbal ability on the part of females does not mean that males could not, with proper compensatory training, reach the same level. Thus one might conclude from the data regarding sexual differences not that we ought to assign career-roles along sexual lines, but that we owe each group compensatory training as a corrective for its shortcomings, so that in the end the only determinant of social role will be individual interest and desire. The point here is simply that differences alone do not show that our society ought to be constructed so as to exploit those differences; we might equally well conclude that society ought to attempt to correct them or compensate for them.

This is, I am sure, radically incomplete as a catalog of weaknesses in the inference from data regarding sexual differences to recommendations regarding social roles. But it is sufficient to show that the argument with which we began is a simple non sequitur as it stands. We have assumed that the data at issue are suitably hard data revealing genuinely fundamental differences, an assumption challenged in the beginning. But even given that assumption the conclusions generally drawn regarding social roles do not follow. In order legitimately to conclude anything at all regarding the desirability of social role differentiation we must deal with a number of additional and complicating factors. We must consider whether differences ought to be exploited or compensated, we must make explicit and defend assumptions as to how society ought to be, and we need firm evidence rather than armchair speculation as to links between particular characteristics and effectiveness at certain tasks. We must be wary of misreading statistical generalizations as universal claims, and must avoid treating prima facie and partial qualifications for particular roles as if they were sole qualifications. Without these the argument simply falls short, no matter how tight our data regarding sexual differences.

Does this indicate that the data, even if legitimate, shows nothing which might be of significance to social decisions? That would be too strong. If there *are* fundamental sexual differences, that fact may be one of moral importance in deciding how society ought to be. Together with other claims and arguments it *could* even be part of a satisfactory justification of social role differentiation along sexual lines. But no data of this type, however good, would alone dictate the shape our society ought to take.

IV. CONCLUSION

The discussion above has a clear central theme, even if it does not build to a conclusive argumentative climax. Contemporary data regarding sex differences is quite often taken as a justification for social recommendations involving social role differentiation on sexual lines. I have tried to detail a number of objections against the use of such an argument and against some assumptions behind it. The data on which such arguments rest is often data of which we should be suspicious, for a variety of reasons. In cases in which we are significantly ignorant, there may be ethical reasons for preferring a social explanation rather than the fundamental difference on which the standard argument relies. And even where the data is as tight and conclusive as one might like, the conclusion generally drawn is not one which follows in any rigorous sense.

It is not unusual for discussions of sex differences to end with an appeal for further testing. I will not make such an appeal. In light of the deep difficulties of attempting any satisfactory test, in light of the social dangers of a test gone wrong, in light of the inconclusiveness of the best of data for any social purposes, and given the variety of genuinely pressing demands on our social energies, I see little reason for continuing such testing.

NOTES

1. See E.E. Maccoby and C.N. Jacklin, *The Psychology of Sex Differences* (Stanford: Stanford University Press, 1974). A more re-

cent piece on visual-spatial abilities is L.J. Harris, "Sex Differences in Spatial Ability: Possible Environmental, Genetic, and Neurological Factors," in *Asymmetrical Function of the Brain,* ed. M. Kinsbourne (Cambridge: Cambridge University Press, 1979), pp. 405–522.

2. Monte Buchsbaum cites this difference and offers a biochemical explanation in "The Sensoriat in the Brain," *Psychology Today* 11 (May 1978): 96–104.

3. See Diane McGuinness and Karl H. Pribram, "The Origins of Sensory Bias in the Development of Gender Differences in Perception and Cognition," in *Cognitive Growth and Development: Essays in Memory of Herbert G. Birch,* ed. Morton Bortner (New York: Brunner/Mazel, 1979), pp. 3–56.

4. Sandra F. Witelson, "Sex and the Single Hemisphere: Specialization of the Right Hemisphere for Spatial Processing," *Science* 193, no. 4521 (1976): 425–27.

5. Aggression is probably *the* standard sex difference, with more studies to its credit than any other. See E.E. Maccoby, *The Development of Sex Differences* (Stanford: Stanford University Press, 1966) and E.E. Maccoby and C.N. Jacklin, *The Psychology of Sex Differences,* op. cit.

6. The terms "manipulative" and "communicative," and various echoes of the argument, appear in Diane McGuinness and Karl H. Pribram, "The Origins of Sensory Bias," op. cit.

7. Some recent examples include Witelson, "Sex and the Single Hemisphere," McGuinness and Pribram, "The Origins of Sensory Bias," Monte Buchsbaum, "The Sensoriat in the Brain," and informal quotations from Jerre Levy in Daniel Goleman, "Special Abilities of the Sexes: Do They Begin in the Brain?," *Psychology Today* 11 (November 1978): 48–59, 120. A history of this and related arguments appears in Stephanie A. Shields, "Functionalism, Darwinism, and the Psychology of Women: A Study in Social Myth," *American Psychologist* 30, no. 7 (1975): 739–754.

8. Were our data to show no sex differences at all then it might be proposed that we would have a very strong case for there being fundamental differences somehow "compensated" by differential social treatment.

    A distinction is sometimes drawn between biological and psychological sex differences; between height in inches, for example, and tendencies toward aggresion. In what follows I concentrate for the most part on questions of psychological differences, simply because these seem the most interesting. But in most respects the argument would apply equally well to either type of trait, and I am wary of attempting a sharp demarcation between them.

9. One might also distinguish between psychological and behavioral

traits on the grounds that the same psychological traits might have different behavioral manifestations in different settings or within different socially enforced roles. Though I have not relied on this distinction, and though it seems to me to be one very difficult to distinguish in practice, the discussion below of aggression and stress seems to emphasize this importance.

10. From Monte Buchsbaum, "The Sensoriat in the Brain," op. cit.

11. It might be suggested that in such cases the data can be of no help to us at all; that the data cannot decide between competing theories because it is that data which each of the theories is to explain. But this would overlook the dual role of scientific data vis-à-vis scientific theories. That which a theory explains (or seems to explain) is at the same time evidence for the truth of the theory.

    The issue, of course, is which of the competing theories *better* explain the data, a matter involving the complexities and subtleties of breadth, ties with other bodies of theory and simplicity.

12. The argument has the general form of Pascal's wager, and like Pascal's wager shows strictly not that a particular alternative is true but that a particular alternative ought to be believed, or that one ought to act as if it is true. In "The Subjection of Women," J.S. Mill comes at least close to this form of argument in maintaining that given natural sex differences, there would be no need to enforce socially distinct roles. Since what women "can do, but not so well as the men who are their competitors, competition suffices to exclude them from . . ." we have nothing to lose in acting as if there are no fundamental differences. But the argument presented here differs from Mill's in a number of major respects. A convenient abridgment of Mill's essay is included in *The Feminist Papers,* ed. Alice R. Rossi (New York: Bantam Books, 1974), pp. 196–238.

13. Whether the loss of efficiency we risk in each case is the same is, perhaps, a more complicated question. Depending on how we (wrongly) treat certain differences and on what effects our incorrect treatment in fact has, these might not balance out. I am obliged to David Pomerantz for bringing this complication to my attention.

14. It should be noted, however, that all possible forms of treatment of social differences as if they were fundamental may not involve equal degrees of injustice. Exploitation of merely social differences as if they were fundamental, for example, may be a more extreme case than attempted correction of social differences as if they were fundamental.

15. Were these prospective losses *only* characteristic of (3), we might still argue that they fail to balance out the radical injustice of (2). But that would call for a more complex argument concerning the assignment of various weights to various social goals, which I have not attempted to provide here.

16. Consider, for example, a hypothetical sample such as the following, using W_1 through W_5 to represent five women and M_1 through M_5 to represent five men:

W_1	.75	M_1	1.0
W_2	.75	M_2	1.0
W_3	.75	M_3	.5
W_4	.75	M_4	.5
W_5	.75	M_5	.5
Average:	.75	Average:	.70

The average score for women is .75, and for men is a mere .70. But those two individuals who score highest are male, and if we have two openings best filled by highest scorers, with no other considerations at issue, they will best be filled by these two men.

17. Consider, for instance, the following sample:

W_1	.85	M_1	.85
W_2	.75	M_2	.85
W_3	.75	M_3	.85
W_4	.75	M_4	.85
W_5	.65	M_5	.10
Average:	.75	Average:	.70

Let us suppose that we have an opening which demands a high score, and that we have set .80 as a specific requirement. Our chances of drawing a satisfactory candidate from the pool on the left are 1/5, from a randomly mixed pool are 5/10, and from the pool on the right are 4/5, despite the fact that the average score for the right hand column is lower than the average for that on the left.

18. The sample in footnote 16 is one in which the highest score is not a woman's. A sample in which the lowest score is not a man's, though the average male score is lower, can easily be constructed:

W_1	1.0	M_1	.70
W_2	.5	M_2	.70
Average:	.75	Average:	.70

The following sample is one in which the score of the majority of men is higher than the score of the majority of women:

W_1	.75	M_1	.80
W_2	.75	M_2	.80
W_3	.75	M_3	.80
W_4	.75	M_4	.55
W_5	.75	M_5	.55
Average:	.75	Average:	.70

For a somewhat simpler discussion of statistical frequencies and sex differences, see Joyce Trebilcot, "Sex Roles: The Argument From

Nature," in this volume, pp. 40–48. The general spirit of Trebilcot's discussion and mine are, I think, very similar.

19. Interestingly enough, "branching quantifiers" appear quite frequently in trying to represent the data. Some of the difficulties and ambiguities of grammatical and logical forms are made clear in Jon Barwise, "On Branching Quantifiers in English," *Journal of Philosophical Logic* 8 (1979): 47–80.

20. An example taken from Diane McGuinness and Karl H. Pribram, "The Origins of Sensory Bias." In "Sex Differences in Mental and Behavioral Traits," *Genetic Psychological Monographs* (1968), J.E. Garai and A. Schienfeld classify those abilities which favor females as "clerical skills" (pp. 169–299).

Part IV
"Androgyny"

Introduction

A. PSYCHOLOGICAL "ANDROGYNY"

We have seen that there is reason to doubt that any Group X and Group Y psychological sex differences can be shown definitively. But let us suppose that there are such differences and that we should, on ethical grounds, act on the assumption that they are caused by environmental rather than biological factors. Let us suppose further that a society is undesirable if the majority of females have only Group X traits and the majority of males have only Group Y traits.[1] We could then conclude that by altering the environment of persons, it would be possible to create a society in which psychological traits are ideally distributed among persons.

But what would an ideal distribution of psychological traits be? Some have answered this question by advocating an ideal of *androgyny* for society. JOYCE TREBILCOT reviews the two types of androgyny ideals commonly found in the literature on this topic. One type, which she calls "monoandrogynism," envisions the perfect society as one in which everyone has both the morally acceptable[2] "masculine" and the morally acceptable "feminine" psychological traits. A "polyandrogynist" ideal, in contrast, would be a society in which everyone has a choice between selecting either (a) some combination of morally acceptable "masculine" (Group Y) and "feminine" (Group X) traits, or (b) only morally acceptable "feminine" (Group X) traits, or (c) only morally acceptable "masculine" (Group Y) traits. Trebilcot argues that if these two ideals are the only options available for an ideal society, polyandrogynism would be preferable because it provides greater freedom of choice for all individuals. MARY ANNE WARREN argues that there is no sharp distinction between the two ideals as defined in terms of psychological traits, however, and defends androgyny against a number of anti-feminist and feminist criticisms. ROBERT PIELKE responds to a further objection, that androgyny might eliminate sexual desire in persons.

The terms "feminine" and "masculine" as applied to psychological traits mean something quite different from those terms as applied to persons. Here again, however, the meanings can vary from author to author. Mary Anne Warren construes advocates of androgyny to be relying on the normative senses of the terms as applied to psychological traits in defining "androgyny." In their normative senses, "masculine" and "feminine" mean "more natural or desirable in males (females) than females (males)." Another way to interpret the terms would be in a descriptive use in which they mean "characteristic of and peculiar to males (females)." Joyce Trebilcot relies on yet a third sense in her definitions of androgyny, in which "masculine" and "feminine" mean "have been traditionally assigned to males (females)."

These terms, however, may raise serious problems for advocates of androgyny. If the terms are used by these advocates in either of the first two senses above, what is actually being advocated is that females and males of the future should have traits which are now more desirable in one sex than the other (the first sense above) or which are now characteristic of and peculiar to one sex (the second sense above). But if it is a myth that morally acceptable Group X (Y) traits are desirable only in females (males) — as Sandra Bem has argued — or a myth that they are characteristic of and peculiar to females (males) now — a view suggested in Part III — commitment to androgyny seems to involve commitment to a falsehood.[3] What is worse, the myth that sex and gender either are or ought to be linked in any way is the very one that androgynists wish to dispel.

It has been suggested that this problem of self-defeating terminology can be resolved if androgyny advocators place the terms "feminine" and "masculine" in quotes to signal their awareness of a false element in their definitions. It is not certain, however, that this device will actually solve the problem. For if what one really believes is that sex and gender are not and ought not now be linked in any way, but rather that Group X and Y traits are *human* ones (ones everybody has at one time or another), then what one is really proposing is a future society in which we all have the psychological traits we now have except for the morally objectionable ones. But surely something is lost here; almost anyone could agree to *that* ideal. Thus difficulties regarding the terms "feminine" and "masculine" seem to be difficulties regarding not merely the letter but the spirit of androgynous ideals that are expressed in terms of psychological traits. An alternative defense of this view is presented by ELIZABETH LANE BEARDSLEY in what follows.

Many have construed such consequences of advocating androgyny to be so disastrous that they have suggested abandoning use of the term altogether. This suggestion has a good deal of practical merit; even when the concept is altered to avoid the above problems, the very history of the notion may lead users of the term "androgyny" to misconstrue it in terms of some older definition. Andrea Dworkin[4] and others, however, seem to have used the term successfully while making it quite clear that they mean something almost opposite to what many androgynists appear to have been committed to. But no matter what the final decision is about the use of the term "androgyny," the negative results of the earlier definitions do not entail that the *program* of the androgyny defender has to be abandoned, particularly at such an early stage of the concept's contemporary development.

B. BEHAVIORAL ANDROGYNY

One way to salvage the program of the androgyny defender would be to distinguish sharply between psychological traits and overt behavioral activities, applying "masculine" and "feminine" to behavioral activities rather than to real or imagined psychological traits. In this view, a commitment to androgyny would entail a commitment to an ideal of men's and women's *behaving* in ways different from ways we do now by virtue of accepting roles other than current sex roles. Commitment to mono-androgynism would be advocation of an ideal society in which females and males engage in some combination of behavioral roles now engaged in primarily by females or primarily by males. Commitment to polyandrogynism would be advocation of an ideal society in which females and males have a choice between selecting only "feminine" roles, only "masculine" roles, or some combination of "feminine" and "masculine" roles. "Feminine" and "masculine" roles are not to be construed as ones which are now in fact selected by all (or even most) females or males, but would be construed as ones which are now engaged in for the most part by females or males.

That there are now such roles in our society is not a matter of dispute. The role of childrearer, for example, is overwhelmingly assumed by females, although not all females engage in it and some males do. The role of upper-level corporate manager is overwhelmingly assumed by males, although not all males have such a role and some females do. The role of synchronized swimmer is for the most part assumed by females, the role of football player by males, and so on. So advocating these androgynous ideals requires commitment to no falsehood nor even to a suspected falsehood; it amounts simply to the claim that we should eliminate a social structure in which behavioral roles are to a large extent divided along sexual lines. In what follows, LINDA NICHOLSON critically examines some theories from the history of philosophy regarding women's so-called proper work roles. JANICE MOULTON and FRANCINE RAINONE argue that the sexual division of labor in our current society is unjust and must be radically revised.

VIRGINIA HELD advocates a form of monoandrogynism with respect to raising children, currently a "feminine" activity where "feminine" is defined as above. In those cases where both mother and father accept the responsibility for raising their children, she argues, both are obligated to divide equally all the tasks involved rather than assign most to the woman as is the current practice. Since it is clear that men are as capable as women of performing such tasks, there is no reason in advance for ruling out their actually doing so on the grounds of some claimed psychological or physical difference between women and men.

If monoandrogynism is extended to the sphere of the public workplace it would entail a drastic overhaul of current corporate business structure. For example, although the role of secretary is now a "feminine" one in the above sense of the term and the role of corporation president a "masculine" one, monoandrogynists would have to advocate each person's selecting both what are now "masculine" and now "feminine" roles. So a woman or man might spend half the day as corporation president, the other half as secretary. Some might argue that such a system would be inefficient, particularly in sales oriented businesses, since it would entail not only large groups of persons moving from one job role to the next in a matter of hours, days, or weeks, it would also entail customers' being served by one person at one time, another at another time. However, there seem to be equally strong reasons[5] for construing such a system as increasing efficiency by allowing greater flexibility; it would not trap women with executive competencies solely behind secretarial desks and it would not force males with good clerical aptitudes to adopt solely executive tasks. To the extent that people of both sexes have a spread of both talents and interests, monoandrogyny in the marketplace would increase efficient use of them. Polyandrogynism as extended to the public workplace would not as obviously suffer from objections on grounds of inefficiency, because it would allow for one and the same person to perform a given role for extended periods of time and yet would allow for more males and more females accepting those roles previously reserved for members of the opposite sex.

Neither monoandrogynistic nor polyandrogynistic ideals are as obviously defensible when successful performance of the activity in question relies almost exclusively on having certain physiological features.[6] There is reason to believe that, statistically speaking, women are shorter than men, have a different oxygenation rate, muscle and hip structure, etc., and that such differences favor women in more successful performance of sports such as synchronized swimming, ballet, and balance beam and favor males in more successful performance of sports such as football. For these reasons, both JANE ENGLISH and BETSY POSTOW hold that although there are no moral grounds for banning women from "masculine" sports or men from "feminine" ones there may be grounds for women in particular to question the desirability of engaging in "masculine" ones.[7] Instead, they suggest that a more fruitful course of action for women in sports would be promoting participation in and developing more "feminine" sports.

Strangely enough, most discussions of behavioral androgyny have centered almost exclusively on talk about work activities, even though there is room for further examination of the concept in relation to sports, as Postow shows. But other activities also seem particularly ripe at this time for our discussions. JANE MARTIN, for example, offers ideas on how our educational system might have to be revised in order to realize a truly androgynous future.

NOTES

1. Sandra Bem has argued that any person who has strictly "feminine" (Group X) or strictly "masculine" (Group Y) psychological traits functions poorly in diverse situations. See her "The Measurement of Psychological Androgyny," *Journal of Consulting and Clinical Psychology* 42 (1974): 155–62.
2. Morally objectionable psychological traits, such as being murderous or pugnacious, are not ones most androgyny defenders wish to see in an *ideal* society.
3. Trebilcot's definition does not require commitment to a falsehood, for even if we all now have all the traits in both Groups X and Y, it is clear that society makes no bones about *assigning* Group X traits to females, Group Y traits to males. However, since this assignation is a mistake on the part of society, the concept of psychological androgyny defined in terms of it is at best awkward to use in that its use suggests at least tacit assent to the mistake.

    Another problem with the definition is that it remains at least as vague as the notion of "morally acceptable" psychological traits; *which* traits end up getting counted as acceptable depend, of course, on what ethical theory is provided along with the androgyny definition. It may be of interest to note here that society at large finds unacceptable traits such as wildness and witchiness, for example, whereas on at least one current feminist theory, such traits are not only acceptable, they are desirable, in women. See, for example, Mary Daly's *Gyn-Ecology: The Metaethics of Radical Feminism* (Boston: Beacon, 1978). If no "masculine" traits end up getting counted as morally acceptable, the concept of androgyny altogether self-destructs. I am grateful to Joyce Trebilcot for these latter insights.
4. See, for example, her *Woman Hating* (New York: E.P. Dutton and Co., 1974). By "androgyny" she means the abolition of the very notions of masculinity and femininity.
5. I am indebted to Patrick Grim for this point.
6. Note that there are very few, if any, public or private workplace activities that could plausibly be claimed now to have this property, due in part to the development of tools and machines designed to decrease, if not eliminate, the necessity for great physical exertion in the workplace.
7. What Postow means by "masculine" is different from the way it is being used in this Introduction to Part IV and from the way it is

defined by Trebilcot. This should be taken into account when comparisons and contrasts between the various viewpoints are classroom-discussed. Further discussion of the question as to whether women have a moral reason to withdraw support from "masculine" sports can be found in Mary Vetterling-Braggin's "One Form of Anti-Androgynism" and B.C. Postow's "Masculine Sports Revisited," both forthcoming in the (Canadian) *Journal of the Philosophy of Sport,* and in Patrick Grim's "Sports and Two Androgynisms" available from Grim at the Department of Philosophy, SUNY, Stony Brook, New York 11566.

Part IV A
Psychological
"Androgyny"

Joyce Trebilcot

Two Forms of Androgynism

Traditional concepts of women and men, of what we are and should be as females and males, of the implications of sex for our relationships to one another and for our places in society, are not acceptable. But what models, if any, should we adopt to replace them? In this paper I consider just two of the alternatives discussed in recent literature—two versions of androgynism.

In discussing these two views I follow the convention of distinguishing between sex (female and male) and gender (feminine and masculine). Sex is biological, whereas gender is psychosocial. Thus, for example, a person who is biologically female may be—in terms of psychological characteristics or social roles—feminine or masculine, or both.

Although what counts as feminine and masculine varies among societies over time, I use these terms here to refer to the gender concepts traditionally dominant in our own society. Femininity, on this traditional view, has nurturing as its core: it

Reprinted by permission of the *Journal of Social Philosophy,* vol. VIII, no. 1 (January, 1977), and the author.

This paper was written in 1974 and read at a session sponsored by the Society for Women in Philosophy at the Pacific Division conference of the American Philosophical Association in San Diego in March of 1975. My thanks to Mary Anne Warren and the late Jane English for their comments on the paper at that meeting and especially to Kathryn Baer (formerly Coordinator of the Women's Studies Program at Washington University) for discussions of this topic.

centers on the image of woman as mother, as provider of food, warmth, and emotional sustenance. Masculinity focuses on mastery: it comprises the notion of man struggling to overcome obstacles, to control nature, and also the notion of man as patriarch or leader in society and the family.

The first form of androgynism to be discussed here takes the word "androgyny" literally, so to speak. In this word the Greek roots for man (*andros*) and woman (*gyne*) exist side by side. According to the first form of androgynism, both feminine and masculine characteristics should exist "side by side" in every individual: each woman and man should develop personality traits and engage in activities traditionally assigned to only one sex. Because this view postulates a single ideal for everyone, I call it monoandrogynism, or, for brevity, *M*.

Monoandrogynism, insofar as it advocates shared roles, is now official policy in a number of countries. For example, the Swedish government presented a report to the United Nations in 1968 specifying that in Sweden, "every individual, regardless of sex, shall have the same practical opportunities not only for education and employment but also fundamentally the same responsibility for his or her own financial support as well as shared responsibility for child upbringing and housework."[1]

Closer to home, Jessie Bernard, in her discussion of women's roles, distinguishes the one-role view, according to which woman's place is in the home; the two-role pattern, which prescribes a combination of the traditional housewife-mother functions and work outside the home; and what she calls the "shared-role ideology" which holds "that children should have the care of both parents, that all who benefit from the services supplied in the household should contribute to them, and that both partners should share in supporting the household."[2]

Caroline Bird in her chapter "The Androgynous Life" writes with approval of role-sharing. She also suggests that the ideal person "combines characteristics usually attributed to men with characteristics usually attributed to women."[3]

The psychological dimension of *M* is stressed by Judith M. Bardwick. In her essay "Androgyny and Humanistic Goals, or Goodbye, Cardboard People," she discusses a view according to which the ideal or "healthy" person would have traits of both genders. "We would then expect," she says, "both nurturance and competence, openness and objectivity, compassion and competitiveness from both women and men, as individuals, according to what they were doing."[4]

The work of these and other writers provides the basis for a normative theory, *M,* which prescribes a single ideal for everyone: the person who is, in both psychological characteristics and social roles, both feminine and masculine.

The second form of androgynism shares with the first the principle that biological sex should not be a basis for judgments about the appropriateness of gender characteristics. It differs from the first, however, in that it advocates not a single ideal but rather a variety of options including "pure" femininity and masculinity as well as any combination of the two. According to this view, all alternatives with respect to gender should be equally available to and equally approved for everyone, regardless of sex. Thus, for example, a female might acceptably develop as a completely feminine sort of person, as both feminine and masculine in any proportion, or as wholly masculine. Because this view prescribes a variety of acceptable models, I call it polyandrogynism, or *P.*[5]

Constantina Safilios-Rothschild supports *P* in her recent book *Women and Social Policy.* In this work she makes a variety of policy recommendations aimed at bringing about the liberation of both sexes. Liberation requires, she says, that individuals live "according to their wishes, inclinations, potentials, abilities, and needs rather than according to the prevailing stereotypes about sex roles and sex-appropriate modes of thought and behavior." Some persons, she adds, "might *choose* to behave according to their sex's stereotypic . . . patterns. But some women and some men may *choose,* if they are so inclined, to take options in some or all of the life sectors now limited to the opposite sex."[6]

Carolyn Heilbrun's work also suggests *P.* In *Toward a Recognition of Androgyny* she writes, "The ideal toward which I believe we should move is best described by the term 'androgyny.' This ancient Greek word . . . defines a condition under which the characteristics of the sexes, and the human impulses expressed by men and women, are not rigidly assigned. Androgyny seeks to liberate the individual from the confines of the appropriate." Androgyny suggests, Heilbrun says, "a full range of experience open to individuals who may, as women, be aggressive, as men, tender; it suggests a spectrum upon which human beings choose their places without regard to propriety or custom."[7]

This second form of androgynism focuses on a variety of options rather than on the single model of the part-woman/part-man (that is, of the androgyne in the classic sense). It is ap-

propriate, however, to extend the term "androgynism" to apply
to it; for, like *M,* it seeks to break the connection between sex
and gender.

For both forms of androgynism, the postulated ideals are best
construed so as to exclude aspects of traditional gender concepts
which are morally objectionable. Femininity should not be taken
to include, for example, weakness, foolishness, or incompetence. Similarly, tendencies such as those to authoritarianism
and violence should be eliminated from the concept of
masculinity. Most importantly, aspects of the gender concepts
which prescribe female submissiveness and male domination
(over women and over other men) must, on moral grounds, be
excluded from both the single ideal advocated by *M* and the
range of options recommended by *P.*

Either form of androgyny may, in the long run, lead to major
changes in human attributes. It is often suggested that the androgyne is a person who is feminine part of the time and
masculine part of the time. But such compartmentalization
might be expected to break down, so that the feminine and
masculine qualities would influence one another and be
modified. Imagine a person who is at the same time and in the
same respect both nurturant and mastery-oriented, emotional
and rational, cooperative and competitive, and so on. I shall not
undertake here to speculate on whether this is possible, or, if it
is, on how such qualities might combine. The point is just that
androgyny in the long run may lead to an integrating of
femininity and masculinity that will yield new attributes, new
kinds of personalities. The androgyne at this extreme would
perhaps be not part feminine and part masculine, but neither
feminine nor masculine, a person in whom the genders disappear.

I turn now to the question of which of these two forms of androgynism is more acceptable. I am not concerned here to
evaluate these positions in relation to other alternatives (for example, to the traditional sexual constitution of society or to
matriarchy).[8] For the sake of this discussion, I assume that
either *M* or *P* is preferable to any alternative, and that the problem is only to decide between them. Let us first consider this
problem not as abstract speculation, and not as a problem for
some distant society, but rather as an immediate issue for our
own society. The question is then: Which form of androgynism
is preferable as a guide to action for us here and now?

Suppose we adopt *M*. Our task then is to provide opportunities, encouragement, and perhaps even incentives for those who are now feminine to be also masculine, and conversely. Suppose, on the other hand, that we adopt *P*. Our task is to create an environment in which, without reference to sex, people choose among all (moral) gender alternatives. How can this best be accomplished? What is required, clearly, is that the deeply-entrenched normative connections between sex and gender be severed. Virtually everyone now, in formulating preferences for the self and in judging the appropriateness of gender characteristics for others, at least on some occasions takes it, consciously or otherwise, that the sex of the individual in question is a relevant consideration: that one is female tends to count in favor of a feminine trait and against a masculine one, and conversely. In order to break this connection, it must be shown that masculinity is acceptable for females and femininity for males. There must, then, be opportunities, encouragement, and perhaps even incentives for gender-crossing. But this is what is required by *M*. Hence, under present conditions, the two forms of androgynism prescribe the same course of action — that is, the promotion of gender-crossing.

The question, "Which form of androgynism is preferable here and now?" then, is misconstrued. If one is an androgynist of either sort, what one must do now is seek to break the normative connections between sex and gender by bringing about gender-crossing. However, once the habit of taking sex as a reason for gender evaluation is overcome, or is at least much weaker and less widespread than it is today, then the two forms of androgynism do prescribe different courses of action. In particular, on *M* "pure" gender is condemned, but on *P* it is accepted. Let us consider, then, which version of androgynism is preferable for a hypothetical future society in which femininity and masculinity are no longer normatively associated with sex.

The major argument in favor of *P* is, of course, that because it stipulates a variety of acceptable gender alternatives it provides greater gender freedom than *M*. Now, freedom is a very high priority value, so arguments for *M* must be strong indeed. Let us consider, then, two arguments used to support *M* over *P* — one psychological, one ethical.

The psychological argument holds that in a society which is open with respect to gender, many people are likely to experience anxiety when faced with the need, or opportunity, to

choose among different but equally acceptable gender models.
Consider the words of Judith M. Bardwick:

People need guidelines, directions that are agreed upon because they
help each individual to know where one ought to go, how one can get
there, and how far one is from one's goal. It is easier to sustain frustration that comes from knowing how far you are from your objective or
what barriers are in your way than it is to sustain the anxiety that comes
from not being sure about what you want to do or what others want you
to do. It will be necessary, then, to develop new formulations by which
people will guide their lives.[9]

Bardwick says that anxiety "comes from not being sure about
what you want to do or what others want you to do." But in a
society of the sort proposed by P, the notion that one should
seek to please others in deciding among gender models would be
rejected; ideally "what others want you to do" in such a society is
to make your own decisions. Of course there is still the problem
of not being sure about what *you* want to do. Presumably, under
P, people would provide one another with help and support in
finding suitable life styles. Nevertheless, it could be that for
some, choosing among alternatives would be anxiety-producing.
On the other hand, under M, the lack of approved alternatives
could produce frustration. Hence, the argument from anxiety
should be paired with an argument from frustration. In M,
socialization is designed to make everyone androgynous (in ways
similar, perhaps, to those which have traditionally produced exclusive femininity and masculinity in our own society), and
frustration is part of the cost. In P, socialization is directed
toward enabling people to perceive, evaluate, and choose among
alternatives, and there is a risk of anxiety. We are not now in a
position to decide whether the frustration or the anxiety is
worse, for there are no data on the numbers of people likely to
suffer these emotions nor on the extent of the harm that they are
likely to do. Hence, neither the argument from anxiety nor the
argument from frustration is of any help in deciding between the
two forms of androgynism.

I turn now to a more persuasive argument for M, one which
claims that androgyny has universal value. This argument supports M not, as the argument from anxiety does, because M
prescribes some norm or other, but rather because of the content
of the norm. The argument holds that both traditional genders
include qualities that have human value, qualities that it would
be good for everyone to have. Among the elements of femininity, candidates for universal value are openness and respon-

siveness to needs and feelings, and being gentle, tender, intuitive, sensitive, expressive, considerate, cooperative, compassionate. Masculine qualities appealed to in this connection include being logical, rational, objective, efficient, responsible, independent, courageous. It is claimed, then, that there are some aspects of both genders (not necessarily all or only the ones I have mentioned) which are desirable for everyone, which we should value both in ourselves and in one another. But if there are aspects of femininity and masculinity which are valuable in this way—which are, as we might call them, virtues—they are *human* virtues, and are desirable for everyone. If Smith is a better person for being compassionate or courageous, then so is Jones, and never mind the sex of Smith or Jones. Hence, the argument concludes, the world envisioned by *M,* in which everyone or nearly everyone is both feminine and masculine, is one in which life for everyone is more rewarding than the world advocated by *P,* in which some people are of only one gender; therefore we should undertake to bring about *M.*

The argument claims, then, that both genders embody traits that it would be valuable for everyone to have. But how is this claim to be tested? Let us adopt the view that to say that something is valuable for everyone is, roughly, to say that if everyone were unbiased, well-informed, and thinking and feeling clearly, everyone would, in fact, value it. As things are now, it is difficult or impossible to predict what everyone would value under such conditions. But there is an alternative. We can seek to establish conditions in which people do make unbiased, informed, etc., choices, and see whether they then value both feminine and masculine traits.

But this reminds us, of course, of the program of *P. P* does not guarantee clear thought and emotional sensitivity, but it does propose an environment in which people are informed about all gender options and are unbiased with respect to them. If, in this context, all or most people, when they are thinking clearly, etc., tend to prefer, for themselves and others, both feminine and masculine virtues, we will have evidence to support the claim that androgyny has universal value. (In this case, *P* is likely to change into *M.*) On the other hand, if "pure" gender is preferred by many, we should be skeptical of the claim that androgyny has universal value. (In this case we should probably seek to preserve *P.*) It appears, then, that in order to discover whether *M* is preferable to *P,* we should seek to bring about *P.*

In summary, we have noted the argument from freedom,

which supports *P*; arguments from anxiety and frustration, which are indecisive; and the argument from universal value, whose analysis suggests the provisional adoption of *P*. As far as I know, there are no additional major arguments which can plausibly be presented now for either side of the issue. Given, then, the problem of deciding between *M* and *P* without reference to other alternatives, my tentative conclusion is that because of the great value of freedom, and because in an atmosphere of gender-freedom we will be in a good position to evaluate the major argument for M (that is, the argument from the universal value of androgyny), *P* is preferable to *M*.

Of course all we have assumed about the specific nature of the hypothetical society for which we are making this judgment is that the connection between sex and gender would be absent, as would be the unacceptable components of traditional gender concepts, particularly dominance and submission. It might be, then, that particular social conditions would constitute grounds for supporting *M* rather than *P*. For example, if the society in question were hierarchical with leadership roles tightly held by the predominantly masculine individuals, and if leaders with feminine characteristics were more likely to bring about changes of significant value, it could reasonably be argued that *M*, in which everyone, including leaders, has both feminine and masculine characteristics, would be preferable to *P*. But such considerations are only speculative now.

NOTES

1. Official Report of the United Nations on the Status of Women in Sweden, 1968. Quoted in Rita Liljeström, "The Swedish Model," in *Sex Roles in Changing Society,* Georgene H. Seward and Robert C. Williamson, eds. (New York: Random House, 1970), p. 200.
2. Jessie Bernard, *Women and the Public Interest* (Chicago: Aldine, 1971); and idem, *The Future of Marriage* (New York: Bantam Books, 1972). The quotation is from the latter book, p. 279.
3. Caroline Bird, *Born Female* (New York: Pocket Books, 1968), p. xi.
4. Judith M. Bardwick, "Androgyny and Humanistic Goals, or Goodbye, Cardboard People," in *The American Woman: Who Will She Be?* Mary Louise McBee and Kathryn A. Blake eds. (Beverley Hills, Calif.: Glencoe Press, 1974), p. 61.
5. "Monoandrogynism" and "polyandrogynism" are perhaps not very happy terms, but I have been unable to find alternatives which are

both descriptive and non-question-begging. In an earlier version of this paper I used "A_1" and "A_2" but these labels are not as perspicuous as "*M*" and "*P*." Mary Anne Warren, in "The Ideal of Androgyny" (unpublished) refers to "the strong thesis" and "the weak thesis," but this terminology tends to prejudice judgment as to which view is preferable. Hence, I use "*M*" and "*P*."

6. Constantina Safilios-Rothschild, *Women and Social Policy* (Englewood Cliffs, N.J.: Prentice-Hall, 1974), p. 7; emphasis hers.

7. Carolyn Heilbrun, *Toward a Recognition of Androgyny* (New York: Harper and Row, 1973), pp. 7–8.

8. My current view is that we should work for the universal realization of women's values; but that is another paper. (For some arguments against the use of the term "androgyny" in feminist theory, see, for example, Mary Daly, "The Qualitative Leap beyond Patriarchal Religion," *Quest: A Feminist Quarterly,* vol. 1, no. 4 (Spring, 1975), pp. 29ff. and Janice Raymond, "The Illusion of Androgyny," *Quest,* vol. 2, no. 1 (Summer 1975).

9. Bardwick, op. cit., p. 50.

Mary Anne Warren

Is Androgyny the Answer
to Sexual Stereotyping?

The term "androgyny" derives from the Greek words for male
and female, and suggests a state intermediate between masculinity and femininity. To many feminists androgyny has come to
represent escsape from the prison of gender—that is, from
socially enforced preconceptions of ways in which women and
men ought to differ in their psychology and behavior. Androgyny, in this feminist sense, has nothing to do with physical
hermaphroditism, a biological anomaly in which a person's body
fails to develop in an unambiguously feminine or masculine
manner. What the feminist androgynists (i.e., advocates of androgyny) recommend, rather, is *psychological* androgyny, the
combination in a single person, of either sex, of so-called
feminine and masculine character traits.

Thus, an androgyne is a person who is able to be both rational
and emotional, strong and nurturant, assertive and compassionate, depending on the demands of the situation. Her
character, or his, defies the limitations imposed by the traditional stereotypes of femininity and masculinity. Androgynists
maintain that such a balanced and flexible character structure is
vastly preferable, from both the individual's point of view and
society's, to the extreme one-sidedness represented by the traditional images of the strong, rational, unemotional male on the
one hand or the weak, emotional, irrational female on the other.
I want to examine this feminist ideal of androgyny, what it

means and what can be said for and against it. For it is a useful and suggestive concept, but poses some difficult practical and conceptual problems.

I. FEMININE AND MASCULINE STEREOTYPES

To understand the concept of androgyny as an ideal of human character development for both sexes, we must first consider what it means to call a particular character trait "feminine" or "masculine." It is standard practice in most (though not all) patriarchal cultures, including our own, to associate a certain range of psychological characteristics with the female sex, and a different range of characteristics with the male sex. These associations are not only descriptive, but normative in effect. To call a trait feminine, for instance, is generally not only to imply that it is found more often or to a greater degree in women, but also to imply that this situation is proper and desirable.

Of course, it is possible to speak of certain undesirable character traits, such as dishonesty, as feminine, without thereby implying that women *ought* to be dishonest. But when women are urged to remain or become more feminine, it is not such so-called feminine vices which they are asked to cherish, but rather the so-called feminine *virtues.* A society's way of assigning diverse virtues to the two sexes is central to its conception of gender and gender roles. In our own culture, it is standard to speak of such virtues as gentleness, nurturance, empathy, compassion, intuitiveness, and the capacity to express emotions as feminine, while virtues such as strength of will, independence, courage, rationality, and the capacity to control emotion are regarded as masculine. The distinction implies — at least in the minds of conservative thinkers — that women ought ideally to cultivate all and only the "feminine" virtues, and men the "masculine" ones.

Traces of this particular sexual categorization of human virtues may be found very early in the Western philosophical tradition. Plato argued against any such sexual dichotomy with respect to virtues, maintaining that virtue, as virtue, is the same regardless of the age or sex of the person in whom it is found.[1] Aristotle, on the other hand, held that because the two sexes have different social roles to play, their virtues must also differ A man's role, according to Aristotle, is to take part in public life, to support his family financially, and to rule with a firm hand over his wife, children, and slaves; the woman's role is to look after her husband's possessions, manage his household, and bear and rear his children. Consequently, Aristotle concluded, while it may be true that both women and men require the virtue of courage, for instance, it will not be the same kind of courage in the two cases: what men require is the courage to command, while women require only the courage to obey.[2]

Nevertheless, Plato and Aristotle knew nothing of the full-blown dichotomy of "masculine" and "feminine" virtues with which we are confronted today. Neither would have thought of suggesting that women have or ought to have superior powers of intuition, or that women are naturally better at understanding other people's emotions and expressing their own. These particular notions seem to have arisen much later, probably during the Enlightenment period. It was then that the process of industrialization gradually withdrew most economically productive labor from the home, thus increasingly making men wage earners, and women unpaid domestic laborers. It is probably not an accident that this sharpening of the sexual division of labor coincided with the appearance of new popular and philosophical rationalizations of that sexual division.

Before the wage labor system made financially remunerative work a male monopoly and domestic work the female "sphere," it had been the habit of most philosophers to justify male supremacy simply by appealing to women's presumed mental and physical inferiority, or to Eve's wickedness and the divine punishment which it supposedly brought upon all women. But when women, especially middle-class women, were relegated to unpaid domestic labor, they were also assigned a new mission, that of providing their husbands and children with all of the understanding and emotional support which they were unable to find in the increasingly impersonal world outside the home. If women were to be assigned this difficult new role, then it was necessary, or at least convenient, to cultivate the view that they possessed special intuitive and expressive capacities which men lacked.

This, at least, is one possible explanation for the proliferation of elaborate theories about the difference between masculine and feminine psychology which occurred during the eighteenth and nineteenth centuries. This process continues today. Psychologists, sociologists, novelists, theologians, sociobiologists, and writers of advice manuals are constantly attempting to capture the elusive essence of femininity or (less often) masculinity. Women are still warned that their struggle for equal rights may endanger their femininity, and men are still stigmatized as weak or unmanly if they behave in ways considered proper for women.

II. THE CONCEPT OF ANDROGYNY

It is against this background that the feminist concept of psychological androgyny has arisen. Supporters of androgyny argue that to be confined to *either* the feminine or the masculine modes of behavior is to be less than what a complete and competent human being ought to be. It is quite obvious, for instance, that in order to perform well in a wide range of situations it is necessary to be *both* rational and intuitive. How else will one be able to balance a checkbook at one moment and comfort an unhappy child at another? Only a person with both the so-called feminine virtues and the so-called masculine virtues will be able to function adequately in the full range of situations with which persons of both sexes are confronted.

Androgynists maintain, therefore, that human competence and self-development require the transcendence of sexual stereotypes. Like Plato, androgynists insist that what is virtuous in one sex is equally virtuous in the other. If men should be strong, rational, and independent, then so should women; and if women should be gentle and nurturant, then so should men. Empirical support for this position has come from research psychologists such as Sandra and Daryl Bem. The Bems' research shows that androgynous persons succeed in a wider range of situations than do exclusively "masculine" or "feminine" persons. They conclude that psychological androgyny is more conducive to competence and maturity than is a predominantly "masculine" or "feminine" character structure.[3]

Thus, androgyny is held up as a sex-neutral standrad of successful human development. But androgyny suggests not only a new standard for individual psychological development, but also a thorough reorganization of domestic, political, and other social institutions. In an androgynous society the two sexes would be equally involved in rearing children, in economic production, and in political, scientific, artistic, and other pursuits of the kind formerly considered masculine. The elimination of the feminine and masculine stereotypes may make it possible to greatly reduce the economic and status differentials between different social roles; but to the extent that such differences remain, they will no longer be based on sex or other morally irrelevant factors.

There are many objections which have been raised against this ideal of psychological androgyny. Some originate from the antifeminist camp and are directed primarily against the ultimate goal of the androgynists, i.e., a society free of the sexual stereotyping of human character and social roles. Other objections originate from within the feminist camp and are directed against the feasibility of androgyny as a means of approaching that goal, rather than against the goal itself. It will be useful to look at some objections of both sorts, before asking whether there is anything persuasive to be said against the ideal of androgyny.

III. ANTIFEMINIST OBJECTIONS

Antifeminists frequently claim that the dichotomy between feminine and masculine roles and traits of character *cannot* be altered, because it is based on certain natural and inevitable psychological differences between women and men. It used to be held—and still is, occasionally—that the most important of these differences is that men are more *rational* than women, i.e., that they have superior capacities for intellectual analysis and deliberation. Now that the results of intelligence and achievement tests have refuted this claim, we find a number of psychologists and sociobiologists holding that the essential difference is that men are naturally more *aggressive* than women. Steven Goldberg, for instance, argues that the male hormone testosterone gives men a greater propensity for aggressive behavior, and a greater need for power and status.[4] For this reason, Goldberg claims, it is for women's own good that they be taught to cultivate their special feminine abilities, rather than be encouraged to compete with males in areas where male aggressiveness will make women the losers in most cases.

This argument fails for both moral and empirical reasons. From a moral point of view, even if it were true that males are naturally and inevitably more aggressive, on the average, than females, it would hardly follow that they deserve to hold most of the high status, well-paid, or otherwise attractive positions in most of our social and political institutions, still less that the status quo is socially beneficial. Androgynists point out that it is precisely the undue concentration of social power in the hands of "masculine" men that has brought the world to its present sorry state.

Goldberg's argument is equally weak empirically. There is a good deal of evidence that in our society males do tend to behave more aggressively than females, but a shortage of evidence that this situation is either natural or inevitable. The existence of societies such as those descibed by Margaret Mead, in which men are *not* generally more aggressive than women seems to stand as conclusive proof that male aggressiveness is not natural or inevitable.[5] Some argue for the naturalness of male aggression by pointing to the social behavior of other animal species, e.g., the male-supremacist baboons. But this argument is useless, since not only is it foolish to assume that what is natural for baboons must also be natural for humans, but there is also evidence that even among baboons, male and female behaviors are determined, at least in part, not by the genetic structure of the species, but by the particular environment and, as it were, the *culture* of a given group of animals.

There is also very little evidence that the male hormone tends to produce an aggressive disposition in humans. The research results which are cited in support of this claim are invariably subject to more than one interpretation. For example, it has been claimed that men who have an extra Y chromosome, and hence an extra quantity of testosterone, are more often convicted of violent crimes than are genetically normal men. But XYY men are often mentally retarded and/or physical abnormal (e.g., very tall), and thus their antisocial tendencies (if they do in fact have such tendencies) could just as well be due to these factors as to their male hormones.[6]

To give another example, Money and Ehrhardt report that a group of genetic females, who through medical error were prenatally exposed to excessive amounts of testosterone, have grown into girls whose behavior is more "tomboyish" than that of the girls in the control group, who were not prenatally exposed to the male hormone.[7] But again, this result has many possible explanations. For one thing, these girls were *physiologically* masculinized to various degrees, a fact which may have influenced their attitudes and those of their parents. This suggests that the so-called tomboyishness or fondness for physical activity which these girls showed may be *more* natural than the more "feminine" behavior of the girls in the control group; the particular medical and social histories of the androgenized girls may have, in some way, interfered with the usual socialization processes which produce "feminine" girls.

These examples illustrate the unpersuasive character of the evidence used to argue for the existence of natural and inevitable psychological differences between the sexes. Nevertheless, it is important to realize that the androgynist does not need to insist that there are absolutely no such differences. It remains an open question whether our traditional conceptions of femininity and masculinity might represent an exaggeration or a distorted reflection of some genuine biologically-based psychological difference between the sexes. But the crucial point is not that sexual biology has no direct influence upon masculine or feminine psychology (which is probably false), but rather that *whatever* effect it may have, the influence of society is still more powerful.

The truth of this claim is demonstrated not only by anthropological studies such as Mead's, but by psychological studies of individuals within our own culture. Some infants are born with ambiguous genitals and may be assigned to the "wrong" sex, and reared as boys when their chromosomal sex is female, or vice versa. It is known that in such cases the sex of assignment, that is the sex according to which an individual is reared, is a much more powerful determinant of that person's gender identity and character structure than either the chromosomal structure or the hormonal environment.[8] Thus, a genetic male reared as a female will generally develop a character considered to be well within the normal "feminine" range.

This being the case, whatever effects sexual biology may prove to have upon human behavior, they clearly *can* be overriden by social influences, and thus cannot be used to show that psychological androgyny is an impossible ideal. Political and ideological realities may make it less than certain that an androgynous society *will* be achieved, but it is a genuine possibility.

Another antifeminist objection to the ideal of androgyny is that "masculine" and "feminine" virtues are, in some way, incompatible. It is often assumed, for instance, that the exercise of reason, especially in very difficult and abstract fields of thought, is inconsistent with having a normal range of human emotions. The analytic powers of *Star Trek's* Mr. Spock, it is thought, could not have been developed except at the expense of his emotional life. Conversely, women are warned by Jungian and Freudian psychoanalysts and advocates of Total Womanhood that too much intellectual activity will destroy their feminine intuition and their ability to feel and express emotions.

But this is nonsense. The least reflection shows that the human capacities which are sexually stereotyped as incompatible opposites are, in reality, complementary. Reason and emotion, for instance, are not naturally opposed psychic forces; they are (more or less) distinct but equally basic capacities which are shared by all normal persons. Some emotions are more rational than others, that is, more justified under the circumstances, and some processes of reasoning arouse more emotion than others. But there is no more necessary or essential conflict between reason and emotion than there is between sight and hearing. Reason and intuition are not incompatible either; sometimes it is more rational to trust one's intuitions than not to. The belief that reason and emotion, or reason and intuition, are mutually exclusive capacities — such that we must each choose between them — is one of the most pernicious of the myths associated with our particular system of sexual stereotypes. The traditional masculine/feminine dichotomy creates an entirely false dilemma: it requires us to say *either/or* when what we need to say is *both/and*.

There is one other antifeminist objection which is worth mentioning. Many people fear that a world of psychological androgynes would be *boring*. They think that if the sexes were not trained to think and act differently they would become completely indistinguishable, or worse, that everyone would become exactly like everyone else.[9] The absurdity of this objection is that of supposing that an increase in freedom would lead to greater uniformity. We are born unique, and sexual stereotyping can only make us less so. As for women and men becoming indistinguishable, physiology alone makes this a very remote possibility.

These seem to be the major antifeminist objections to the ideal of androgyny. None are very persuasive. The feminist objections may, however, turn out to be more serious.

IV. FEMINIST OBJECTIONS

Some feminists worry that androgyny might become a new normative stereotype, a mold into which both sexes are ruthlessly pressed. Margaret Mead warns against this possibility, though she does not use the term "androgyny."[10] Joyce Treblicot distinguishes between two forms of androgynism, one of which she considers a threat to human freedom.[11] The first—monoandrogynism—treats androgyny as an ideal to which everyone ought to aspire, while the second—polyandrogynism—merely claims that every individual should be free to develop whatever type of character she or he pleases, whether feminine, masculine, or androgynous. Treblicot opts for the second, because it appears to allow more scope for individual freedom, and because she believes that it is not (now) possible to prove that an androgynous character structure is necessarily or invariably preferable to a strictly feminine or masculine one.

I would argue, however, that this sharp distinction between mono- and polyandrogyny is misguided. Properly understood, the two approaches are not inconsistent. Whether it makes more sense to speak of androgyny as a new normative ideal or simply as a liberation from the old sexual stereotypes depends upon the context, i.e., upon the particular sexual stereotypes under discussion. The polyandrogynist approach is most appropriate with respect to "feminine" or "masculine" traits which are largely matters of personal style and preference, and which have little direct moral significance. Thus, a hearty, extroverted personality is often considered to be masculine, while a more shy, reserved, and soft-spoken manner is considered more proper for females; yet it seems unreasonable to suggest that everyone ought to speak at the same moderate volume or to exhibit the same moderate degree of extroversion. There is surely room for personal variation in such matters, even in the ideal society. What is important is that no one be made to feel abnormal for possessing psychological traits that are traditionally associated with the other sex.

When we turn to the more important "feminine" and "masculine" *virtues,* however, the case is very different. Consider the question of whether it is better to be rational or empathic—or both. If rationality and empathy are both genuine virtues, then it is odd to view the three choices as equally desirable. It can plausibly be argued that to have *either* virtue without the other is to be flawed as a moral agent. The same point can be made with respect to many other pairs of "feminine" and "masculine" virtues, e.g., courage and compassion, rationality and intuition, emotional control and emotional expression, and so forth. Other things being equal, it is always better to have more virtues than fewer; this is especially true where—as in these cases—the absence of one virtue is apt to reduce the value or effectiveness of another.

I conclude, therefore, that if we are to be androgynists at all, we ought to be monoandrogynists with respect to the so-called masculine and feminine virtues. Fortunately, this in no way implies a reduction of individual freedom of choice. It is no part of the androgynists' purpose to advocate authoritarian or oppressive methods of inculcating moral virtues. Their point is simply that all individuals ought to be helped and encouraged—not forced—to develop the full range of human virtues. There is no reason to suppose that this can only be done by methods which place undue limitations upon individual freedom. Rousseau argued that (at least in the case of males) moral virtues develop best in a climate of relative freedom and self-determination.[12] The androgynist may well agree with him—while adding, of course, that the same thing is true of females. Whatever our pedagogical methods, if we succeed in enabling some individuals to develop a wider set of virtues then we will, to that extent, have *expanded* their freedom, by increasing the range of situations with which they are equipped to deal.

We need not fear, therefore, that the androgynists will seek to impose a restrictive unisex standard of dress, behavior, or personality. But there are other feminist objections to androgynism. Some feminists have pointed out that in the past the ideal of androgyny has often been presented as one which applies only or primarily to men.[13] Men have often longed to "get in touch" with the so-called feminine aspects of their own nature, while at the same time looking askance at the prospect of women developing their so-called masculine capacities. For instance, Jung—in spite of the apparent symmetry of his theory of the masculine *animus* in women and the feminine *anima* in men—is much more enthusiastic about the integration of "feminine" traits into the masculine psyche than he is about the converse. He warns that an excess of rationality in women will damage their femininity and endanger the creative talents of the men around them,[14] but provides no parallel warning about the danger of too much "femininity" in men.

There have been many antifeminists who have advocated psychological androgyny for the male sex only. But this is no objection to the androgynous ideal which is proposed by some contemporary feminists, since they have made it quite clear that they intend to recommend androgyny as a goal for both sexes alike. It is perfectly clear that equality between the sexes will be impossible so long as only one sex is liberated from the traditional sexual stereotypes. If women became androgynous while men remained as deficient as ever in the so-called feminine virtues, or if men became androgynous while women failed to achieve the "masculine" virtues, the male-dominant power structure will almost certainly persist. The very logic of the feminist concept of androgyny, or sex-role transcendence, requires that it be equally applicable to both sexes. It should not, therefore, be condemned by association with other, more androcentric conceptions of androgyny.

Another, and quite interesting, feminist objection is that androgynism seems to endorse heterosexuality as the only valid life-style. Catherine Stimpson argues that by idealizing the union of "feminine" and "masculine" traits within each individual, androgynism implicitly suggests a rejection of homosexual relationships between individuals.[15] But this is a misconception; androgynists advocate the *intrapersonal* union of "feminine" and "masculine" character traits, not (necessarily or exclusively) the sexual union of males and females. Far from implying that homosexual relationships are in some way inferior, androgynism undermines one of the primary rationales for heterosexuality—i.e., the notion that a viable sexual relationship requires that the parties be of different sexes in order that the "masculine" virtues of the one may complement the "feminine" virtues of the other. Androgynism places the complementary virtues within each individual, thus obviating this particular reason for seeking sexual union only with persons of the opposite sex. It is also reasonable to predict that, to the extent that the old stereotypes are replaced by an androgynous ideal of human character, lesbianism and male homosexuality will cease to be so deeply stigmatized, because they will no longer be associated with "mannishness" in women or "effeminacy" in men.

Other feminists object to the ideal of androgyny on the grounds that it is utopian and visionary rather than pragmatically useful. For instance, Cynthia Secor argues that androgyny is useless as a feminist goal because it provides no clue as to how we can actually bring about a society in which androgynous women and men are valued as highly as "masculine" men. It is, she says, "a goal without any road map for getting there; a moral imperative without strategic directions."[16] Others have argued that while psychological androgyny may be a fascinating idea, it is not one which will "play in Peoria." But this objection is somewhat premature. Many strategies are being developed for the promotion of psychological androgyny, including new forms of psychological therapy, the creation of androgynous role models for both sexes, and a determined attack on all the countless ways in which our social institutions act to preserve the old sexual prejudices. The problem is not so much that we don't know *what* to do as that the task is so enormous.

I have saved for last what I think is the most serious feminist objection to the ideal of androgyny. It might be argued that the concept of psychological androgyny is self-defeating; while it suggests the elimination of the sexual stereotyping of human character, it is in itself formulated in terms of the very concepts of "femininity" and "masculinity" which it urges us to abandon.[17] Is it not at least mildly paradoxical to urge people to cultivate both "feminine" and "masculine" virtues, while at the same time holding that virtues ought not be sexually stereotyped? Would it not be simpler just to say that rationality, courage, and so forth are *not* masculine traits in any legitimate sense of the term, in spite of the traditional presumption to the contrary? To go on calling these traits "masculine," even in the process of urging women to develop them, seems to risk encouraging the assumption that it is, after all, easier and more natural for men to do so.

There are several responses to this objection. It is obvious that the feminist androgynists do not *intend* to lend any support to the old sexual stereotypes. If they speak of "feminine" or "masculine" character traits, it is only to call attention to the lie that these traits are, in truth, more natural or more desirable in one sex than in the other. Furthermore, there are various linguistic devices which can be used to avoid creating the impression that one thinks, e.g., that rationality is *really* a masculine trait. These include being very careful to speak only of the *so-called* feminine or masculine traits, or enclosing the words "feminine" and "masculine" in quotation marks to indicate that this use of the terms—though traditional and therefore convenient—is a reflection of myth rather than reality.

But, the skeptic may reply, does this really absolve the androgynist of the charge of *seeming* to endorse the old stereotypes? Isn't there something problematic about the very word "androgyny," whose etymology and current meaning both suggest a state intermediate between maleness and femaleness, and hence somewhat contrary to nature? The point of this objection may be illustrated by an analogy. Suppose that in a certain society character traits are racially, rather than sexually, dichotomized. Black persons play most of the high-status roles, and traits like rationality, courage, and strength of will are traditionally spoken of as negroid traits. White generally occupy subordinate positions, and traits like cooperativeness, humility, and industry are thought of as caucasian. Suppose that the whites rebel against this situation, and arrive at the insight that the racial stereotyping of human character traits is nothing more than a flimsy rationalization for the unjust distribution of power and privileges in their society. Some of them might express this insight by advocating "psychological mulattoism," or, the combination of both negroid and caucasian virtues in each individual.

The question is, would the concept of psychological mulattoism be a useful one for these rebels, or would it be more apt to lead only to further confusion? They could be very careful to speak only of *so-called* negroid or caucasian traits, or to confine these terms within quotation marks. This would help, but one can't help suspecting that the use of the term *mulattoism* would still tend to foster the assumption that what was advocated was in some way unnatural or "against the grain" for both blacks and whites. Confusion between psychological and genetic mulattoism would be apt to persist. Would it not be better simply to attack the myth that rationality and the rest are *negroid* traits, rather than calling a rational white person a psychological mulatto? The former strategy would surely be less confusing, and probably more conducive to racial pride as well.

In response to this objection, it might be pointed out that the concept of androgyny is only a provisional one. Once the old stereotypes of femininity and masculinity have thoroughly broken down, and people find it bizarre to speak of rationality as masculine or intuition as feminine, the concept of psychological androgyny will have served its purpose and will no longer be needed. In the meantime, however, if we want to persuade people to abandon their old assumptions about women and men, we must speak to them in language they will understand. Most people at least *understand* the claim that it is better to have both feminine and masculine virtues than virtues of only one sort. To understand it *fully,* and to understand and accept the arguments for it, is to realize that the old norms of masculine and feminine behavior no longer make sense, if they ever did.

This response suggests that the concept of psychological androgyny should be viewed as no more than a stepping stone toward clearer and more accurate theories of human personality and development. When androgynism is viewed in this light, it is difficult to oppose. It does not claim to be the only viable strategy for breaking down false and destructive sexual stereotypes; but it is an approach which is proving useful for a great many theorists, researchers, and individual women and men in research of personal freedom.

At the same time, it is important to be aware of the dangers inherent in even the provisional use of the concept of androgyny. The most serious danger is that of forgetting that psychological androgyny is only a metaphor. The traits being combined are not *really* feminine or masculine, that is, not naturally, inevitably, or desirably the monopoly of either sex. June Singer's book, *Androgyny,* illustrates the danger of taking the metaphor of androgyny too literally.[18] Singer is a Jungian psychoanalyst who accepts Jung's definition of the feminine principle as Eros, or human interconnectedness, and the masculine principle as Logos, or rationality. She describes the feminine and masculine principles as conflicting ontological forces, cosmic rivals which generate a duality inherent in all being. Singer says that these rival forces must be balanced within each individual, and she calls this state of balance, androgyny.

Singer's version of the ideal of androgyny is almost the antithesis of femininst androgynism. Singer, like the antifeminists, believes that males are naturally and properly ruled by the masculine principle, and females by the feminine principle. Like Jung, she thinks that men should remain predominantly "masculine," even while integrating the feminine elements of their psyche, and vice versa for women. Thus, the traditional sexual stereotypes are upheld, even while the strictures they impose are slightly loosened.

The fact that there are antifeminists who speak of themselves as androgynists should in no way discredit the feminist androgynists. It does, however, demonstrate that androgyny is a rather *dangerous* metaphor; not only is its status *as* a metaphor easy to overlook, but its apparent implications when it is taken too literally are inconsistent with its real purpose. Even when we are fully aware that rationality is not *really* a masculine trait, we may be misled by the dualistic model which androgynism retains into believing that, for instance, reason and intuition, or reason and emotion, are sharply distinct and naturally opposed mental processes which require a special effort to combine successfully. This can lead to viewing psychological androgyny as a difficult juggling act, in which one is constantly forced to reconcile powerful opposing elements within oneself. The truth is that this juggling act is largely a myth. It is natural and virtually inevitable that human beings of both sexes will *both* reason and have emotions, and that there will be a constant interplay between the two not-so-distinct processes. In the same way, it is natural for a person sometimes to think in a linear or analytic fashion, and sometimes in an intuitive or nonlinear fashion. What is artificial is the notion that *combining* these diverse capacities is more difficult than *separating* them. This is exactly the myth that the feminist androgynists are attempting to destroy; so perhaps it cannot be held against them that their theory has often been misinterpreted. Still, the *imagery* of androgyny is more misleading than one wishes it to be.

V. CONCLUSION

In summary, it seems that the worst that can be said about the feminist concept of psychological androgyny is that it is somewhat subject to misinterpretation. In its favor, it must be said that it is one of the more promising attempts to conceptualize the process of overcoming sex role stereotyping, at both the individual and the social level. It provides a framework by which we can begin to understand how these traditional ideas about proper feminine and masculine behavior have shaped and misshaped us. It directs attention to a much neglected set of moral and conceptual issues, issues which will have to be resolved as part of the struggle for equality between the sexes. Thus, it is a useful concept, so long as its provisional and metaphorical status are kept in mind.

One may hope, however, that the day is not too far distant when the concept of androgyny will have served its purpose and become obsolete. The sooner the old sexual stereotypes have been forgotten, the sooner we will be able to be comfortable with our natural human differences (both those between the sexes and those *within* each sex), whatever these may turn out to be. When that day comes, few people will be very much attracted by, or even attach much meaning to, the suggestion that they ought to be more feminine or more masculine, or that they should try to be both at once. Whatever their personal characteristics, they will have no doubts about their sexual identity. This is the outcome which the ideal of androgyny points us toward, but which the concept of androgyny itself cannot adequately describe.

NOTES

1. Plato, *Meno,* excerpted in *Woman in Western Thought,* ed. Martha Lee Osborne (New York: Random House, 1979), pp. 16–17.
2. Aristotle, *Politics,* excerpted in *Women in Western Thought,* op. cit., p. 43.
3. Masculinity and femininity are measured through a self-rating test called the Bem Sex Role Inventory. This test treats masculinity and femininity as independent variables, such that one can score high in both or low in both. (Only those who score *high* in both are considered to be psychologically androgynous.) See Sandra Bem, "Probing the Promise of Androgyny," in *Beyond Sex-Role Stereotypes,* ed. Alexandra G. Kaplan and Joan P. Bean (Boston: Little Brown and Co., 1976), pp. 48–61.
4. Steven Goldberg, *The Inevitability of Patriarchy* (New York: William Morrow Co., 1973).
5. Margaret Mead, *Sex and Temperament in Three Primitive Societies* (New York: William Morrow and Co., 1965; first published in 1935).
6. For a good discussion of the research on XYY males, see Hilary Lips and Lee Colwill, *The Psychology of Sex Differences* (Englewood Cliffs, N.J.: Prentice-Hall, 1978).
7. John Money and Anke Ehrhardt, *Man and Woman, Boy and Girl: The Differentiation and Dimorphism of Gender Identity from Conception to Maturity* (New York: Mentor Books, 1974).
8. See Money and Ehrhardt, op. cit.; also see Robert Stoller, *Sex and Gender, Volume I: The Development of Masculinity and Femininity* (New York: Jason Aronson, 1974).
9. See Robert McCracken, *Fallacies of Women's Liberation* (Boulder, Colo.: Shields Publishing Co., 1972), p. 144.
10. Mead, op. cit., pp. 313–18.
11. Joyce Treblicot, "Two Forms of Androgynism," in *Feminism and Philosophy,* ed. Mary Vetterling-Braggin, Frederick A. Elliston,

and Jane English (Totowa, N.J.: Littlefield, Adams and Co., 1977), pp. 70–78, pp. 161–69 in this volume.

12. Jean Jacques Rousseau, *Emile* (London: J.M. Dent and Sons, 1963; first published in 1762).

13. See Barbara Charlesworth Gelpi, "The Politics of Androgyny," *Women's Studies* 2, no. 2 (1974): 151–60.

14. Carl Gustav Jung, *The Relations Between the Ego and the Unconscious* (Princeton: Princeton University Press, 1966), pp. 297–98.

15. Catherine Stimpson, "The Androgyne and the Homosexual," *Women's Studies* 2, no. 2 (1974): 237–48.

16. Cynthia Secor, "Androgyny: An Early Reappraisal," *Women's Studies* 2, no. 2 (1974): 164.

17. See Janice Raymond's "The Illusion of Androgyny," *Quest* II, (Summer 1975), for a good statement of this objection. Also see Carol Ochs, *Behind the Sex of God* (Boston: Beacon Press, 1977), pp. 127–29.

18. June Singer, *Androgyny: Toward a New Theory of Sexuality* (Garden City, N.Y.: Anchor Press, 1976).

Robert G. Pielke

Are Androgyny and Sexuality Compatible?

Proponents of androgyny as a social ideal must respond to a
number of serious and challenging objections. Among them are
the claims that androgyny would be detrimental to mental
health,[1] that it would covertly endorse a traditional and
therefore sexist heterosexuality[2] and further, that it would actually require universal masculinization.[3] The literature abounds
with discussions on these and related topics.[4] An unspoken, and
perhaps even unconscious, objection however, is a fear that androgyny would in some way be incompatible with sexuality, and
it is this objection which I intend to explore in what follows. To
my knowledge, no advocate of androgyny has attempted to do
this, yet I feel that it just might be the underlying basis for most
if not all, of the other objections.[5] If this fear is the fundamental
problem, a satisfactory response would inevitably make androgyny a much more attractive style of life.

My initial intuition is that the fear of androgyny being incompatible with sexuality is completely unfounded, and that on the
contrary androgynous people would enjoy a quantitative and
qualitative enhancement of their sexuality. In order to see
whether this would in fact be the case, it will first be necessary to
clarify the concept of androgyny itself as far as it is possible.
Then, after a brief characterization of sexuality, the precise
nature of the fear will have to be examined and shown to be
groundless. It should then be apparent that androgyny is not

only compatible with sexuality but is also likely to enhance it significantly.

I

Androgyny is an exceedingly tricky concept for its literal meaning continues to raise questions. A mixture of male and female traits (*andros* means man and *gyne* means woman) tells us nothing about how those traits are to be mixed, their desirable proportions, if all traits are equally valuable, whether a variety of mixtures is possible, or even if these traits are psychological, behavioral, physiological, or all three. Clearly, the first task for anyone discussing androgyny is to specify precisely what meaning the term is to have. Fortunately, a consensus is emerging so that debates about the merits of androgyny need not become fruitlessly stalled at this preliminary stage. The distinction drawn by Joyce Trebilcot between monoandrogyny and polyandrogyny, for example, has advanced the meaning of androgyny considerably,[6] and I plan to make use of this distinction in describing how I understand the term.

Trebilcot's first category, monoandrogyny (M), is understood by advocates as a single ideal for everyone. Monoandrogynous people would thus adopt most of the psychological characteristics and social roles which have been traditionally assigned to both masculine *and* feminine genders.[7] These hitherto bifurcated traits would thus exist simultaneously in the very same person. What comes immediately to mind is the term "unisex," most often used pejoratively. There are, however, quite a few people who seem to consider this desirable, at least according to Trebilcot. Her second category, polyandrogyny (P), derives from the proposal that "not a single ideal but rather a variety of options including 'pure' femininity and masculinity as well as any combination of the two" be available regardless of a person's biological sex.[8] Again, there are a number of supporters for this as a social ideal.

The underlying connection between the two, as she rightly points out, is an attempt to break the connection between sex and gender. This means bringing into play a fundamental moral principle, namely, "that biological sex should not be a basis for judgments about the appropriateness of gender characteristics."[9] It seems to me that proponents of androgyny (whatever its meaning) *must* affirm this in some way, otherwise their efforts would involve self-contradiction. A second, more specific, moral principle is also brought into play by Trebilcot, but this one is *not* logically entailed by either M or P. It is the notion that gender traits which are morally objectionable ought to be "excluded from both the single ideal advocated by M and the range of options recommended by P."[10] Now, as it happens, I agree with her on this, but she has provided no argument for this moral assertion; neither has she given any basis for judging which traits are objectionable and which are not. Although this might first appear to be a trivial objection, it is by no means obvious (to everyone) which traits are morally desirable and which are not. Some, such as courage and nurturance have a positive connotation. But others, such as aggressiveness and modesty, are questionable. Conceivably, advocates of androgyny could propose combinations of traits which would offend nearly everyone's moral sensibilities.

I strongly feel that there *are* independent moral arguments for ruling out such offensive traits as submissiveness, foolishness, incompetence, and weakness for women, and dominance, authoritarianism, and violence for men (the very ones Trebilcot mentions). I don't feel that it is necessary to develop them here, for others have done so at length elsewhere.[11] Suffice it to say that an advocate of androgyny must specify and provide a defense for which traits are morally acceptable options (P), or which ones can legitimately be used in constructing a single ideal (M). But regardless of what moral norm is used to exclude offensive traits, it must be applied universally so as to avoid arbitrariness. Thus if a trait is desirable it ought to be adopted, if it is undesirable, it ought to be discouraged, but if it is *neither,* it ought to be up to the individual as to whether to adopt it or not. This triple distinction between right, wrong, and obligatory (often overlooked in ethical disputes) allows the freedom of choice argument implicit in P as well as the argument from virtue implicit in M. The task is simplified considerably, however, when M and P are examined more closely. For they turn out to be pretty much the same, if not identical, as they are actually dealt with by Trebilcot. Hence the confusing situation will never arise wherein traits found morally acceptable, or even obligatory, for one version of androgyny are not also found acceptable for the other.

Given the norms to break the connection between sex and gender and to exclude offensive traits, one other criterion must be kept in mind: the logical (and perhaps empirical) requirement of consistency or noncontradiction. Together, these three criteria form the necessary preconditions for a single version of androgyny. With regard to the third criterion, it would make no logical or empirical sense to construe as obligatory traits which contradict one another, or even to consider as permissible traits which would conflict with obligatory traits. The most meaningful way to conceptualize obligatory (or desirable) traits is to understand them as virtues (and the undesirable ones as vices). In accordance with the basic norm to break the link between sex and gender, virtues and vices must be seen as *human,* not sex-linked, dispositions. As such, the virtues would necessarily be compatible, since it would clearly be absurd for a moral theory to encourage dispositions which, if acted on, would contradict one another.[12] However, not all traits are either obligatory or forbidden, having more to do with personality than with character.[13] Admittedly, while it is enormously difficult to decide which traits are optional, it should nevertheless be obvious that, whatever they are, they are permissible if and only if they do not conflict with any of the virtues. (Again, the three-fold distinction is crucial.) Although Trebilcot seems to recognize the possibility that some traits might not be compatible, she declines to speculate on what practical effects this logical limitation might have.[14] Others, however, have not been so reluctant. Ann Ferguson points out that "as we presently understand these [masculine and feminine] stereotypes, they exclude each other," and she then proceeds to illustrate their logical and empirical incompatibilities.[15] Carrying the point further, Janice Raymond says that "one would not put master and slave language or imagery together to define a free person," clearly pointing out the absurdity of such a proposal.[16]

While there are certainly many other traits which would be disqualified on grounds of inconsistency, it should be rather obvious that neither M nor P can include certain traditionally feminine and masculine gender characteristics (which include virtues and vices as well as other kinds of traits). In other words, when properly understood, androgyny rules out genderization as we have come to know it. Whatever else it might affirm (and this would depend on a moral assessment of character and personality traits), it would reject "pure" femininity and masculinity as well as many combinations of the two. Nevertheless, within certain logical and moral (including nonsexist) limitations, it would still permit a real choice among some combinations.

II

In dealing with the phenomenon of human sexuality, it must be kept in mind that many physiological, psychological, and behavioral factors are involved in a very complex interrelationship. Attempts to understand the phenomenon philosophically have differed, often dramatically, making conceptual clarity difficult, if not impossible.[17] For the purpose of this paper, however, sexuality may be understood simply as a certain kind of desire and/or the behavior intended to satisfy it. Most important is the fact that sexual desire, so specified, is not something which is subject to choice; it is a major component in the struggle of all life-forms to survive. Commonly characterized as a need or an appetite, it functions as a primary motivating force in human life (if not the basic one). Further, while this desire certainly has biological or physiological roots, the objects of desire and the activities undertaken to fulfill it are socially defined.[18] Thus sexual desire is logically and empirically independent of both the objects of desire as well as sexual behavior itself. Consequently, while sexual activity and the choice of objects are open to the varying influences of differing societies and cultures, humans inevitably *will* have sexual desire for *some* object or objects and *will* try to act accordingly (barring physical and/or psychological impairments).

The fear that androgyny would inhibit or even abolish our sexuality is typically expressed in emotive outbursts such as, "if women (or men) were to act like men (or women), then I wouldn't want anything to do with them," or "I can't get turned-on to somebody who looks and behaves like me," or simply "vive la difference!" Implicit in these remarks and others like them is a belief that a sex-based gender differentiation is essential for sexual attraction or desire. The fear is that a society *un*differentiated by gender would somehow result in the permanent inactivity or possibly the destruction of the sex drive itself. After all, so the rhetorical claim seems to go, when the objects of desire are no longer specifically identified, can the desire long remain? Opposing gender traits alone are apparently thought to be responsible for eliciting sexual desire (which is perhaps thought to lie dormant until awakened); so to obviate such differences might destroy the mechanism of arousal itself. Presumably, the sex drive is regarded as totally passive, waiting to be triggered by gender-traits different from those of the agent. If there is no opportunity for this to happen, not only will the drive never be activated, it might actually atrophy. The aphorism, "use it or lose it" only makes sense in this context. (Interestingly enough, there is seemingly no female equivalent for this warning. No doubt this omission stems from the sexist notion that arousal, initiation, intercourse and orgasm have traditionally been understood in a stereotypically masculine fashion.)

Another related fear is that the loss of differentiated sex roles would remove the guidance and direction that such roles provide. Many people perceive this as a distinct threat. In societies where rigid gender differentiation is maintained, all expressions of sexuality are rigorously channeled through sex roles. This includes prescribing who are to be considered desirable partners, how to attract them, how to recognize favorable and unfavorable reactions, what constitutes acceptable and satisfying physical activity, how to perform such activity and for what purposes. Nothing is left to chance; everything is laid out in a pattern to be followed. When confronted with forces as powerful as the sex drive, this affords the individual a great deal of security and comfort. To remove these patterns would, accordingly, cause considerable distress. Without their guidance, the sex drive could not identify a suitable object, know what to do with one or why. As a result, sexuality could be expected to diminish or even die. Again, the underlying assumption seems to be that the sexual drive is passive, awaiting specific gender-traits to trigger it!

In responding to these two related fears, I want to avoid relying on the obvious rejoinder, namely, an analogy to our appetite for food. It would go something like this: even if all food looked and tasted the same, we'd still get hungry and often eat ravenously. But this analogy does as much harm to my case as any good it might do, for it grants a point which androgynists need not and should not grant. It concedes the implicit accusation that everyone would look and act alike if the connection between biological sex and gender (sex roles) were broken. As we have already seen, this is not what proponents of androgyny as M or P actually favor. On the contrary, within certain logical and moral (including nonsexist) parameters, there would be a considerable variety of options available. Even if a wide variety of traits were deemed obligatory (and hence virtuous), there would still be numerous permissible traits which would ensure individuality. Granted, none of them would be tied to biological sex; but if this is used as an objection, it is different from the ones being considered here. No matter how androgyny is initially construed, as long as the three preconditions are met, there would be enormous variations in how people are disposed to look and act.

A better response to these two fears would begin by pointing out that they only make sense in a thoroughly genderized context, one in which biological sex is the basis for gender differentiation. It is obviously the case in such societies that if a "woman" ceases playing her assigned role and instead plays that of a "man" (or some deviant role), most (if not all) "men" would not find her appealing; they've been programmed to find only "women" appealing. The same is true in reverse, of course. However, in a society in which the connection between traits and sex has been broken and there are a variety of morally acceptable role options, the problem of "women" acting like "men" would never arise. There would be no prescribed patterns of sexual expectations, and activities; therefore, the sex drive would not be held to any rigid paths in seeking satisfaction. Anything moral would go! If this kind of situation is considered threatening, then so be it; if androgyny is morally desirable, then any loss of direction and guidance will simply have to be endured. Besides, it is highly questionable if such a loss would occur. What would be abandoned is gender, not morality, and moral guidance would seem to be quite sufficient for countering any putative, psychological threat. So to the extent that both versions of the fear presuppose a "unisex" understanding of androgyny, they are unfounded.

Even more significant is the misconception of sexuality that both assume. The idea that the sex drive is passive, waiting to be activated by gender-traits opposite those of the agent, is naive and based, in all probability, on an antiandrogynous ideology, and not on any kind of evidence. The only evidence that I'm familiar with supports the idea that sexual desire is both logically and empirically independent of a sexual object. The choice of this object may, of course, be culturally determined; but it need not be. Without sex roles to prescribe which objects should be of interest to us, the sex drive would still survive. The object has nothing whatsoever to do with the drive; it has everything to do with its satisfaction, in that *some* object (real or imagined) seems to be needed. But this hardly rules out androgyny as an ideal. Thus to the extent that both versions of the fear assume a passive interpretation of sexual desire, they are, again, unfounded.

Being unfounded, the original claim that sexuality (i.e., sexual desire as well as any activity which would tend to fulfill it) is incompatible with androgyny is clearly false. Furthermore, there is every reason to believe that an androgynous society would actually enhance sexuality, both quantitatively and qualitatively. Since the traditional sex roles (gender) have served to *restrict* the sex drive in every conceivable way, their removal would inevitably serve to encourage a much freer and more abundant sex life than ever before. This being the case, the overall *quality* of sex must similarly increase, just as the unlimited availability of food would enhance our ability to make better judgments about taste. Whether or not this increase in quantity and quality would be desirable is another question, but it's hard to imagine an argument against it. In fact, it should provide a rather convincing argument why androgyny ought to be adopted!

While these fears have been shown to be illusory, there is at least one genuine problem that arises during an attempted transition to androgyny. Those persons who are conscientiously attempting to move beyond gender differentiation, while living in a society with traditional sex-roles, are caught in a particularly difficult situation. They are almost always misunderstood by androgynists and nonandrogynists alike. Traditional societies will simply not permit its members to be perceived as not playing some kind of sex role (even though it might be a deviant sex role, e.g., "butch," "dyke," "queen," or "macho-man"). Most often such people are viewed as transsexuals or, more crassly, "queers." Only another androgynist has the capacity to make an accurate interpretation, but this is certainly no guarantee. When it comes to expressions of sexual interest, for example, there is just no way to be confident whether a sexual overture is androgynous or not. Aside from some obvious types of genderized behavior, an overture by itself gives no clue. Visually inspecting and appreciating another person's body is consistent with any social form.

The fact that such a problem arises, however, is further evidence that androgyny is not incompatible with sexuality. Indeed, the more the problem surfaces, the greater the probability that androgynous individuals are increasing their sexual activities. If this is so, people who have feared androgyny may be persuaded to convert to the androgynous ideal.

NOTES

1. For example, Ronald A. LaTorre, *Sexual Identity* (Chicago: Nelson-Hall, 1979), argues that sexual differentiation is vital for a person's mental health, although such a society need not be sexist (pp. 145–46).
2. For example, Catherine Stimpson, "The Androgyne and the Homosexual," *Women's Studies* 2, no. 2 (1974): 237–47. "It [androgyny] fails to conceptualize the world and to organize phenomena in a new way that leaves 'feminine' and 'masculine' behind" (p. 242).
3. For example, Janice Raymond, "The Illusion of Androgyny," *Quest: A Feminist Quarterly* 2 (Summer 1975): 57–66, defines her ideal society as one of "Integrity," which seeks to go beyond one that is gender-defined. The androgynization of our present society would be no more than its masculinization! (pp. 61–64).
4. A massive, but already long out-dated list was compiled by Nancy Topping Bazin, "The Concept of Androgyny: A Working Bibliography," *Women's Studies* 2, no. 2 (1974), an issue of the journal which was devoted exclusively to this subject. June Singer's *Androgyny: Toward a New Theory of Sexuality* (New York: Anchor/Doubleday, 1976), aside from providing a multicultural perspective, also has a worthwhile bibliography.
5. Although I do not plan to argue for the validity of this assertion at this time, it should be obvious that I regard the "sex drive" as paramount in explaining human behavior.
6. Joyce Trebilcot, "Two Forms of Androgynism," in *Feminism and Philosophy,* ed. Mary Vetterling-Braggin, Frederick Elliston, and Jane English (Totowa, N.J.: Littlefield, Adams and Co., 1977), pp. 70–78, pp. 161–69 in this volume.
7. Ibid., pp. 71–72, pp. 162–63 in this volume.
8. Ibid., p. 72, p. 163 in this volume.
9. Ibid.
10. Ibid., p. 73, p. 164 in this volume.
11. Aside from virtually everything written in the area of feminism, see especially Thomas Hill, "Servility and Self-Respect," in *Today's Moral Problems,* 2d ed., ed. Richard Wasserstrom (New York: Macmillan, 1979), pp. 133–48.
12. Mary Anne Warren makes this point in *The Nature of Women* (Point Reyes, Calif.: Edgepress, 1980), pp. 18–19.

William Frankena, in *Ethics,* 2d ed. 13. (Englewood Cliffs, N.J.: Prentice-Hall, 1973), p. 63, relies on this division in order to distinguish between virtues and vices on the one hand and different kinds of traits on the other. He also sees abilities and skills as personal attributes and thus in some way related to character and personality traits. The inevitable confusion which results detracts from this otherwise fascinating book.

14. Trebilcot, op. cit., p. 73, p. 164 in this volume.
15. Ann Ferguson, "Androgyny as an Ideal for Human Development," in Vetterling-Braggin, Elliston and English, op. cit., p. 46.
16. Raymond, op. cit., p. 61.
17. See for example, Sara Ruddick's "Better Sex," Thomas Nagel's "Sexual Perversion," and Robert Solomon's "Sex and Perversion," all in *Philosophy and Sex,* ed. Baker and Elliston (Buffalo, N.Y.: Prometheus, 1975); and Alan Goldman's "Plain Sex," in *Philosophy and Public Affairs* 6 (Spring 1977): 267–87.
18. Peter Berger relates an amusing, imaginary but quite accurate tale about how this social process occurs. He follows a couple from the moment they meet through courtship, marriage, children and old age. See his *Invitation to Sociology* (New York: Anchor, 1963), pp. 35–36 and 85–92.

Elizabeth Lane Beardsley

On Curing Conceptual Confusion:
A Response to Mary Anne Warren

To "escape from the prison of gender" is to reach the free land of humanity and personhood. It is doubtful that this can be accomplished by espousing androgyny. I shall argue that the androgynous ideal makes access to the free land more difficult in two fundamental respects, and that these considerations count decisively against accepting that ideal.

The first respect concerns the dichotomy of masculinity and femininity. There my arguments would so closely parallel those considered by Warren toward the end of her paper that I need not set them forth. Suffice it to say that her presentation of what she calls "the most serious feminist objection to the ideal of androgyny" is so compelling that it calls for the rejection of the ideal. Androgyny is not only "self-defeating," but self-defeated.

An interesting question is why Warren herself maintains that the ideal of androgyny retains some value. It is, she says, "not . . . the only viable strategy for breaking down false and destructive sexual stereotypes but . . . an approach which is proving useful. . . ."[1]

The answer appears to lie in her belief that people who are suffering from conceptual confusions must be spoken to "in a language they will understand."[2] At least at the beginning of a program of conceptual therapy, she thinks, this should be done. Warren also believes that such measures should be only temporary and that their temporary nature can be assured by making it clear that one speaks only of "so-called 'masculine' and 'feminine' traits," never of "masculine and feminine traits."

An alternative strategy for communicating with people who are suffering from conceptual confusion is to speak to them in a language they will *come to* understand. It seems to me less important that they understand the new language at once than that, when understanding is attained, no new confusions will have been introduced or old ones reinforced. Let us cure conceptual disease by methods which are abrupt, but in the end more humane.

Where degenderization of language is called for, the most effective tactic is, I have argued elsewhere,[3] a direct use of sex-neutral terms where these exist. Where they do not, terms originally genderized can eventually be brought to sex-neutral status by applying them, without footnotes or fanfare, to both males and females. ("Colleen Dewhurst and Derek Jacobi are fine actors.") That the acquisition of sex-neutral force by terms once genderized will occur only gradually is doubtless true. We should not infer from this, however, that the transformation must be *approached* gradually. Language-users mired in habits of genderization will, at first, take the locutions produced by contextual degenderization to be incorrect. But their attention will have been captured, and explanations, if requested, can be supplied. In any case, the new locutions will, if repeated, lose their air of novelty and of seeming incorrect.

It is admittedly easier, though not easy, to alter language habits than to alter complex attitudes. Nevertheless, what I have said about the proper cure for linguistic confusion seems to apply mutatis mutandis to more basic conceptual confusion. Perhaps a certain trait, say rationality, is thought to be widely perceived as "masculine," while another trait, say empathy, is thought to be widely perceived as "feminine." The remedy seems to be to note of a female that she is rational or of a male that he is empathic. This tactic requires, of course, a supply of rational females and empathetic males. To argue that this requirement is hard to meet would be grotesque, and needs no rebuttal here.

I have argued that access to the free land of humanity and personhood is impeded by the ideal of androgyny, through the reliance of the latter on its adoption, however temporary, of the masculine/feminine dichotomy. Here the slogan should be, not "Reculer pour mieux sauter," but "Sauter sans reculer." I turn now to the second respect in which androgyny is an ill-adapted cure for conceptual confusion.

This concerns the dichotomizing of whatever traits are taken to count as "masculine" or "feminine." Warren discusses chiefly the rational/intuitive pair. Again, her discussion is so cogent that it need not be repeated in detail. Yet if her discussion were less closely linked to androgyny it would be even more forceful. The point she makes with respect to the two capacities of reasoning and responding emotionally has a much broader application than is given to it in the context of her paper. What she says is worth repeating:

> It is natural and virtually inevitable that human beings of both sexes will *both* reason and have emotions and that there will be a constant interplay between the two not-so-distinct processes. . . . What is artificial is the notion that combining these diverse capacities is more difficult than separating them.[4]

This fine passage calls for no comment, I think, other than to note that a different significant point could be made by simply omitting the words "of both sexes." Part of the problem with androgyny is that it fosters the tendency to dichotomize in general, so that not only are humans classified as "masculine" and "feminine," but also as "rational" and "intuitive/empathic," "aggressive" and "submissive," or whatever. There are prisons other than that of gender from which one may need to escape. As philosophers, e.g., we have all suffered from the dichotomizing of "clarity" and "profundity."

The ideal of androgyny thus seems to pose barriers of two kinds to those who wish to enter the free land of humanity and personhood. It is at best awkward,[5] and at worst ungrateful,[6] to claim that a writer who had previously advanced the philosophic understanding of persons has now taken a step in the opposite direction. Yet I believe that in defending the ideal of androgyny (even with serious reservations) this is what Warren has done. The cure she finds in some respects acceptable is worse than the disease.

NOTES

1.   Mary Anne Warren, "Is Androgyny the Answer to Sexual Stereotyping?", p. 183 in this volume.

2. Ibid., p. 182 in this volume.
3. In "Degenderization," in *Sexist Language: A Modern Philosophical Discussion,* ed. Mary Vetterling-Braggin (Totowa, N.J.: Littlefield, Adams and Co., 1981).
4. Warren, op. cit., p. 184 in this volume.
5. Warren's paper "On the Moral and Legal Status of Abortion" has been much (and properly) admired.
6. In E.L. Beardsley, "Degenderization," op. cit., I express my own indebtedness to Warren.

Part IV B
Behavioral Androgyny

Linda Nicholson

Women's Work: Views From The History of Philosophy

I. INTRODUCTION

When sex difference theorists talk about women having "feminine" psychological traits, they are usually referring to traits they consider to be either *characteristic* of women (i.e., traits they believe to be held by all, or at least most, women) or to traits they believe *proper* or desirable for women to have. At least four questions, therefore, arise in response to such ascriptions of "feminine" to psychological traits: (1) whether all or most women do, in fact, have such traits, (2) whether only women (and not men) do, (3) if only women do, whether this is due to some biological feature(s) that women have which men do not, and (4) if it is not the case that only women have such traits or that the cause is not biologically linked if they do, whether it is proper or desirable for women to develop these traits anyway.

But for the most part, sex difference theorists do not confine themselves to the ascription of the term "feminine" to psychological traits; they also quite liberally apply it to certain tasks such as childrearing and housekeeping. The difference in the ascription is that in calling certain tasks "feminine," the theorists are generally not interested in the questions whether all or most women, or only women and not men, perform such tasks. Rather they generally call such tasks "feminine" because they believe that it is either necessary or desirable that women do these jobs. Thus, in the ascription of "feminine" to certain tasks, a different set of questions arise: (1) whether such tasks must, in fact, be performed by all or most women (and no men), (2) if so, whether this is because all or most women have certain features, biological or other, that men do not have which directly or indirectly make it necessary that women, but not men, perform the tasks, and (3) if not, whether it is proper or desirable for women to perform these tasks anyway. Positive answers to questions (1) and (3) would entail that it is correct to apply the term "feminine" to certain types of labor. In this paper, I shall first try to show the different answers given to these questions by key philosophers of sex difference theory and secondly to determine whether there exists any explanatory pattern for the differences.

II. ARISTOTLE

Deviating from chronology, I wish to begin with Aristotle and follow with Plato. Aristotle's arguments serve as a useful starting point for discussion in that they provide a clear example of a consistent justification of a sexual division of labor. In the following remarks Aristotle is saying what was widely held in the Greece of his time:

... the courage of a man is shown in commanding, of a woman in obeying. All classes must be deemed to have their special attributes; as the poet says of women.
  'Silence is a woman's glory,' but this is not equally the glory of man.[1]

For Aristotle, these 'oughts' follow from nature. A woman's very soul is different from that of a man's:

Now it is obvious that the same principle applies generally, and therefore almost all things rule and are ruled according to nature. But the kind of rule differs; — the freeman rules over the slave after another manner from that in which the male rules over the female, or the man over the child; although the parts of the soul are present in all of them, they are present in different degrees. For the slave has no deliberative faculty at all; the woman has, but it is without authority, and the child has, but it is immature.
  For although there may be exceptions to the order of nature, the male is by nature fitter for command than the female, just as the elder and full-grown is superior to the younger and more immature.[2]

As Christine Pierce has pointed out, there is no necessary connection between the "natural" and the "inevitable" or even "the good."[3] Roaches, tornadoes, and bacteria are all "natural" phenomena. They are also phenomena which human beings attempt to eliminate. Thus even if one agreed with Aristotle that "the male is by nature fitter for command than the female," this does not lead to the conclusion that it is necessary or desirable that men command. One might, for example, want artificially to increase women's commanding abilities or diminish men's. Aristotle, however, believes in the desirability of the rule of those who are by nature "most fit" for rule:

For that some should rule and others be ruled is a thing not only necessary, but expedient; from the hour of their birth, some are marked out for subjection, others for rule. . . . And it is clear that the rule of the soul over the body, and of the mind and the rational element over the passionate, is natural and expedient; whereas the equality of the two or the rule of the inferior is always hurtful. The same holds good of animals in relation to men; for tame animals have a better nature than wild, and all tame animals are better off when they are ruled by man; for then they are preserved. Again, the male is by nature superior, and the female inferior; and the one rules, and the other is ruled; this principle, of necessity, extends to all mankind.[4]

In sum, Aristotle supports the status quo by claiming not only that it is a manifestation of the "natural order of things," but also that this "natural order" is itself more desirable than any conceivable alternative. One can question this position on several grounds. First, it is obviously questionable whether women are "by nature" inferior to men. Even if it were the case in Aristotle's Greece that women did not possess the same abilities as men, Aristotle has provided no argument establishing any necessary connection between such a lack of capacities and "womanhood." As John Stuart Mill, a theorist I will discuss later, points out, since there is such overwhelming evidence of the social obstacles to women's development, a heavy burden of proof rests on the claim of women's "natural inferiority." Secondly, as I have already noted, what is "natural" is not necessarily inevitable or unchangeable. Even if it were the case that women were "naturally" less competent than men, we might still attempt to change this fact of nature by increased schooling for women (if we were interested, for example, in increasing the supply of competent people in the labor market). Ultimately there is the question of social goals; in this case, it is the question of whether we believe social inequality to be desirable or not. From Aristotle's perspective (i.e., the perspective of the ruler) that "some are marked out for subjection, others for rule" is desirable, but this position is certainly questionable (particularly, although not exclusively, from the ruled's point of view).

III. PLATO

For Plato, that which exists does not necessarily represent that which is desirable. The point of *The Republic* was to portray a society more desirable than that which Plato encountered. The ideal society which Plato constructed in that treatise allowed for women performing public roles unheard of in Plato's Greece. In Plato's Republic, the guardian class did contain women and thus they carried out the highest and most important functions of that society. Moreover, within the guardian class there was no sexual division of labor. What led Plato to adopt such a position? It is worthwhile to reproduce those passages in *The Republic* where he makes the argument justifying women as guardians:

"Now," said I, "take the male and female sex; if either is found to be better as regards any art or other practice, we shall say that this ought to be assigned to it. But if we find that they differ only in one thing, that the male begets and the female bears the child, we shall not take that difference as having proved any more clearly that a woman differs from a man for what we are speaking of; but we shall still believe that our guardians and their wives should practice the same things." . . . Then, my friend, no practice or calling in the life of the city belongs to woman as woman, or to man as man, but the various natures are dispersed among both sexes alike; by nature the woman has a share in all practices, and so has man, but in all, woman is rather weaker than man."[5]

What is apparent from these passages is that Plato is *not* claiming that there are no differences between men and women. All that he is arguing is that the properties which do differentiate men and women are not relevant to the performance of those duties required of a member of the guardian class. What also should be stressed is that this argument does not commit Plato to a position on sexual equality. Plato did not believe that a woman's reproductive capacity, or that which distinguishes her as a woman, should determine her life activities. However, he did believe that women generally were inferior to men.[6] The compatibility of these two positions can be illustrated in a contemporary argument for sexual equality in tryouts for professional basketball. While women are generally shorter than men, not all women are. Therefore, those women who are of the minimum height required for playing basketball on a given team ought to be allowed to play, other factors being equal. Similarly for Plato, while women generally are inferior to men and thus incapable of the tasks required of a guardian, this did not preclude the possibility of some women being equivalent in capacity and thus fully qualified.

What is interesting about the above argument is that it fits so well Plato's needs for his ideal society as a whole. Plato only abolishes a sexual division of labor among the guardian classes; among other classes the traditional division of labor between men and women is maintained. Thus if Plato required an argument which attacked the traditional division of labor only for one group within the society, he constructed the one most fitting. Susan Okin has argued that this perfect fit is not surprising, that Plato needed an argument to allow for the rejection of the conventional division of labor for the guardian class alone because of prior decisions concerning the way of life for the guardian class. In particular, Plato's prior abolition of private property and the family for members of the guardian class made necessary an abolishment of women's conventional roles within that class. Plato was aware of the danger of abolishing women's activities within the family without giving them alternative employment. That it was the abolition of the family which led Plato to emancipate female guardians and not vice versa, Okin argues, is evidenced in his maintenance of the traditional division of labor for other classes where the family is maintained but where the above arguments could also be applied. Finally, she notes that in *The Laws,* despite Plato's increasing conviction on the potential capabilities of the female sex, he is more conservative than in *The Republic* in maintaining traditional sex roles. This can be accounted for, she argues, by the reintroduction of the family and private property in that work.[7]

Okin's argument is in accord with other recent theory which has argued for a historical connection between the nuclear family and a rigid sexual division of labor associated with female subordination. Marilyn Arthur, for example, has argued that the control of women which existed in fifth century B.C. Athens can in large part be accounted for by the transition in Greece in the eighth and seventh centuries B.C. from a tribally/aristocratically organized society, where property was controlled and distributed through the extended kin, to a democracy, where property was transmitted through the more nuclear family residing in the individual oikos or household. This transition was accompanied by the emergence of the polis representing male heads of household qua heads of household. The oikos thus became an important political and economic entity. Maintaining its integrity and the legitimacy of its head's, heirs became crucial. What developed was an increased control over women's sexuality and of her activities generally.[8] Thus what Arthur points to is a historical connection between a concern for the integrity of the family and a control and limitation of women's activities, in particular, a restriction of women's activities to the household. Such a connection does appear borne out in the difference in Plato between activities appropriate for women of the guardian class who exist outside of a nuclear family and all other women. It might also explain the difference between Aristotle and Plato as the difference between a theorist endorsing the family and the activities of women associated with it and a theorist advocating the elimination of this institution for a small class of people.

In sum, Plato's position on women's capacities and tasks is quite problematic unless it is put in the context of a framework such as that provided by Okin. Plato argued that there was nothing in a woman's biology that prevented her from performing equivalent tasks to a man. He used this argument as a basis for allowing women to become guardians. If, however, biology is not destiny for a female guardian, then biology cannot be destiny for any other woman either. Even granting Plato's assumption that women were generally inferior to men, this does not justify a division of labor organized around gender; criteria of competence alone should suffice. Thus Plato's argument that the biological differences between men and women do not entail a gender-organized division of labor requires that he attack such a division of labor for everyone, not only for members of the guardian class. That he does not make this attack for those outside of the guardian class must therefore be explained by his commitment to family life for such people.

IV. LOCKE

There is a widespread, though not frequently articulated, theory that women's equality to men has gradually increased with the progress of time. In the cave, man ruled with a heavy, if not yet iron, club. The march of history, representing an overall march toward greater enlightenment and equality for all, has been accompanied by greater equalization between the sexes. A different, more sophisticated theory would hold that while it is wrong to believe in any gradual increase in sexual equality, democracy, at least in its most recent manifestations, has contributed toward equalizing the sexes. Similarly, one might expect that exponents of modern democratic theory (who usually argue for an increase in human equality) would be highly sympathetic to increased equality between the sexes. I would now like to examine the work of two theorists, John Locke and Jean Jacques Rousseau, both major exponents of modern democracy, in order to explore this relation between democratic theory and sexual equality.

An initial examination of Locke's statements on women's place would tend to support the thesis that modern democracy represents an advance for women. Within the home, while Locke does place "ultimate authority" with the man, he also appears to argue for a high degree of equality between husband and wife in determining their own affairs and the affairs of their children.

82. But the Husband and Wife, though they have but one common concern, yet having different understandings will unavoidably sometimes have different wills too; it therefore being necessary, that the last Determination, i.e., the Rule, should be placed somewhere it naturally falls to the Man's share, as the abler and the stronger. But this reaching out to the things of their common Interest and Property, leaves the Wife in the full and free possession of what by contract is her peculiar right, and gives the Husband no more power over her Life, than she has over his. *The Power of the Husband* being so far from that of an absolute Monarch, that the *Wife* has, in many cases, a Liberty to *separate* from him, where natural Right, or their Contract allows it, whether that Contract be made by themselves in the state of Nature, or by the Customs or Law of the Country they live in; and the Children upon such Separation fall to the Father or Mother's lot, as such Contract does determine.[9]

52. It may perhaps be assured as an impertinent Criticism in a discourse of this nature, to find fault with words and names that have obtained in the World: And yet possibly it may not be amiss to offer new ones when the old are apt to lead men into mistakes, as this of *Paternal Power* probably has done, which seems so to place the Power of Parents over their children wholly in the *Father,* as if the *Mother* had no share in it, whereas if we consult Reason or Revelation, we shall find she hath an equal title.[10]

What is noteworthy about these arguments is that the equality which Locke appears to grant women seems to follow directly from his democratic theory and particularly from his description of the family as a contractual unit:

78. *Conjugal Society* is made by a voluntary Compact between Man and Woman and tho' it consists chiefly in such a Communion and Right in one anothers Bodies, as is necessary to its chief End, Procreation; yet

it draws with it mutual Support, and Assistance, and a Communion of Interest too, as necessary not only to unite their Care and Affection, but also necessary to their common off-spring, who have a right to be nourished and maintained by them, till they are able to provide for themselves.[11]

Locke does argue that the conjugal unit has a biological basis, i.e., the dependency of a woman on the support of another person during the extended period of childrearing. However once these natural requirements are satisfied, there appears no reason for marriage not to be treated like any other contractual union.

81. But although these are Ties upon *Mankind* which make the Conjugal Bonds more firm and lasting in Man, than the other species of Animals; yet it would give one reason to enquire, why this *Compact,* where Procreation and Education are secured, and Inheritance taken care for, may not be made determinable, either by consent, or at a certain time, or upon certain conditions, as well as any other voluntary Compacts, there being no necessity in the nature of the thing, nor to the ends of it, that it should always be for life.[12]

Lorenne Clark takes a skeptical position on such passages. She points out that Locke's belittling of the absolute power of the father and the husband is only undertaken where he wishes to undermine the concept of patriarchal government.[13] Apart from those passages where Locke attacks a patriarchal model of the family as a justification for patriarchal government, he is quite conservative on the status of women. For example, there is the assumption throughout the *Treatises* that the natural place of women is in the family. Talk of single women does not appear in either work.[14] We could supplement Clark's point here by noting that Locke's arguments justifying the existence of the family, that women need the protracted support of men during pregnancy and childrearing, would seem to imply that pregnancy is incapacitating and childrearing an all-consuming task.

Women's activity thus seems to Locke to be limited to those traditionally associated with the home and family. Moreover, once within the family, women appear to have rights different from those of men outside the family. Thus, as Clark also notes, whereas Locke does not assume that any natural differences between men mitigate against their equality "in respect of jurisdiction in dominion one over another," Locke uses the argument of women's "natural" inequality with respect to men to justify men's ultimate authority over women.[15] Marxists have long criticized liberalism for not extending the notion of equality from the political sphere to the economic sphere. Similarly, feminists might argue that Lockean democratic theory stops at the door of the home.

V. ROUSSEAU

One could argue that the failure of Locke's democratic theory with regard to women is mainly a failure of omission. True, Locke does speak of the ultimate authority of men in the home. True, Locke does seem to imply that most of a woman's life is necessarily spent producing and raising children in the confines of the family. On the other hand, Locke by and large does not speak very much of women concerning either their rights or their tasks. The same, however, cannot be said of Rousseau who has a lot to say about what a woman ought to do:

In the union of the sexes each contributes equally to the common aim, but not in the same way. . . . One ought to be active and strong, the other passive and weak. . . . Once this principle is established, it follows that woman is made specially to please man. . . . The first education of men depends on the care of women. Men's moral, their passions, their tastes, their pleasures, their very happiness also depend on women. Thus the whole education of women ought to relate to men. To please men, to be useful to them, to make herself loved and honored by them, to raise them when young, to care for them when grown, to counsel them, to console them, to make their lives agreeable and sweet—these are the duties of women at all times, and they ought to be taught from childhood.[16]

In ministering to the needs of a man, a woman must be sure to satisfy what is for Rousseau a most crucial need, that a man be sure he is father to his wife's children.

The strictness of the relative duties of the two sexes is not and cannot be the same. When woman complains on this score about unjust man-made inequality, she is wrong. This inequality is not a human institution—or, at least, it is not the result of mere prejudice but of reason. It is up to the sex that nature has charged with the bearing of children to be responsible for them to the other sex. Doubtless it is not permitted to anyone to violate his faith, and every unfaithful husband who deprives his wife of the only reward of the austere duties of her sex is an unjust and barbarous man. But the unfaithful woman does more; she dissolves the family and breaks all the bonds of nature. In giving the man children which are not his, she betrays both. She joins perfidy to infidelity. I have difficulty seeing what disorders and what crimes do not flow from this one. If there is a frightful condition in the world, it is that of an unhappy father who, lacking confidence in his wife, does not dare to yield to the sweetest sentiments of his heart, who wonders, in embracing his child, whether he is embracing another's, the token of his dishonor, the plunderer of his own children's property. What does the family become in such a situation if not a society of secret enemies whom a guilty woman arms against one another in forcing them to feign mutual love.[17]

From the above we can see that for Rousseau the differences in duties between men and women follow from nature in conjunction with reason. The dictates of nature make woman the childbearer. Given this fact, social harmony in turn requires of the woman strict sexual fidelity in conjunction with other behavioral dictates:

It is important then, not only that a woman be faithful but that she be judged to be faithful, by her husband, by those near her, by everyone. It is important that she be modest, attentive, reserved, and that she gives evidence of her virtue to the eyes of others as well as to her own conscience. If it is important that a father love his children, it is important that he esteems their mother. These are the reasons which put even appearances among the duties of women, and make honor and reputation no less indispensable to them than chastity. There follows from these principles, along with the moral difference of the sexes, a new motive of duty and propriety which prescribes especially to women the most scrupulous attention to their conduct, their manners, and their bearing. To maintain vaguely that the two sexes are equal and that their duties are the same, is to lose oneself in vain declaiming; it is to say nothing so long as one does not respond to these considerations.[18]

The duties which Rousseau expects of a woman can be summarized in the overriding obligation that she keep the family together. Thus when Rousseau attacks Plato's elimination of a sexual division of labor among the guardian class, he notes that this elimination follows from Plato's elimination of the family.

In his Republic, Plato gives women the same exercises as men. I can well believe it! Having removed private families from his regime and no longer knowing what to do with women, he found himself forced to make them men.[19]

For Rousseau, Plato's elimination of the family was irrational even given Plato's end, the creation of a strong state. An elimination of the family, Rousseau says, harms rather than helps the state:

. . . as though there were no need for a natural base on which to form conventional ties; as though the love of one's nearest were not the principle of the love one owes the state; as though it were not by means of the small fatherland which is the family that the heart attaches itself to the large one; as though it were not the good son, the good husband, and the good father who make the good citizen.[20]

What Rousseau is missing in his criticism of Plato is that the state constructed by Plato in *The Republic* was a very different kind of state from that endorsed by Rousseau himself. It was suggested earlier that there might be a connection between a democratically organized society based on representation by male heads of households and an importance and concern given to the integrity of the individual household unit. One manifestation of this concern would be a greater control over women's sexuality and activities than might be required in a more aristocratically-organized society where property and power are distributed and transmitted through the line or extended kin network as opposed to the nuclear family. Thus, a political theorist who endorsed an aristocratically-organized society might be more sympathetic to women's equality, at least for some women, than one might otherwise expect. This hypothesis was brought forth to help account for Plato's deviation from accepted Greek practice in his vision of the duties and position of women in the guardian class in his ideal society. Since Plato's ideal society was more aristocratic than democratic and since it did eliminate the family for the guardian class, this could explain the fact that some women in Plato's ideal society could be liberated from the position of the citizen wife in the democracy of classical Athens. For the same reasons, a political philosopher whose theory was in other respects highly democratic might be less than sympathetic to women's equality. Thus one could at least account for the conjunction of Rousseau's democratic theory in the political realm and his position on sexual inequality within the family, an otherwise contradictory conjunction. I do not wish to suggest that there is any necessary connection between democratic theory and an espousal of a strong nuclear family and a subordinate position of women. The theorist whom I shall next consider, Jóhn Stuart Mill, could easily serve as a counterexample to such a thesis. Rather, all I wish to suggest is a compatibility between democratic theory and sexual inequality made understandable by the importance of the individual household unit in at least certain conceptions of, and perhaps certain historical exemplifications of, a democratic state.

VI. JOHN STUART MILL

John Stuart Mill's position on women's work is light years away
from that of Rousseau's. Mill strongly argued against those laws
which existed in nineteenth-century England (with similar
counterparts in the United States) which made the wife a subordinate and unequal partner in the marriage relation, laws which
denied a married woman rights of property and which denied
her rights to the control of children. More relevant to the concerns of this essay, he also strongly argued against those laws
and social prohibitions which denied a woman entrance to any
occupation she chose. Like Plato, he argued that the qualifications of any particular woman could not be deduced from the
capabilities of women in general. Mill claimed that any decision
over who was to fulfill a particular job should be decided by fair
competition open to all regardless of sex. In this way, society
would insure that any particular job was performed by the most
qualified, guaranteeing social efficiency as well as satisfying the
demands of social justice. Mill says,

For if performance of the function is decided either by competition, or
by any mode of choice which secures regard to the public interest, there
needs be no apprehension that any important employments will fall into
the hands of women inferior to average men, or to the average of their
male competitors. . . . Is there so great a superfluity of men fit for high
duties, that society can afford to reject the service of any competent person? Are we so certain of always finding a man made to our hands for
any duty or function of social importance which falls vacant, that we
lose nothing by putting a ban upon one half of mankind, and refusing
beforehand to make their faculties available, however distinguished they
may be? And even if we could do without them, would it be consistent
with justice to refuse to them their fair share of honour and distinction,
or to deny to them the equal moral right of all human beings to choose
their occupation (short of injury to others) according to their own
preferences, at their own risk?[21]

Mill not only argued for free and open competition, but also
that women's present capabilities might be a function of environmental factors and could thus possibly be changed in a differently ordered society. His position is even more radical than
Plato's. Plato believed in free and open competition, but women
in general were naturally inferior to men. Mill, on the contrary,
argued that what women are "by nature" is impossible to say:

I do not say, as they will continue to be; for as I have already said more
than once, I consider it presumption in anyone to pretend to decide

what women are or are not, can or cannot be, by natural constitution. They have always hitherto been kept, as far as regards spontaneous development, in so unnatural a state, that their nature cannot but have been greatly distorted and disguised; and no one can safely pronounce that if women's nature were left to choose its direction as freely as men's, and if no artificial bent were attempted to be given to it except that required by the conditions of human society, and given to both sexes alike, there would be any material difference, or perhaps any difference at all, in the character and capacities which would unfold themselves.[22]

In spite of the above, Mill cannot be considered a feminist, at least by late twentieth-century standards. Mill believed a woman should be an equal partner with her husband in marriage. He also believed that a woman should be free to enter any occupation for which she was qualified. However, Mill did not believe that a woman, unlike a man, could choose both marriage and an occupation outside of marriage. Mill argued that for a married woman to take on an occupation in addition to marriage would inevitably result in poor child care and household management as there would be no one to relieve her of these tasks. Thus, he claimed that a woman's choice of marriage was equivalent to that of a man's choice of a profession, requiring the renunciation of many other activities.

Like a man when he chooses a profession, so, when a woman marries, it may in general be understood that she makes choice of the management of a household, and the bringing up of a family, as the first call upon her exertions, during as many years of her life as may be required for this purpose.[23]

What Mill clearly could not see, as indeed could few others in the nineteenth century, was that child care and household management need be no more binding to a married woman than to a married man.

Mill's claim that married women ought to stay at home would seem to imply that many women ought to stay at home. If we can assume that Mill believed childbearing should take place within marriage and if he also believed that this was an activity necessarily engaging a high percentage of the female population, two widely held premises of his and our society, the consequence would be that many women in Mill's view, should be homemakers. But this conclusion is in effect no different from Plato's. In other words, while Mill's views appeared to represent an advancement over Plato's, in actuality there may be no advancement at all. Mill, unlike Plato, allows for the possibility that all or many women could, in a well-ordered society, attain the capabilities required for the performance of occupations traditionally thought to be masculine. Thus it would appear that Mill allows for the possibility of the elimination of a sexual division of labor per se. On the other hand, he also accepts the traditional division of labor within the family which in addition carries the consequence of prohibiting married women from taking on jobs outside of the family. The consequence, therefore, for the sexual division of labor, is in effect no different in Mill's ideal society than it was in Plato's. In both cases many women are to stay home managing the household and taking care of children. While some women could deviate from this assignment, they were exceptions. What is interesting is that for both Mill and Plato the exceptions are unmarried, with Mill their being "single women" and with Plato their existing with their male counterparts outside of a traditional family.

VII. ENGELS

One of the few pre-twentieth-century theorists to have critically examined the situation of women in light of women's roles within the family is Frederick Engels. Engels, in *The Origin of the Family, Private Property and the State,* employed the anthropological work of Lewis Henry Morgan to argue for the existence of an early form of social organization where women enjoyed a certain supremacy.[24] While there was a certain sexual division of labor such that men had principle responsibility for obtaining food and while there was a loose form of monogamy between men and women resulting in what Engels describes as the "pairing family," neither this division of labor nor this family form were, for Engels, comparable to the modern sexual division of labor nor to the modern monogamous family. The crucial difference was that the "pairing family" existed within a larger communistic type of household in which most or all of the women were related by blood. That this larger family unit, the 'gens,' was organized around the female line provided the material foundation for the supremacy of women and it was common in "primitive" times. This supremacy ended as a consequence of economic changes resulting from the transformation of the society from one based on hunting and gathering to one based on agriculture, the domestication of animals, and the breeding of herds. The transformation made possible a surplus of wealth or at least more than what was required for simple maintenance. That man's position in the division of labor grew in importance with this accumulation of wealth created tensions for the traditional form of inheritance:

Thus on the one hand, in proportion as wealth increased it made the man's position in the family more important than the woman's, and on the other hand created an impulse to exploit this strengthened position in order to overthrow in favor of his children the traditional order of inheritance. This, however, was impossible so long as descent was reckoned according to mother right. Mother right, therefore, had to be overthrown, and overthrown it was. . . . The overthrow of mother right was the *world historical defeat of the female sex*. The man took command in the home also; the woman was degraded and reduced to servitude; she became the slave of his lust and a mere instrument for production of children.[25]

From this transformation emerged the patriarchal family and its progeny, the modern monogamous family. Both, according to Engels, are characterized by a high degree of control of female sexuality and by a significant difference between the ways in which male and female labor is viewed:

In the old communistic household, which comprised many couples and their children, the task entrusted to the women of managing the household was as much a public, a socially necessary industry as the procuring of food by the men. With the patriarchal family and still more with the single monogamous family, a change came. Household management lost its public character. It no longer concerned society. It became a *private service;* the wife became the head servant, excluded from all participation in social production. Not until the coming of modern large-scale industry was the road to social production opened to her again—and then only to the proletarian wife. But it was opened in such a manner that, if she carries out her duties in the private service of her family, she remains excluded from public production and unable to earn; and if she wants to take part in public production and earn independently, she cannot carry out family duties.[26]

Engels, unlike Mill, does not accept a division of labor which puts the woman in the home and the man in the social realm of industry. Such a division of labor contributes to the subordination of women to men and must be abolished for sexual equality:

In the great majority of cases today, at least in the possessing classes, the husband is obliged to earn a living and support his family, and that in itself gives him a position of supremacy without any need for special legal titles and privileges. Within the family he is the bourgeois, and the wife represents the proletariat. . . . And in the same way, the peculiar character of the supremacy of the husband over the wife in the modern family, the necessity of creating real social equality between them and the way to do it, will only be seen in the clear light of day when both possess legally complete equality of rights. Then it will be plain that the first condition for the liberation of the wife is to bring the whole female sex back into public industry and that this in turn demands that the characteristic of the monogamous family as the economic unit of society be abolished.[27]

Thus, unlike Mill, Engels sees sexual inequality within the home as a consequence of a sexual division of labor which places women at home, outside of and yet dependent upon, the monetary economy. Further, the elimination of this inequality requires an elimination of the sexual division of labor per se. Thus only when women work in the public realm with and alongside of men can women achieve any true form of equality. Moreover, also unlike Mill, Engels believes that a further necessary condition for such equality is the elimination of the monogamous family as an economic unit of society. This type of family, based on the transference of private property to the heirs of its male head, requires the control of female sexuality and consequently women's activities generally. Though Engels does not attack monogamy per se and indeed argues for the possibility of true "individual sex love" after property is socialized,[28] he does believe in its incompatibility, when economically motivated, with sexual equality. In sum, in conjunction with Engels' attack on a sexual division of labor is his belief in the need to eliminate the monogamous family as an economic unit.

VIII. CONCLUSION

In comparing Plato and Aristotle, I introduced the thesis that Plato's rejection of a nuclear family for members of the guardian class might account for his rejection of the sexual division of labor for members of that class. Similarly, the endorsement of the nuclear family by both Locke and Rousseau seemed in both cases central to their acceptance of a sexual division of labor. Moreover, their beliefs in the necessity of a sexual division of labor and their beliefs in sexual inequality generally seemed compatible, rather than imcompatible, with their democratic theory, given an importance of the family in certain forms of a democratic state. Finally, when I turned to Mill and Engels, the issue of the family again appeared the crucial variable in regard to both philosphers' positions on the sexual division of labor. While Mill, like Plato, does allow for any woman to perform any job for which she is qualified, and even goes further than Plato in noting the probable social determinants of existing capabilities, he does not believe that a married woman, unlike a married man, can be both married and have an occupation outside of marriage. The consequence of this position seems to be that for Mill, as for Plato, there can be no conjunction of the family and an elimination of a sexual division of labor. Only Engels, who also attacks the monogamous family, at least when economically motivated, maintains an explicit rejection of a sexual division of labor per se. The glaring conclusion of these philosophers thus seems to be: where there is family, there women shall be.

The connection I am thus suggesting is between an endorsement of a sexual division of labor and an endorsement of the family, particularly in its nuclear form. This conclusion is broad, and should not obviate the important differences between the content of the sexual division of labor among even those theorists who endorse it in principle. That Locke believes that the appropriate place of married women is at home does not mean that he is thereby committed to the same pronouncements on the activities of a married woman as is Rousseau. Even Rousseau and Aristotle, who appear similarly conservative on the activities of women, must differ in giving content to such activities, if only because of the important economic differences between classical Athens and eighteenth-century France. That activity of raising children must inevitably be different in such different societies. Thus what I have examined in this essay has been the extent to which different theorists have been committed to the idea of a sexual division of labor per se. I have not explored in depth the differences which might, for example, exist between Aristotle and Rousseau on what specific tasks that women, as opposed to men, should perform. Also, I have employed a broad concept of a "nuclear family" thereby ignoring the differences which again must exist within this type of family. Lawrence Stone in his history of the English family from 1500-1800 notes important differences even within the modern English nuclear family in this period, particularly those between what he describes as the "Restricted Patriarchal Nuclear Family" and the "Closed Domesticated Nuclear Family," the latter being characterized by greater equality and autonomy of husband and wife.[29] Nevertheless, though I have painted a conclusion in broad strokes, I believe it may prove helpful to further thought on this topic. That in the history of philosophy there appears a connection between an endorsement of a sexual division of labor and an endorsement of the family may indicate possible connections between these institutions as they have existed in practice.

NOTES

1. *Nichomachean Ethics,* 1260a in *The Basic Works of Aristotle,* ed. Richard McKeon (New York: Random House, 1941), p. 1145.

2. *Nichomachean Ethics,* 1259b in McKeon, op. cit., p. 1143.

3. Christine Pierce, "Natural Law Language and Women," in *Sex Equality,* ed. Jane English (Englewood Cliffs, N.J.: Prentice-Hall, 1977), p. 133.

4. *Politics,* 1254b in McKeon, op. cit., p. 1132.

5. *The Republic,* 454B–456A in *Great Dialogues of Plato,* trans. W.H.D. Rouse, ed. Eric Warmington and Philip G. Rouse (New York: New American Library, 1956), pp. 252–53.

6. As Susan Okin points out, even in *The Republic* before Plato introduces the idea of including women as guardians, he argues that impressionable young guardians are to be prevented from imitating the female sex in their characteristic traits. As she also notes, Plato's account of the origins of the human race in *The Timaeus* presents a hierarchy of goodness and rationality in which women are placed midway between man and beasts. Susan Moller Okin, *Women in Western Political Thought* (Princeton: Princeton University Press, 1979), p. 23 and p. 26.

7. Ibid., pp. 41–42.

8. Marilyn Arthur, "'Liberated' Women: The Classical Era," in *Becoming Visible: Women in European History,* ed. Renata Bridenthal and Claudia Koonz (Boston: Houghton Mifflin, 1977), pp. 7–8.

9. John Locke, *Two Treatises of Government,* ed. and with an introduction and apparatus criticus by Peter Laslett. Rev. ed. (New York: Cambridge University Press, 1960), p. 345.

10. Ibid., p. 364.

11. Ibid., p. 362.

12. Ibid., p. 364.

13. Lorenne Clark, "Women and Locke: Who Owns the Apples in the Garden of Eden?" in *The Sexism of Social and Political Theory: Women and Reproduction from Plato to Nietsche,* ed. Lorenne M.G. Clark and Lynda Lange (Toronto: University of Toronto Press, 1979), p. 22.

14. Ibid., p. 20.
15. Ibid., p. 19.
16. Jean-Jacques Rousseau, *Emile,* intro., trans. and notes by Allan Bloom (New York: Basic Books, 1979), pp. 358 and 365.
17. Ibid., p. 361.
18. Ibid., pp. 361–62.
19. Ibid., p. 362.
20. Ibid., p. 19.
21. John Stuart Mill, *The Subjection of Women,* intro. Wendell Robert Carr (Cambridge, Mass.: MIT Press, 1970), pp. 51–52.
22. Ibid., p. 57.
23. Ibid., p. 48.
24. Frederick Engels, *The Origin of the Family, Private Property and the State,* intro. and notes by Eleanor Burke Leacock (New York: International Publishers, 1972), p. 113.
25. Ibid., pp. 119–20.
26. Ibid., p. 137.
27. Ibid., pp. 137–38.
28. Ibid., pp. 138–46.
29. Lawrence Stone, *The Family, Sex and Marriage in England 1500–1800* (New York: Harper and Row, 1977), pp. 7–8.

Francine Rainone and Janice Moulton

Sex Roles and the
Sexual Division of Labor

Previous arguments for the elimination of sex roles do not confront the question of why women in particular are disadvantaged by sex roles. Instead of facing that question, the arguments are sex neutral. They are directed toward any possible system of sex roles. Often they tend to be defensive. Concentrating on countering the claim that sex roles are good or necessary, they attempt to demonstrate that nothing terrible would happen if there were no sex roles. In order to pacify and appeal to traditionalists, these arguments often go on to show that interests of males as well as females would be served by such a change. The values of traditional liberal theory are invoked to support these claims: it is argued that individual freedom for both males and females would be enhanced and opportunities made more equal if sex roles were abolished.

We would like to give a different account of the problem of sex roles. We will argue that the problem is not that sex roles restrict freedom but that sex roles and the sexual division of labor are used in patriarchal societies to oppress women.

In the first part of this paper we will argue that if an increase

The authors wish to thank G.M. Robinson and A. Ferguson whose helpful comments improved earlier drafts of this paper. They also wish to thank each other and to point out that each is convinced that she is not responsible for the mistakes of the final draft.

in freedom and opportunity is the reason to eliminate sex roles, then all roles should be eliminated. But all roles should not be eliminated; roles are necessary and essential to any society as well as basic prerequisites of freedom and opportunity. In the second part of this paper we argue that sex roles are wrong because they buttress a sexual division of labor (SDL) which oppresses women, consigning them to positions subordinate to men. We conclude that under certain circumstances the key to attacking women's oppression is attacking the SDL. In the final part of the paper we consider a number of strategies for such an attack.

I.

Dictionaries define a role as a part, an office, a duty, or a function. In addition to roles that people assume, there are roles that people (and other things) just *have,* sometimes by choice and sometimes not. There are actors' roles and advisory roles, personal and professional roles, child, parent, and adult roles. The term "role" is used so broadly that nearly any pattern of behavior or function in a group or system can be called a role.

To say that there are sex roles is to say that females perform and are expected to perform functions different from those of males. In some societies (ancient Greece and 20th-century Arab countries, for example) sex roles dictate who does the shopping and who does the cooking. In other societies one sex is expected to do neither. In our culture women, not men, are expected to raise children; men, not women, are expected to repair cars; and a woman is expected to earn less money and be neither taller nor older than her husband.

It is not sufficient for a behavior pattern or function to exist in a society for it to be a role; there must be expectations or standards about the behavior for it to be a role. Thus there might be a pattern of behavior or function performed in a society that people were unaware of and about which there were no expectations or standards. Such a pattern could not be called a role. On the other hand, there might be unrealistic or impossible expectations that no one, or hardly anyone, ever met. But the role would still be characterized by the expectations and not by what people actually did.

Where there are expectations and standards in a society, there will be rewards and penalties for not fitting some patterns or carrying out some functions. Some penalties may be just the withholding of desired rewards while in other cases social and legal sanctions may exist for insuring conformity. The restrictions on freedom and opportunity that these penalties produce have been the subject of debate in previous discussions of sex roles.

It is certainly true that sex roles limit individual freedom and opportunity, but so do roles other than sex roles. One must be qualified to fill certain roles. There are legal restrictions on who may fill particular roles and penalties for playing disallowed roles. Immigrants cannot be President; convicted felons cannot get gun permits. In addition, freedom and opportunity are further restricted because having one role can prevent a person from having another. Just as society tells us that men are not supposed to act like women, it also tells us that adults are not supposed to act like children and that lawyers are not supposed to dress like jazz singers. One cannot simultaneously take a vow of silence and be on a debating team, have two nine-to-five jobs, be a boxer and a concert pianist, nor be a member of a city council and live in another city.

So sex roles are not alone in imposing limitations. The arguments used against sex roles will apply to any roles whatever: roles *in general* impose limitations on the people who are in them and roles come with expectations about conduct, style, behavior, and so on that incur sanctions when not met.

One could try to avoid this conclusion by arguing that sex roles are objectionable because they are not freely chosen whereas other roles are not objectionable because, although they restrict freedom, they have been freely chosen. However, there are a great many occupations and social roles that are not freely chosen, but rather are determined by economic necessity, social pressures, or ignorance about alternatives. Many roles are chosen with little information about the actual requirements of the roles. For example, stage entertainment is a role that attracts many people, but the actual working conditions of most performers are usually unknown by aspiring stars—low pay, job insecurity, road travel, and long periods away from home. Parenting is a social role which many people find satisfying, although it involves costs and responsibilities many people are unaware of before the fact; therefore parenting is not always freely chosen. It is not easy to make any distinction between roles chosen freely and roles that are not. Influences such as early childhood experience (e.g., exposure, or lack of exposure, to team sports, musical training, or role models) often determine the roles one has in later life. It is not clear that Wanda Landowski's being a harpsichordist was more freely chosen than was her being a woman. Distinguishing acceptable roles from sex roles cannot be done that simply.

One could try to make the distinction between acceptable roles and sex roles by claiming that with equal opportunity and greater dissemination of job information, occupational and social roles could be freely chosen in the future, but that sex roles are determined from birth and so cannot be freely chosen. Yet there are roles other than sex roles which are assigned to people because of properties or situations they could not have chosen that do not seem unjustified. Grandparents may be eager for their roles but they may have no choice about acquiring grandchildren. The weakest player may be assigned right field or catcher regardless of a desire to play shortstop. The blind cannot be truck drivers nor the mentally handicapped school teachers. Inheritance laws (which both liberals and conservatives traditionally support) favor genetic relationships that one has no choice about. Laws punish adults more severely than children for some misdeeds. Yet certainly one does not choose to be an adult or a child. So it does not seem that lack of free choice, per se, is what makes a role wrong.

One could try to distinguish sex roles from acceptable roles by claiming that the acceptable roles are restrictions on occupational roles while sex roles are restrictions on persons. Restrictions on occupational roles include training and licensing requirements, rules in games and sports, and they are justified by the purpose they serve. But restrictions on persons as persons are not justified. This distinction will not work, for restrictions on occupations are also restrictions on persons, namely the persons who have those jobs and who must do certain things, and the persons who do not have those jobs and therefore must not do certain things. A person not accepted to medical school can never legally prescribe certain drugs and that is a restriction on that person whether she or he wanted to be a doctor or not. Moreover this ignores the attempted justification of sex roles that claims that women and men ought to have different roles because women are better qualified than men to do certain jobs, whereas men are better qualified than women to do others. That is, this distinction ignores the extent to which sex roles are job roles and how important that is for this issue.

If freedom cannot be used to distinguish sex roles from other roles, then it looks as if one is stuck with a dilemma. Either freedom and opportunity are not the grounds for the elimination of sex roles, or one must conclude that all roles are wrong—that in order to guarantee individual freedom there should be no roles at all. Existentialists, such as the early Sartre, seem to have embraced the second alternative. Sartre seems to claim that a person can never truly be a waiter—but can only imitate the actions of other waiters. You can never be an authentic waiter, for by adopting that role, you cut out all the other possibilities in yourself. You reduce yourself to the requirements of the role, thus presenting the role as though it were your entire being. Since it is not your entire being, you are being untrue to yourself by acting out a role.

Sartre objects not to the existence of roles per se, but rather to anyone's ever adopting or accepting a role. According to him, social expectations, past behavior, and moral values do not determine our actions and to suppose that they do is self-deception, bad faith. Recognition of our total freedom will produce nausea and anxiety, but nonetheless Sartre exhorts us to face our freedom and not to succumb to bad faith. There are several problems with this view.

Even if we accept Sartre's premises, we might well conclude that bad faith is preferable to the anxiety and nausea of freedom. Sartre's injunction not to accept roles is just another attempt to coerce us, to create a role—the existentialist role. If we are really totally free, then there is no reason why we should choose nausea over self-deception. The real problem in this case is that we are not free to choose: if we believe Sartre is right we are stuck with the anxiety of our freedom; the comfort of self-deception is not an option.

But we ought to question Sartre's premises as well. Are we really that free? We know that there are social expectations and sanctions related to roles. Often not accepting a role is unavoidably an act of rebellion, a violation of social expectations. And we are not free to ignore this, to pretend to ourselves that our rebellious actions are independent isolated events unrelated to anyone else, that they are not rebellious. That others see what we do, in a certain way affects the way we see it too. And it is not just rebellions, but the whole way we view the world—our concepts and assumptions and ambitions—that is largely determined by the society we live in. Sartre's view of freedom presupposes an extreme individualism that ignores how much our past experience constrains and directs even what we consider as future possibilities.

Where Sartre argues that the acceptance of a role constitutes bad faith and a denial of our freedom, we will argue that roles are essential to our freedom because they provide information about what to expect when one chooses to do something, that it is only with roles that informed choices are possible. On our view it is impossible to imagine a society in which there are no roles at all and the demand that they be abolished or that we ignore them when acting is incoherent.

As the world is now, everyone fills more than one role. We are neighbors to some, children to others. We are workers and hobbyists and members of organizations or households. A person may be an alto in the choir, treasurer of an organization, and play short-center for the softball team. In order to eliminate these roles, we would have to eliminate rules and positions in games, functions in organizations and social groups, professional responsibilities, and all social expectations that could result in disapproval or punishment.

Suppose there were no roles. How could we then decide what specific activities to undertake, what is worth training for, or whether some activities will be rewarded well in the future? If there were no roles, then there would be no expectations about patterns of behavior and functions and therefore no reason to believe that a person's current actions or situation are part of, or prerequisites for, particular future actions or situations. We could not require an education, apprenticeship, or practice in order to become an X (driver, teacher, scuba diver) because that would amount to a role restriction. And if we went to school, served an apprenticeship, or practiced with the aim of becoming an X in this society-without-roles, we would be deluded. If there were no roles, no one would be able to gain an advantage by special training to fulfill some X, for that would restrict the people who had not trained to be Xs. We could not say that something was done well or ill because that would impose sanctions, restrictions on the way something was done; it would show that we had standards and expectations about doing X well. Work done toward as goal produces expectations which can, and very often will, be exhibited by rewards for some and punishments for others. If there were no roles, we could never decide between occupations or hobbies on the grounds that one appeared to involve more interesting activities or more pay than the other, or that it attracted more praise or respect than the other; for all these attributes are part of the rewards and punishments that are supposed to be eliminated. If we chose occupations based on knowledge or beliefs of what we would do in those jobs, we would be using role expectations to make our decisions. Surely such a view of the world is both undesirable and impossible. There will always be different things to do, with training required for some; and there will always be expectations about performance with praise for success and penalties for failures.

The same benefits that roles provide for adults are also crucial to children. They are essential to successful childrearing. Roles provide patterns, give us information about casual relationships between our social activities (if I do this, I will be able to do that, or I am likely to get that), and make it possible to plan our future, that is, to consider what *sorts* of people we want to be, what *sorts* of things we want to strive for. If there were no roles there would be no way of predicting that doing this now is a step toward something else, that it will cause certain social reactions, or that it will permit certain social relations. In order to choose courses of action, to make plans, to try to achieve something, there must be guides, ideals to aspire to, restrictions on future possibilities so that some behaviors make some possibilties more likely and others less likely.

Consider the following analogy. Our theories and beliefs about the world affect our perceptions by restricting what we perceive, so that we see things one way and not another. But this restriction is what allows us to understand and make sense of the world, by organizing our experience and relating it to other things. Similarly, roles constitute restrictions. They limit our freedom so that some choices are possible and others not. But in so doing, roles provide information about the future—about what behavior is possible, about how behaviors are related, about what treatment to expect from others. And this information is essential for making choices. If we had no theories and beliefs we would not have any coherent perceptions at all, and if we had no roles in our society, we would not have any reasons for making choices at all. The limitations that roles produce do restrict freedom, but without roles there would be no real freedom at all.

If our arguments so far are correct, we have established that all roles limit freedom and opportunity, but that this does not prove them unjustified. In fact, a world without roles would be impossible. This does not mean that every particular role is justified. Far from it. But it does mean that we must show something other than that sex roles limit freedom in order to show what is really wrong with them.

II.

In this part of the paper we shall explore the connection between sex roles and the sexual division of labor (SDL). We shall not argue against sex roles per se or the sexual division of labor per se. We do not intend our argument to be generalizable to sex roles in all cultures or in hypothetical examples. We have argued against the contention that the wrongness of sex roles is traceable to the simple fact that they restrict individual freedom. But we do not deny that sex roles restrict individual freedom. Although restrictions on freedom are often justifiable, we adhere to the principle that restrictions on the freedom of one group ought not to be made for the purpose of perpetuating that group's subordination to another group. We claim that sex roles are morally objectionable when they buttress sexual divisions of labor which perpetuate the subordination of women to men.

Now there are some who would dispute that women *are* subordinate to men. Power-behind-the-throne arguments and surprising statistics about the number of female stockholders are common enough. And of course there are individual exceptions — Thatcher, Ghandi, Meir, Curie. But it seems to us that these are overwhelmed by the statistics about female salaries, world illiteracy rates, legal restrictions on women, lack of women in political offices, and so on.

There could conceivably be sex roles and a division of labor by sex that did not subordinate either sex. We have to show that sex roles do function to give women their subordinate status in society. And in order to do that we have to discuss more specifically what sex roles are.

Sex roles are constituted by social expectations that females ought to do certain things and males ought to do others. As we said earlier, it is not required that females or males actually fill the roles or even that it is possible for them to be filled, as long as the expectations are there. There is no universal agreement about what each sex ought to do, and no single view about what sex roles are. We are going to show how two categories of sex roles working together are used to promote women's subordination.

We will consider two main views of sex roles, "liberal" views that tell us what each sex's primary roles ought to be, but do not rule out the possibility that they can do other things as well, and "traditional" views that specifically rule out certain roles for either sex. Someone might hold a liberal view about women's roles and a traditional view about men's roles, or vice versa. In fact, most people probably hold some vague combination of the two views.

The liberal view of female sex roles can be divided again into two, somewhat inconsistent but nevertheless often held, requirements. The primary responsibility for women on this view is either to be a successful wife and mother, or to be attractive to men in general. Within this view may be a wide range of views about what counts as successful or attractive. The liberal view of women's roles does not directly subordinate women to men. It is the one that is promoted in advertising recently, suggesting that women can be nuclear physicists, professional athletes, work on the Alaskan pipeline, as long as that does not interfere with their roles either as wives and mothers or with their attractiveness.

On the liberal view of sex roles, there is supposed to be nothing in principle to prevent women from doing other things, as long as they do not violate their primary roles. However, success at being a traditional wife and mother demands considerable work in caring for a husband and teaching and caring for children. The work that wives and mothers do is unpaid and has low prestige, and this work leaves less time for other work. Since being a wife and mother is supposed to come first no matter what one's other work is, problems with one's marriage or one's children are often blamed on the other roles and one will be expected to curtail the other roles, making them subordinate to one's job as a wife and mother, which is subordinate to the interests of one's husband and/or children.

Now let us consider the other version of the liberal view of sex roles. Sexual attractiveness is determined by the approval or disapproval of men. This may not seem different from many other roles where success is dependent on others—those of a colleague, employer or supervisor, for example. However, the important difference is that this particular role relegates women *as a group* to a position of being subject to the approval of men, and hence to a lower status.

One might try to deny that this version of female sex roles gives women lower status. After all, many boys and unattached men feel that their success depends on female approval. Both boys and girls in their teenage years may be particularly unhappy because they feel dependent on approval by the other sex. It seems that they will be failures if they are not appreciated by the other sex, and their other accomplishments do not matter. Now if male and female dependence on sexual approval were exactly parallel, then there would be no difference in their status. But males can become respected and appreciated for their other accomplishments and be attractive to females as a *result of* their other accomplishments. But on this view of sex roles, the primary role for females is to be attractive to males and the primary means to accomplish this is to be pretty. Simone de Beauvoir pointed out in *The Second Sex* that women are expected to keep up with fashions, wear a variety of clothing that requires time-consuming care, and spend time and money on cosmetics and hair dressing, and all this leaves women with much less time (as well as less money) to pursue their other roles. The expectation that they do this in addition to other roles handicaps women in competition with men and contributes to their having lesser status. A more significant problem is that being attractive to males is often considered a disqualification for some professional roles and/or an invitation to sexual harassment which makes functioning in the other roles very difficult.

These liberal views of sex roles indirectly create and support a dominance hierarchy which places women on lower levels because they are women. Being successful as a wife and mother requires one to be subordinate to men and spend a great part of one's life doing unpaid, low-prestige work with less time available for well-paid high-prestige work. Being successful at being attractive to men also requires considerable time taken away from other work as well as being subordinate to the opinions and preferences of men in one's primary role. Still the liberal views allow some latitude, and even though they place serious restrictions on women's ability to achieve other things, it is possible on these views to play other roles and still be feminine.

And since women do much more than fill the roles of wives and mothers or be sexually attractive, one could not say that men were dominant over women in general, or that sex roles supported this dominance if women were not subordinate to men in their other roles. After all, they might be peers, colleagues, and even supervisors in their other roles. The subordination of someone in one role might only be one side of the story. Women might be subordinate to men in some roles and dominant to men in others.

And this is where the traditional views of sex roles complement the liberal views, designating certain jobs as suitable for males and other jobs as suitable for females. There are far fewer jobs considered traditionally suitable for females and they are concentrated at the lower ends of scales of pay, power, and prestige. So the 40 percent of the work force that is female is crowded into a very small number of occupations. And these occupations—nursing, clerical, secretarial, teaching (at the lower levels), domestic servant, textile and electronic industries, food services—pay very little and/or require work largely under the supervision of men (nursing and secretarial work are clear examples of the latter).

The usual argument for a sexual division of labor is that women are more suited for certain jobs and men for others. On this view, the function of the division of labor is economic efficiency, and the lower status is a side effect. It may be unfortunate, so the argument goes, that what women are suited for is not worth as much, just as it is unfortunate that what mentally handicapped people are suited for is not worth as much, but that's the way it is.

But let us look at some of the activities of the low-prestige female-assigned occupations and compare them with those of some of the high-prestige male-assigned occupations. If this division of labor were based on economic efficiency we would expect the actual work done to be of very different sorts. The skills and abilities required for female work ought to be different in kind from the skills and abilities required for male work. But are they really so different? It is not thought remarkable for a woman to follow an intricate pattern for a dress or jacket, but reading a blueprint for a building or a road is thought inappropriate for her. Yet both activities require much the same skills: following a graphic representation, keeping note of dimensions and materials, and translating a two-dimensional outline into a three dimensional object. The concepts dealt with by computer scientists might be thought more easily understood by males than females, yet at least two well-known books on computer programming explain the basic principles in terms of an analogy with knitting patterns.[1] We expect women to clean up the various excretions of babies and care for the diseased and dying, but morticians who do the same washing and dressing of the dead are almost always men. Women office workers are expected to manage switchboards, typewriters hooked to computers, photo-duplicating machinery, dictaphones. Women homemakers may operate food processors, floor waxers, microwave ovens, sewing machines and other machinery. But women are not supposed to be good at operating lathes, radial arm saws, or engine tuning equipment. Women assemble most of the electronic equipment produced in this country, but electronic technicians are expected to be men. The list could go on, giving more evidence that there is not a clear division between the activities that women are expected to perform at low or no pay, and those that men are expected to perform.

Perhaps one might think that the assignment of women to subordinate positions is just a side-effect of the beliefs in different abilities of men and women: women are assigned to the jobs that are less important for the society or to the jobs that do not require much training. However it is easy to find examples to show that the importance of a job and the training required for it do not determine the status of the job when it is women's work that is at issue.

Women are responsible for creating the future citizens of the society and for the socialization and early cognitive training of these children. Not much could be more important for a society than that. Nurses, social workers, and school teachers receive more education and training than plumbers and garage mechanics but are usually paid less. And female office workers usually come to their jobs with more of the relevant skills than do male office workers. So it does not look as if women are relegated to occupations that in fact deserve less prestige, but rather that those occupations have less prestige and pay because they are filled by women.

Furthermore, even if it were true that the subjugation of women were a secondary effect of other factors that determined job status, or a secondary effect of an interaction of haphazard factors, objecting to the sexual division of labor because it oppresses women would be no less appropriate. One does not have to attribute a motive or purpose to social structure to condemn it when it has ill effects. We conclude that whatever the factors that determine status, the single most pervasive effect is that when jobs are assigned according to sex, women's jobs have lower status, less power and are subordinate to men's jobs. Since it is not the activities themselves on which sex roles are based, it is not training or other incidental properties that distinguish women's jobs from men's jobs, and the salary differential between women's jobs and men's jobs cannot be explained in terms of training or importance to society, we conclude that the main function of the sexual division of labor which sex roles support is to keep women subordinate to men.

III.

We have argued that one way sex roles keep women in positions subordinate to men is by providing a rationale for an unfair sexual division of labor. But we believe that it is neither sex roles per se nor the existence of a SDL per se that maintains women's oppression. Instead we believe that sex oppression is only one of many interdependent systems of oppression. The systems of race and class oppression are equally important. We begin this section by briefly examining some of the ways that sex roles and the SDL support and/or undermine other systems of oppression. Then we consider the three major strategies proposed for overcoming the unfairness of the SDL in the United States today. We believe that the weaknesses of these strategies are often traceable to the fact that sex oppression is often so inextricably intertwined with other systems of oppression.

Consider competitive industrial societies with a market economy. These societies are characterized by a sharp division between the realm of production and the realm of reproduction,[2] i.e., between work life and family life. A competitive market economy requires an increasingly severe division of labor because, in general, goods are produced more efficiently when the tasks involved in their production are divided among different people. Other things being equal, the more efficiently goods are produced the better their competitive position on the market. With the development of capitalism, which is the primary example of this kind of society, the demands of efficiency dictate that productive labor be carried on outside the home, away from the "distractions" of "personal" life. Child care is a job which requires the constant availability of attention. Such availability is inconsistent with maximum efficiency in production. So in this type of society, as long as women's place in the SDL is to take care of children, their participation in the productive realm must be restricted.[3] But in these societies the locus of authority and control over social resources is the productive realm. Excluding women from this realm and/or restricting their participation in it not only prevents them from achieving the power and control in the society that is available to men, but renders most women financially dependent on men. Dependence of many types is, in turn, seen as part of women's sex role.

Women's sex role and the SDL strengthen the hierarchical class structure of capitalism in a variety of ways. For example, because women are expected to be closely tied to home, they provide a reserve of marginal workers which can be used in the work force when demands for production are high and then bumped back into the home during periods of recession and depression. The SDL crowds women into a very few occupations. This keeps the supply of workers for these jobs high, and the wages correspondingly low. The belief that women's "real" place is in the home makes many women seek only part-time or temporary employment. Such workers do not accrue seniority. Nor do they have to be paid fringe benefits, in most cases. In addition, many women consider their work "temporary" regardless of how long they have been doing it. All these factors tend to keep profits higher than they would be otherwise and to make it more difficult and less likely for women to organize for higher wages and better benefits. In occupations with both male and female workers sexism can retard or even prevent unionization; workers fight each other instead of joining together to fight those who actually control social resources. Furthermore, the belief that women's place is in the home has been used to condition women to be conspicuous consumers. In the name of being a "good homemaker" the advertising industry dupes women into buying many unnecessary and even useless products. And of course in order to be properly feminine women require a stunning variety and number of accoutrements, from cosmetics and feminine deodorant spray to the latest in fashion designer jeans. As a result consumption is one of women's major roles in the economy.

We have listed some of the ways sex roles and the SDL strengthen class oppression and keep profits high. This helps explain why male capitalists would support sex roles and the SDL, but it cannot explain why men in other classes do too. Nor does it fully explain the persistence of sex roles and the SDL. This is because although capitalism requires, for example, a reserve of marginal workers, there is no feature intrinsic to capitalism that requires that *women* constitute this reserve. In the United States both male and female members of minority races are also part of the reserve. And racism is surely as divisive as sexism. Since the persistence of racism and sexism tends to keep wages low in occupations with significant numbers of women and/or minority workers, one would expect male workers to be anti-racist and anti-sexist. They often are, but at least as often they are not. Our point is, in part, that since sex roles and the SDL predate capitalism we cannot attribute their perpetuation to capitalism alone. To understand why working class males often support sex roles and the SDL we need to look for some feature common to all patriarchal societies whether or not they are capitalist.

It is commonplace to note that from society to society there are wide variations in the specific tasks the sexes perform. Within the same society, sex roles differ along race and class lines and may vary dramatically from one historical period to another. But whatever else women do—and this "else" has always been considerable—they are expected to raise children and/or to satisfy the emotional and sexual needs of men. Despite cultural variations, women's role as mothers and/or emotional-sexual caretakers of men is virtually universal. When women are otherwise dependent on them, males are able to control female labor-power within the family. The advantages that result from their privileged position in the family (for example, clean laundry, hot dinners, sexual services, and sympathy) provide a motivation for men to maintain their domination over women.[4] We are not suggesting that all men always act on this motivation, or that it is always in their interests to do so.

We are suggesting two things. First, the fact that both men and women are caught in multiple systems of oppression must be taken into account when formulating strategies for fighting any one of those systems. For example, it is in the interests of many men to press for higher wages for women, both because that would tend to increase men's wages in the same occupations and because it would directly financially benefit men who are married or associated with women whose wages would be increased. But it doesn't follow that it is in these same men's interests to press for equal distribution of child care, for example. This brings us to our second point. It we are correct that the basis of the SDL is women's role as mothers and caretakers of men, then attempts to change or eliminate sex roles which do not alter that aspect of women's role will not alter the balance of power between men and women.[5] If we see the basis of the SDL as a fundamental mechanism for perpetuating male domination, then we can formulate two rules about changes in sex roles. First, changes in the female sex role can be made quite easily in response to changes in the economy and pressure from women for equality. And these changes, while they might improve the conditions of women's lives to some extent, can also be used to mask the fact that women are still subordinate to men, albeit in a different way. Second, changes which will threaten the *basis* of the SDL (women's mothering and caretaking of men) will be resisted vigorously.

If we are correct, many of the contradictory aspects of women's sex roles are functional for maintaining women's oppression, rather than just irrational. Race, class, cultural and historical variations in sex roles overwhelmingly serve to support rather than weaken the SDL. For example, the change from Victorian morality to the flapper era liberated women from many oppressive restrictions on their sexuality. But it was used as "proof" that full sexual equality had been achieved. But it actually transformed women from sexless beings into sex *objects*; it did not allow them to be active sexual subjects exploring and satisfying their sexual desires however they chose. To give a different example, when women are needed in the labor force the female ideal becomes the working mother. But national systems of child care are not established. Nor is there a corresponding shift in male ideals. In addition, the image of the working mother is that of a privileged, at the minimum comfortably well-off, woman. This ignores the fact that most women in this country have to work, and do not conform to this image.[6] It hides the fact that most women in the work force are still channeled to a very small assortment of low-paying jobs, and men may be expected to "help" in the home (when they are present) but are not expected to assume equal responsibilities there. If our hypotheses are correct, then strategies for achieving sexual equality by changing the SDL will not be successful unless they include attempts to change the basis of the SDL.

Three major strategies for changing the SDL have been proposed. One strategy is to attempt to get women into "male" jobs. this might be called the "add and stir" approach. Since proponents of this strategy believe that a major barrier to sexual equality is that women control so few social resources, they believe that women must be added into positions of greater power and dominance over resources. One way to accomplish this has been to use government powers through affirmative action programs. One of the difficulties with these programs is that they do not address the fact that the influence of sex role socialization prevents women from even becoming applicants for certain jobs. Another difficulty is that even if there were no resistance to these programs, given the way that they are currently structured, it would take an unconscionably long time for them to be effective.[7] There are three other serious difficulties with this strategy.

Firstly, merely having men and women do the same work is not enough. In many cases where men and women are trained to do the same thing, the women are relegated to lower status positions. In college teaching women have only token representation, if at all, in the high ranks or high status positions. Most female college teachers are to be found in small colleges or at low ranks. Women and men hired for maintenance jobs are routinely assigned different duties. In industry, males who do secretarial work are sometimes called clerks and command higher wages for less skill.[8] As more women move into a profession, hierarchies and status differences can be created where there were none before so that women can continue to have lower status than men in that profession.

In addition, identical work by men and women is perceived differently. Not only are papers and accomplishments rated lower if thought to be by women than by men, but the same activities are perceived differently. A Washington hostess will be perceived as fulfilling feminine social functions: nurturing, facilitating communication, helping people make contacts. A male performing the same deeds, hosting gatherings for famous people, will be perceived as fulfilling a political rather than a social function: manipulating power, engineering deals, being diplomatic. So merely having women and men do the same work is not enough.[9]

Moreover, feminists do not want men's work to remain the "same." A dilemma confronts feminist organizers. In order to create sexual equality women need to gain control of social resources. They cannot do this without doing "men's work." Men's work in the institutions by means of which social resources are controlled (for example, banks and governmental agencies) is based on a hierarchical power structure, domination and exploitation. Working in these institutions requires acting in accordance with these values, at least to some extent. But acting in accordance with these values strengthens the bases of oppression rather than weakening them.

Finally, from our point of view this strategy is incomplete. We cannot end the sex segregation of the labor force unless there is a national system of affordable, quality child care. A woman who purchases child care services does not necessarily weaken the SDL, even if those services enable her to work in a non-traditional job. The system can absorb a large number of token women able to afford child care without altering the balance of power. This brings us to the second strategy for changing the SDL.

This strategy is to establish government-run government subsidized child care facilities. Women cannot participate equally with men in production unless they are relieved of their child-rearing duties by some form of collectivized child care. But we should be wary of leaving the early training and possible indoctrination of children to government agencies. Moreover, where this solution has been instituted (whether or not it is government controlled) child care remains a low-paying low status job performed almost exclusively by women. Thus it reinforces the basis of the SDL. It also reinforces the class oppression of the child care workers.

A third strategy seeks to overcome this deficiency by involving men in child care, either privately or in state run facilities. But it is not clear that women should give up their control, limited as it is, over child-rearing, until they have political and economic power. They cannot be sure that loss of this control will not be used to further weaken their position in society unless they are involved in the economic and political decisions that restructure child care. We are not claiming that these strategies are necessarily useless or self-defeating. We are emphasizing the point that creating sexual equality will require a total transformation of society. This transformation cannot be accomplished piecemeal; attempts at change can each be coopted if they are not coordinated. If we are right, the time has come to examine methods of coordinating the enormous amount of feminist organizing going on in this country. One way to do this would be to create a national feminist political party. We cannot discuss this or any other option here. But we hope that our work will stimulate others to engage in debate over which of all the possible options would be the most effective.

NOTES

1.   The books are Douglas Hostadter, *Gödel, Escher, Bach* (New York: Vintage Books, 1979), pp. 149–150 and Margaret Boden, *Artificial Intelligence and Natural Man* (New York: Basic Books, 1977) pp. 9–12.

2.   We are using the terms "realm of production" and "realm of reproduction" nontechnically. We are not taking a stand on such questions as whether housewives produce surplus value and/or contribute to the GNP.

3.   Two points should be made clear here. First, we are not assuming that there are no working mothers! We are claiming that women's role as the primary caretakers of children cuts down on their ability to compete with men effectively on the job market. Second, we are not assuming that a capitalist economy always reinforces patriarchy.

4.   For an analysis of the benefits men get from hierarchically structured families see Ann Ferguson, "Women as a New Revolutionary Class" in *Between Labor and Capital,* ed. Pat Walker (Boston: South End Press, 1979), pp. 279–309. For an analysis of men's resistance to changes in the SDL see Heidi Hartmann, "Capitalism, Patriarchy, and Job Segregation by Sex," in *Capitalism Patriarchy and the Case for Socialist Feminism,* ed. Z. Eisenstein. (New York: Monthly Review Press, 1979), pp. 206–247. Her view of the SDL is similar to our own.

5.   This point could be expressed in terms of individual psychology. The attitudes and behavior required by sex roles are the sort of things that could be chosen if society were organized differently. In that respect, sex roles differ from roles which depend on characteristics such as height. However, sex roles are manifestations of gender identity. And while changes in sex roles result in changed attitudes and behavior, they do not result in changes in gender identity. Because gender identity is fixed so early in life, it is not a matter of individual choice. But it is a matter of social choice, or it could be. By changing the factors that fix gender identity, a society could change or perhaps eliminate gender. Chodorow (*The Reproduction of Mothering*) and others have suggested that women's gender identity is a result of their mothering role in society. We do not have the space in this paper to examine the implications of these views for our own position.

6.   One of the major arguments against women's suffrage was that women who voted would lose their femininity. In a 1912 speech Rose Schneiderman exposed the fallacy and class bias of this argument.

>   We have women working in the foundries, stripped to the waist. . . . They . . . stand for thirteen or fourteen hours in

the terrible steam and heat with their hands in hot starch. Surely these women won't lose any more of their beauty and charm by putting a ballot in a ballot box once a year than they are likely to lose standing in foundries or laundries all year round.

Quoted in C. Hymowitz and M. Weissman, *A History of Women in America* (New York: Bantam, 1978), p. 278.

7. See Virginia Held, "Reasonable Progress and Self-Respect," *Monist* 57, 1 (January 1973): 12–27.

8. This is the practice at, for example, Burroughs Wellcome's Research Center in Raleigh, N.C.

9. Of course nothing can be done to equalize the division of reproductive work, short of ceasing it altogether. The only remedy would be to recognize that making babies is a form of work to be valued and rewarded like other forms of production. But this might not change the value accorded such work. One might argue that anti-abortion advocates are trying to exploit the reproductive workers of the world, trying to get them to do that work against their will and without compensation. One can imagine women proclaiming, "If the world wants babies, let it pay a fair market price for them."

Virginia Held

The Obligations of
Mothers and Fathers

Possibly, the continued existence of humanity will require that
we cease to turn "mothering" into an activity filled only by
mothers. If it is true that the human personality is formed very
early in life, and if it is true that our social practice of making
mothers but not fathers the primary caretakers of small children
forms the male personality into one in which the inclination
toward combat is overdeveloped and the capacity to feel for
others is stunted, our survival may depend on a reorganization
of parenting. instead of forming girls into human beings with a
weak sense of self and a diminished ability to assert their independence, and forming boys into human beings "whose nurturant capacities . . . have been systematically curtailed and
repressed,"[1] we ought to transform the social institution of
parenting into one performed equally by women and men.

The extent to which parenting is *not* tied to biology but is instead a social construction can be suggested by considering the
entirely different meanings we give to the sentences "he fathered

I am grateful to Sissela Bok, Sandra Harding, Onora O'Neill, William Ruddick,
and Mary Vetterling-Braggin for their helpful comments.

the child" and "she mothered the child." Mothers *need* not be the ones who "mother," and we may have urgent reasons to turn the parenting done by fathers and mothers into entirely similar activities. But I shall not consider these arguments in this article. Nor shall I take up questions concerning the raising of children in homosexual households.

Rather, I shall consider the arguments for a change in parenting practices based on principles of equality applied to parents. I shall discuss the rights of children to care, but not rights to any particular personality, though on these grounds as well as on grounds of our concern for humanity in general, the argument for equal parenting may be decisive. If, as Nancy Chodorow writes, "the very fact of being mothered by a woman generates in men conflicts over masculinity, a psychology of male dominance, and a need to be superior to women,"[2] both girl and boy children may have rights to equal parenting. But my arguments will deal with a different issue: What does a commitment to considering female and male parents as persons of equal human worth require as applied to parenting?

Over and over, one encounters the argument: if a woman chooses to become a mother, she must accept a recognized set of responsibilities and obligations that are quite different from the responsibilities and obligations of being a father. In the eyes of many people, a father is expected to contribute some of his income for the expenses his child makes necessary. A mother is expected to give up whatever other work may interfere with her availability to care for her child and to take full care of the child—cheerfully and contentedly, to whatever extent, and as long as the child needs it. And if it is thought that the child will develop problems due to early separations from a parent, it is the mother who will be thought responsible for preventing them.

Recent and still existing law, in its characteristically obtuse way in this domain, deals almost entirely with "support" of the child in the sense of paying the bills for the child's food, clothing, shelter, etc. This is thought to be the father's obligation; if he is unwilling or unable to fulfill it, it becomes the mother's. The mother, just by virtue of being a wife, has standardly been expected by the law to "render services in the home," as it is often put, and these services include, incidentally, caring for any children who happen to be in it. As summarized in a legal textbook published not long ago, *The Law of Domestic Relations,* "the husband is to provide the family with food, clothing, shelter, and as many of the amenities of life as he can manage . . . The wife is to be mistress of the household, maintaining the home with the resources furnished by the husband, and caring for the children."[3] And as the author says, in a judgment not yet outdated, "a reading of contemporary judicial opinions leaves the impression that these roles have not changed over the last two hundred years."[4]

A few states have made some changes to bring the law in line with state equal rights amendments. And if the federal Equal Rights Amendment is adopted, it may bring about quite significant changes in the law. But courts will continue to be dominated for a long time by conservative, middle-aged men, and, more importantly, the law seldom enters into the domestic picture until there is a breakdown of a marriage. While the marriage is intact, the law leaves husband and wife great latitude to work out their domestic arrangements; when the marriage falls apart, courts decide how to divide up possessions and obligations. The possibilities of dividing parental obligations equally, even at this point, are only beginning to be explored.[5]

In the attitudes of society, "motherhood" is often taken to be an occupation (though unpaid) which women can perform the way men can be auto workers, or bankers, or professors. In a recent article by a social scientist, one comes across the following view: "Once these successive needs—the physical, the social-affectional, and the equal esteem or dignity needs—are sufficiently gratified, humans are not even then content: they then begin to look for that kind of activity that is particularly suited to them as unique individuals. Whether their competence is to be a ditchdigger, a powershovel operator, a construction foreman, a civil engineer or a building contractor, an architect, a mother, a writer, or a politician—they must do these things when they have become rather sure in the gratification of their even more basic physical, social and esteem needs."[6]

At least the ranking in this list is favorable. In contrast, the skill level thought to be needed by a homemaker, child-care attendant, or nursery school teacher was rated in a recent U.S. Department of Labor publication at only 878 on a scale from 1, the highest skill level, to 887, the lowest (hotel clerks were at 368).[7]

Just how ludicrous it is from the point of view of equality to see motherhood as an occupation can be seen if one substitutes "father" for "mother" in such lists. As we all know, and yet as even a rudimentary sense of equality must protest, women have routinely been asked to choose between parenthood and having an occupation (or another occupation, if one counts parenthood). Men have routinely been expected to be able to enjoy *both* parenthood *and* an occupation (or another occupation).

The common view that motherhood is one occupation among others, but virtually the only one open to mothers not driven to factory or farm labor in addition to motherhood, was shared, one regrets to note, by John Stuart Mill, despite his awareness, quite unusual among philosophers along with nearly everyone else, that women were entitled to equal rights.[8] It has sometimes been suggested that any different view of the occupational possibilities of women had to await the development of industrialization in the nineteenth century or the development of birth control techniques later. But that this is a lame excuse for millennia of exploitation can be seen in the perfectly imaginable alternative view given by Plato, at least in *The Republic*. Plato pointed out to anyone who would notice that whether one bears or begets children is not a relevant basis on which to determine whether one is fit to govern.[9] The same argument could be applied to the whole range of occupations. Instead, the link between giving birth and caring for children is still assumed to be necessary and inevitable.

That so few have been able to imagine, much less support, the notion of both mothers and fathers caring for children and being engaged in other occupations is part of the problem of turning conceptions of equality into practice. But it is unclear, perhaps, what might be required by equality, or what parents who acknowledge each other to have equal obligations toward their children need to do to fulfill these requirements and obligations. It is this question that I shall now try to explore.

I. EQUAL OBLIGATIONS

Must we suppose that equality requires both parents to do approximately the same tasks, taking approximately the same length of time, so that one parent might, for instance, be completely in charge of the children from 6 A.M. to 2 P.M., say, and the other parent completely in charge from 2 P.M. to 10 P.M., say, while both work at paid jobs to support themselves and their children in the hours they are not engaged in child care, and both take turns at whatever getting up in the night is needed?

Are staggered and perhaps shorter work shifts in industry and the professions an obvious objective?

Or should we consider the possibility that if the abilities of the two parents are significantly different, the child is entitled to care "from each according to his or her ability" rather than "from each the same kind of activity for the same length of time"? It has often been supposed that women have greater natural talents for and are more skillful at taking care of small children, and that men have greater natural talents for and are more skillful at obtaining the objects and/or money with which to provide food, clothing, shelter, etc., for the child. It seems highly probable that many differences in skill levels along these lines would disappear if both parents had been brought up as equals from childhood, and if they, as parents, shared both kinds of activities. But if it should happen that some significant differences remained in particular cases, and that a given infant's mother, say, really did have much more talent than the infant's father for making the infant comfortable, happy, friendly, and eager for new experiences, while the infant's father, say, really did have much more talent at earning the family's income, would the parents have an obligation to accept a traditional division of labor, she at home caring and he in the world earning, each working *equally hard* at contributing what they did best to the well-being of the child?

And what about preferences? If one parent greatly prefers to earn an income from outside work, rather than take care of children, should this guide the parents' decisions on how to divide their obligations equally? Or if a child, especially at a given age, greatly prefers being taken care by one parent rather than the other, should the parents accede to the child's wishes? Are such preferences largely the result of the habitual inequalities built into the traditional gender roles of men and women, and the expectations of children raised in sexist societies, and should they on these grounds be discounted? Or can they be legitimate preferences which should be considered when parents try to work out cooperative arrangements?

It is inadequate to consider questions of parental obligation in isolation from the social situation. Societies ought to recognize their obligations to their children. Societies ought to provide adequate levels of part-time and full-time child care, of support for parents who take care of children at home if they choose to, of medical care and education. But measures to do so are, unfortunately, in the United States, a long way off. I shall, in what follows, deal with the equal obligations of parents in terms of *given* levels, however inadequate, of social support. Doing so should certainly not be taken to imply that current social arrangements are satisfactory, only that women and men may often try to do the best they can to respect each other as equal persons within existing social structures. And the questions I shall consider are primarily moral ones. One hopes the law and social arrangements will come to reflect moral requirements, but long before they do, morally concerned persons must deal with these issues and can try to arrive at reasonable solutions of the problems involved. What I am asking, then, is: If individual women and men recognize principles of equality, as most would presumably by now profess to do, and if both really do respect each other as persons of equal worth, entitled to equal liberty[10] and justice, with equal rights to choose how to live their lives, what are the implications of this for their obligations as mothers and fathers?

Much of what is said here may apply to housework apart from child care, but I shall not discuss such applications. The difficulties of deciding how to divide housework equally are much less complex; a willingness to do so goes far, if persons living together agree on what needs to be done. But the restrictions and demands of parenthood raise complications of a different order, since the rights of parenthood raise complications of a different order, since the rights and interests of other human beings are involved, and since small children require someone "on duty" continually. These new complications often disrupt the equitable arrangements that might be worked out apart from children, as when it is assumed that since the mother will be home with the children anyway, she might as well do most of the housework.

Many of the activities involved in caring for children are intrinsically pleasurable. Sometimes, to be with one's child may be much closer to leisure enjoyment than to work. To play with a child for a few hours in the evening after a day of work away from home, for instance, may be a reward, not a burden, of parenthood. But providing much of what children need can be routine drudgery or emotional torment when it is done constantly, repeatedly, because of one's obligations, in a way that consumes nearly all of one's energies and time, as when a mother does nothing else than care for children and household, or a father nothing else than work at a job he hates in order to pay his family's bills. And the burdensome aspects of these activities become all the greater when the person feels that the arrangement placing these burdens on her or on him are unjust, and that it is unfair to be required to bear them.

I shall consider, in what follows, only the obligations parents have to perform various tasks, not the activities they may share with their children for pleasure, and not the feelings with which the tasks are performed. Family and marriage texts have generally asserted that the mother's function is to provide "emotional support," to "keep the family happy," to remain calm amidst the noise and turmoil of the household, to sympathize, to be what is called the family's "heart." The father's function, on the other hand, is to be efficient and strong in dealing with the wider world, to be rational, impartial, just and firm in enforcing discipline, to be what is called the family's "head." I shall restrict the discussion that follows to the performance of specific tasks, without considering whether they include the supplying of adequate psychological or emotional benefits. And the tasks under consideration will be tasks that need doing, apart from whether or not they are done with an acceptable emotional tone or from an appropriate psychological stance.

It would certainly not be adequate to think of the relation between parents and children only or even largely in terms of obligations and rights. Children have rights to care and support, and parents have obligations to supply these when the society does not do so, but it is obviously better for children to receive more from their parents than what the mere fulfillment of the parents' obligations would require. A parent who gives love, concern, and attention to a child because it is a joy to do so is obviously a better parent than one who merely grimly meets his or her obligations to feed and safeguard the child. And it is surely of more value to the child that there be a genuine relationship of mutuality, of shared concern and respect[11] between the man and the women who are the child's parents, than that such a relationship be absent. But I am going to limit discussion here to obligations and their equality. Parents cannot have obligations to feel emotions beyond their control, or to give children everything that would be of value to them. They can be expected to meet their equal obligations.

I shall also not discuss how parental obligations to children arise in the first place. For instance, in a case where birth control measures have failed, where neither parent wants a child, but where society compels them to become parents against their wills through laws forbidding or social practices preventing abortion, do parents have any obligations to this child, or does society alone have them? Or, if one parent wants a child and the other does not, does the parent who wants the child have greater obligations to care for the child if they have one? Possibly, in such a case, the parents might make an agreement specifying their unequal obligations to the child, which child they otherwise might not have. I shall deal only with cases where both parents voluntarily become the parents of a child, are equally responsible for becoming parents, and recognize that they are equally responsible for the child.

II. WHAT DOES EQUALITY REQUIRE?

Children are entitled to support and care. To the extent that, under given social arrangements, the moral obligation to provide these falls on the parents, it falls on them collectively. From the point of view of the child, it may often not matter which parent provides what aspect of support and care in what proportion.

Parents should, first of all, agree on what the child's rights and needs are, and agree on the necessity and relative importance of the tasks that are to be done before they consider which parent should do which tasks. They should try to decide how much the child's preferences will count and in which domains they will count before they discover what the child's preferences are. They should not, for instance, accept those of the child's preferences which require that the mother bear more than her otherwise fair share of the burdens of fulfilling parental obligations, and discount those of the child's preferences which would require the father to do so, although this has traditionally been standard.

Then the parents should proceed from such judgments as "the parents have an obligation to provide w,x,y, and z" to such judgments as "parent A has an obligation to provide w and z," and "parent B has an obligation to provide x and y." How people move from the former judgments to the latter has traditionally not been a matter of reasonable argument, but of little more than social prejudice. Much thinking anew and goodwill are needed to reconcile thinking about the obligations of parents with thinking about the obligations of mothers and fathers in ways that are morally plausible.

In trying to see what equality requires, it is sometimes helpful to consider its application in some other area, close enough to be relevant but different enough to be instructive. Let us consider another family context than the one of parental obligations, a context of two men able to earn income—brothers in this case—having an obligation to support an aged mother unable to be self-supporting.

If the brothers agree that their obligations are equal, what would this require? If one brother is very rich, the other very poor, it is unlikely that they would feel obligated to contribute exactly the same *amount* of money to their mother's support. Would this be a departure from their having an equal obligation? It would seem not, but rather that a requirement to contribute according to ability would be applied equally to each.

Perhaps they might consider that if one contributed more money, the other could contribute more time, visiting the aged mother more often, helping her in her garden, etc. But let us limit the debate to the question of an equal obligation to provide financial support, in terms of some monetary unit.

If, then, the brothers recognize an equal obligation to contribute to financial support, would they have to contribute an equal percentage of their income, if one is rich and the other poor? Or would equality require them to recognize a further aspect of proportionality in their ability to pay, as equality would seem to require rather than oppose a graduated income tax? There might be general agreement that we would hold the latter, although there might be some difficulty in specifying the amount. It would seem plausible that equality of obligation would require that the rich brother should contribute a greater amount *and* proportionately a higher percentage of his income, because the ability to contribute is a relevant factor to consider, a greater ability requires a greater contribution, and as the ability to contribute rises, it is appropriate for the percentage contribution to rise.

The question of the brothers' obligation to earn an income in the first place might be more troublesome. Suppose that one brother has more income because he works many hours, and the other brother has less because he works fewer hours. Both find paid work equally available, and equally unsatisfying, but one brother earns three times as much money as the other because he works three times as many hours a week. We would then have to distinguish actual ability to contribute at a given time, once income, etc., was in hand, and the effort expended, prior to this, to arrive at this actual ability. Then it would not seem that an equal obligation would require the brother who works many hours to contribute three times as much as, or a much higher percentage of his income than, the brother who works few hours, because with an increase of effort, the latter could meet the difference, and contribute, himself, a sum that really would be an absolutely equal amount. If, after that, the brother who works few hours chose leisure over further labor, that would be his right, at least relative to his brother, although if the combined amount contributed by the two for the mother's support left her in extreme and painful poverty, the brother who works few hours might have an obligation to work longer, and the brother who works many hours an obligation to raise the total amount.

If we suppose the earning capacity of the two brothers to be equal, and that they find the labor necessary to earn income equally unsatisfying, we might think that fulfilling their obligations on a basis of equality might require each to provide half of what can be taken to be adequate to fulfill their combined obligation. Then we would be back to an absolutely equal amount, even if one brother is relatively rich and the other is relatively poor.

In considering cases such as these, the following principles would seem plausible: (1) In meeting their obligations, the person with the greater actual ability to contribute ought to make a proportionately larger contribution. (2) Effort is an appropriate factor to consider in deciding on obligations, and obligations concerning effort take priority over obligations based on actual ability to contribute. Thus, as between two persons with an equal actual ability to contribute, one person should not be expected to expend far more effort to achieve this actual ability. And as between two persons making an equal effort, a greater resulting actual ability to contribute requires this person to make a proportionately larger contribution, but if he or she should choose to make a further expenditure of effort, this should not be penalized by a still further increase of contribution.

If we find these principles plausible in the case of the brothers, we might extend them to the case of parental obligations. If the parents decide that the needs of the child require them to earn, say, thirty additional monetary units a week, and if, as would be likely in American society at present, the mother would have to work at a paid job almost twice as long as the father to earn the fifteen units that would seem like an equal share, then equality of obligation would not require her to provide half of the thirty units. However, if the mother wishes to work, her contribution should not be discounted just because an equal effort will bring in less money. Again, if the work the mother would have to do, even if equally paid, would be significantly less satisfying than the work the father would have to do, and would thus be more of an effort to perform, then an equal contribution would not require the mother to expend as much time at such work or to provide as much money for the child from it as the father.

In a different aspect of their obligations, if the parents decide that on a typical day the child should be given breakfast, taken on a two-hour outing with close supervision, given lunch, a rest, a bath, and a story and that the objects the child has scattered about the house should be put away, then equal obligations would not be fulfilled if the mother, because of greater effort, did (or, when appropriate, got the child to do) all these things on the days it was her turn, while the father, because of a lesser effort, managed to get done only two or three of the five on the days, an equal number, it was his turn. But if it really was, at least temporarily, significantly more difficult for him to do these things than for her, he might be required to do fewer of them.

In making these determinations, we could raise the question of whether it is intention or success that should count in establishing when two persons are making "an equal effort." In child-care work, one person may succeed with modest effort in keeping a baby satisfied and occupied, while the other may try much harder and fail. In trying to improve one's position in outside employment, one person may try and repeatedly suffer defeat, and the other may move steadily forward with little effort. But despite the possibilities it may create for deception and self-deception, in the case of meeting one's obligations, it seems to be intention, not success, that should count.[12] But then we must assume sincerity, and that statements such as "but I *am* doing the best I can" will not be used to mask willful inefficiency.

Whenever differences of interpretation arise as to what importance to attach to what, and what guidelines to use to weigh obligations, devices to cut down distortions of perception may be helpful. Parents can try to apply the "roommate test" suggested by Sandra and Daryl Bem, and ask how the tasks would be divided if, instead of being a male/female couple, they were roommates of the same sex.[13] Parents can acquaint themselves with all the tasks, and devise arrangements and divisions of them before knowing which tasks they themselves will perform. They can, for instance, decide whether feeding the children their evening meal should count for more than doing their laundry or count for less, before deciding which parent will do which task. And they can decide whether a typical hour of outside employment is more burdensome or more rewarding than a typical hour of child care before deciding how the hours will be divided. And so on.

Differences of competence can be brought in at a later stage of discussing these arrangements, but here again, procedures to aid impartiality may be helpful. For instance, the parents might agree to evaluate each other's competence rather than their own, and to do so before knowing what arrangements their discussions will recommend. And differences of preference which make some tasks more burdensome to one parent than to the other should be considered only to the extent that the preferences of both parents are considered to an equal degree, including higher-order preferences, such as when a women might say, "I do not now like to give lectures, but I want to get practice at it because I would like to like to."

To the charge that such "counting" of hours and such "calculation" of who is doing how much will spoil the spontaneous and harmonious relation between parents and with children, will turn family affection into the pursuit of selfishness and turn children into products, one can point to centuries of experience. Such charges have always been leveled against workers—factory workers, teachers, secretaries—who have "calculated" how many hours they were working overtime or without pay instead of failing, out of "loyalty," to notice. And such charges have routinely been used against women who have finally begun to recognize that, in addition to working all day like their husbands, whether at home or at paying jobs, they have been doing nearly all the evening housework. Those who have been taken advantage of have always been asked by the beneficiaries to be trusting and altruistic,[14] but the result of acquiescence in arrangements that are unfair is the growth of resentment and mistrust. The response must be that when respect and equality become habitual, calculation becomes unnecessary. Mutuality and sharing are to be sought, but on a basis of equality, not exploitation.

II. CAN WORK BE DIFFERENT BUT EQUAL?

Equality of obligation would certainly not rule out *all* differences in the tasks performed by mothers and fathers. We now have, I think, no reliable empirical knowledge of any genuine differing talents and tendencies of mothers and fathers (except the dispensable and brief capacity of mothers to nurse their infants). We should be very wary of accepting any division of labor between mothers and fathers based on their differing talents at the time they become parents, since these may be due to years of sex-stereotyped preparation, in which boys are encouraged to study and work at various jobs, and girls are expected to babysit and do housework. One significant feature of parenthood is that *neither* parent has much previous training for the work, although this is often overlooked, as it is assumed that the mother will "know what to do," and hence, since it is so much "easier" for her, that she should take care of the children. Anyone who has studied, or experienced, the anxious and helpless feelings that affect women faced with a first newborn baby to care for, or the feelings of guilt and incompetence of mothers not able to handle "smoothly" the outbursts and demands of small children, has every reason to believe that fathers would be equally capable of preparing themselves for child-care work as best they could, and learning fast on the job.[15]

Still, we cannot preclude altogether the possibility that differences of parental ability and preferences between men and women may be significant. It was suggested in a recent article by David Gutmann, a psychologist, that the differences are particularly acute among young parents, and that these differences are more than cultural. He wrote:

. . . the vulnerability and helplessness of infants and young children seem to arouse a sense of chronic emergency in parents even under relatively affluent conditions, and fathers and mothers respond to this sense of emergency in sex-specific ways. Thus, the young father forces even more deeply into his psychic underground the receptive sensuality that might be distracting to him in his instrumental role, and hence potentially lethal to his children . . . the wife becomes an external representation of the "passive" yearnings her husband must give up in order to provide for his family. By the same token the wife concedes to her husband — and figuratively sends out of the house with him — the aggression that might be deadly, in the emotional and even in the physical sense, to her vulnerable offspring. The standard reaction for each sex is to surrender to the other the qualities that might interfere with the provision of its own special form of security. Men, the providers of physical security, give up the sensual dependency that might inhibit their courage and endurance; and women, the providers of emotional security, give up the aggression that might frighten or hurt a vulnerable and needful child.[16]

Even if one were to accept such "facts," one might suppose that they result more from the early upbringings of the parents than from innate psychological dispositions. Or perhaps, faced with the awesome and demanding responsibilities of new parenthood, both parents make extra efforts to conform to what society expects of them—to be, that is, what they have been induced by traditional roles to think of as "good" parents. But Gutmann considers the case for connecting different responses to parenthood with sexual differences to be strengthened by a consideration of what he calls "the sexual reversals that take place in middle-age, as children grow up and take over the responsibility of providing for their own security." As he sees it,

A massive involution takes place in which men begin to live out directly—to own, as part of themselves—the passivity, sensuality, and tenderness, in effect the "femininity," that was previously repressed in the service of productive instrumentality. By the same token, we find (again, across a vast range of societies) the opposite effect in women, who generally become domineering, independent, and unsentimental in late middle life. . . . Grandpa becomes sweet, affable, but rather vague, Grandma becomes toughminded and intrusive.[17]

As a description of our social situation, this is, one must say, ludicrous, since, as one looks around at the leading positions in every important social structure—governmental, economic, legal, educational, etc.—one of its most obvious features is the almost total absence of anyone who is or ever will be a grandmother. So long as the society rewards the outside work of young fathers with promotions, pay raises, seniority, tenure, and career advancement, and asks young mothers to pay so heavily for their years of caring for children at home, to pay for the rest of their working lives with dismally restricted chances for occupational and personal development, the division of function suggested by Gutmann and those sympathetic to his point of view hardly appeals to our notions of equality.

But if, in fact, it suited our empirically given natures better for most of us to be, at different stages of our lives, successively either tenders of children or earners of income, rather than to try to keep the two in balance or to yield to one activity or the other over the whole of our lives, then possibly more mothers than fathers *would* be suited to care for small children, *and* more grandmothers than grandfathers would be suited to run the world. And the requirements of equality between parents would not seem to be violated by life cycles that might be significantly different.

Equality of obligation, then, does not require that both parents perform exactly the same tasks, any more than equal opportunities for occupational attainment require that each person spend his or her working life at exactly the same kind of work. But it does require a *starting presumption* that *all* the tasks connected with supporting and bringing up children should *each* be divided equally. Dividing the tasks equally might be done by having both parents engage in the same activities for the same periods of their lives, as when they both split their days equally between child care and outside work. Or, dividing the tasks equally might be achieved through taking somewhat longer turns, one parent working away from home for a few years for instance, while the other stayed home, and then, for the next few years, reversing the roles. These latter divisions may be especially appropriate for parents who are separated, or who must live separately at times for professional or other reasons. But women should be cautious about relying on agreements to have their years of child care "made up for later." A recent study shows that two-fifths of the divorced, separated, and single mothers legally eligible to receive child support payments from the fathers of their children "have never received even a single payment," and many of those fathers who do provide support do so irregularly and in trivial amounts.[18] Furthermore, fathers who take little part in raising their children in the early years may not be able to develop close relations with them, suddenly, later on. And it may be very difficult for children to adjust to a complete shift of care from one parent to the other at different stages of their childhoods.

Equality of obligations *does* require that every departure from each parent performing the same tasks be justified in terms of relevant criteria and appropriate principles. There must be good reasons, and not merely customs and social pressures, for such departures. Simply being male or female is not a relevant ground for such departures and cannot be the basis for justifiable differences in parental roles. And equality of obligation requires that the choices to perform given tasks at given stages of our lives should be no less voluntary for one parent than for another.

For this principle to be recognized, we would have to abandon not only the view that the obligations of mothers and fathers are unequal, but also the view that they are in *any* way different. *Any* differences in tasks performed would have to be the result of voluntary agreement between the parents, arrived at on the basis of initial positions of equality, such agreements to include provisions for any later reversals of roles equality would require.

Taking care of small children for a few years of one's life is an incredibly interesting and satisfying kind of work, full of joyful as well as exhausting times. If mothers were not expected to pay so heavily in terms of their chances for self-development for choosing this kind of work, few would wish to miss out on it.[19] In fact, women would probably, if given the choice, be glad to agree to more than an equal share of child-care work temporarily in exchange for more than an equal share of occupational opportunity and career advancement later on. But fathers should not be expected to be so foolish as to let mothers get more than their fair share of the best work of young adulthood, and to let grandmothers get more than their fair share of the best work of late middle age. If fathers *would* be that foolish, they would still be *entitled* to equality, and mothers would have an obligation to help them realize it.

NOTES

1. Nancy Chodorow, *The Reproduction of Mothering: Psychoanalysis and the Sociology of Gender* (Berkeley, Calif.: University of California Press, 1978), p. 7. See also Dorothy Dinnerstein, *The Mermaid and the Minotaur* (New York: Harper Colophon Books, 1976).
2. Ibid., p. 214.
3. Homer H. Clark, Jr. *The Law of Domestic Relations* (St. Paul, Minn.: West Publishing Co., 1968), p. 181.
4. Ibid.
5. See Georgia Dullea, "Joint Custody: Is Sharing the Child a Dangerous Idea?" *New York Times* (May 24, 1976), p. 24; and Charlotte Baum, "The Best of Both Parents," *New York Times Magazine* (October 31, 1976), pp. 44–46.
6. Ironically, or appropriately, the quotation comes from an article

called "The J-Curve of Rising and Declining Satisfaction as a Cause of some Great Revolutions and a Contained Rebellion," by James C. Davies, in *The History of Violence in America,* Hugh Davis Graham and Ted Robert Gurr, eds. (New York: New York Times Book, 1969), pp. 693–694.

7. See Ann Crittenden Scott, "The Value of Housework," *Ms.,* vol. 1, no. 1 (July, 1972): 56–59.

8. See John Stuart Mill and Harriet Taylor, *Essays on Sex Equality,* Alice S. Rossi, ed. (Chicago: University of Chicago Press, 1970), esp. pp. 74–75 and 179–180.

9. On the distortions of Plato's argument to which his interpreters have sunk, see Christine Pierce, "Equality: Republic V," *The Monist,* vol. no. 1 (January, 1973): 1–11.

10. See Virginia Held, "Men, Women, and Equal Liberty," in *Equality and Social Policy,* W. Feinberg, ed. (Urbana: University of Illinois Press, 1978).

11. See Virginia Held, "Marx, Sex, and the Transformation of Society," in *Women and Philosophy,* ed. C. Gould and M. Wartofsky (New York: Putnam, 1976).

12. For a discussion, see Michael A. Slote, "Desert, Consent, and Justice," *Philosophy and Public Affairs,* vol. II, no. 4 (Summer, 1973): 323–47.

13. Sandra L. Bem and Daryl J. Bem, "Homogenizing the American Woman," reprinted in *Feminist Frameworks,* Alison M. Jaggar and Paula Rotherberg Struhl, eds. (New York: McGraw Hill, 1978).

14. See Larry Blum, Marcia Homiak, Judy Housman, and Naomi Scheman, "Altruism and Women's Oppression," in Gould and Wartofsky, *op. cit.,* and Virginia Held, "Rationality and Reasonable Cooperation," *Social Research,* vol. 44, no. 4 (Winter, 1977): 708–744.

15. For a perceptive discussion, see Angela Barron McBride, *The Growth and Development of Mothers* (New York: Harper, 1973).

16. David Gutmann, "Men, Women, and the Parental Imperative," *Commentary,* (December, 1973): 62.

17. Ibid.

18. *Search* (Washington, D.C.: The Urban Institute), Spring, 1977.

19. On many of these issues, see Jessie Bernard, *The Future of Motherhood* (New York: Penguin, 1975), and Adrienne Rich, *Of Woman Born* (New York: Bantam, 1977).

Jane English

Sex Equality in Sports

What constitutes equal opportunity for women in sports?
Philosophers have developed three major positions concerning
equal opportunity, but they have focused on fields in which the
sexes are either known or assumed to have equal potentialities.
In sports, some relevant differences between the sexes, though
statistical, do appear to be permanent. All three of the most
widely held views on equal opportunity are deficient when applied to this area. Since there may be other permanent differences between the sexes, in such areas as spatial perception or
verbal ability, it is useful to examine the problems of equal opportunity in sports.

I

One account of equal opportunity identifies it with non-
discrimination. On this view, if we do not pay any attention to
the race of applicants to law school, for example, then our ad-
missions are "color blind" and give blacks equal opportunity.
Admission should be based on characteristics relevant to law
school, such as intelligence and grades, while irrelevant

"Sex Equality in Sports" by Jane English originally appeared in *Philosophy and
Public Affairs,* vol. 7, no. 3 (Spring, 1978), pp. 269–77. It is reprinted here by
permission of Princeton University Press.

characteristics such as sex and race should be ignored entirely. Most philosophers have rejected this account as too weak. If women lack motivation because they never see female lawyers on television, "sex blindness" alone will not provide equal opportunity. Although "formal" equality is necessary for justice, it is not sufficient. These philosophers would permit temporary violations of this ideal, but only in the transition to a just society.

When applied to sports, however, their view proves inadequate. If our sports were made sex-blind, women would have even less opportunity to participate than at present. Given equal incentives and more role models, women would have more interest in athletics, but few would qualify for high school, college, professional, and Olympic teams. Statistically speaking, there are physiological differences between the sexes that are relevant to sports performance. Remedial programs and just institutions cannot obliterate all differences in size and strength. So far from being necessary for equal opportunity, sex-blindness can actually decrease it.

A second account of equal opportunity identifies it with equal chances. Oscar and Elmer are said to have equal opportunity to become brain surgeons if it is equally probable that they will become brain surgeons. Most philosophers have rejected this conception of equal opportunity as too strong. If Oscar is a genius with great manual dexterity and Elmer is uncoordinated and slightly retarded, then they should not have an equal chance to become brain surgeons. Our society is not unjust if it encourages Oscar and discourages Elmer from this profession, because these skills are relevant to the job.

When we turn to women in sports, however, the model of equal probabilities seems to have some merit. Sports offer what I will call *basic benefits* to which it seems everyone has an equal right: health, the self-respect to be gained by doing one's best, the cooperation to be learned from working with teammates and the incentive gained from having opponents, the "character" of learning to be a good loser and a good winner, the chance to improve one's skills and learn to accept criticism – and just plain fun. If Matilda is less adept at, say, wrestling than Walter is, this is no reason to deny Matilda an equal chance to wrestle for health, self-respect, and fun. Thus, contrary to the conclusion in the example of the brain surgeon, a society that discourages Matilda from wrestling is unjust because it lacks equal opportunity to attain these basic benefits.

The third account of equal opportunity calls for equal chances in the sense of equal achievements for the "major social groups." Blacks have an equal opportunity to be lawyers, on this view, when the percentage of lawyers who are black roughly equals the percentage of blacks in the population. Like the "equal pro-babilities" view, this one calls for equal chances, but it interprets this by averaging attainments across the major social groups.

When this third account is applied to sports, it seems to have the undesirable consequence that a society is unjust if less than half its professional football players are women. If we had to provide sufficient incentives or reverse discrimination to achieve this result, it would create a situation unfair to 170-pound males. (They may even clamor to be recognized as a "major social group.") More important, it seems wrong to argue that a low level of health and recreation for, say, short women, is compen-sated for by additional health and recreation for tall women; one might as well argue that women are compensated by the greater benefits enjoyed by men. Rawls and Nozick have argued against utilitarianism by pointing out that society is not a "macro-individual" such that the benefits of some persons cancel out the sufferings of others. But the major social groups are not macro-individuals either. Proponents of the third account have not, to my knowledge, replied to this objection.

Beyond the basic benefits of sport, some athletes reap the fur-ther benefits of fame and fortune. I shall call these the *scarce benefits* of sport. The term is not meant to imply that they are kept artificially scarce, but that it is simply not possible for prizes and publicity to be attained equally by everyone at once. Although everyone has an equal right to the basic benefits, not everyone can claim an equal right to receive fan mail or appear on television. For this, having the skill involved in the sport is one relevant factor. In short, I shall maintain that the second account, equal probabilities, should be applied to the basic benefits; whereas the third model, proportional attainments for the major social groups, should be applied to the scarce benefits. And I shall construct an argument from self-respect for taking the "average" across the major social groups in the case of scarce benefits.

II

The traditional accounts of equal opportunity are inadequate because men and women are physiologically different in ways relevant to performance in sports, What is a fair way to treat physiologically disadvantaged groups? Two methods are in common use, and I shall suggest a third option.

One common method is to form competition classes based on a clear-cut physiological characteristic, such as weight or age, well known to be a hindrance in the sport in question. For example, middleweight boxers receive preferential treatment in the sense that they are permitted to move up and compete against the heavyweights if they desire, while the heavyweights are not permitted to move down into the middleweight class.

Sex is frequently used to form separate competition groups. If we apply the boxing model, several conclusions about this practice follow. Women should be allowed to "move up" and compete against the men if they wish. Since sex is not relevant to performance in all sports, the sport should be integrated when it is not. For example, it is probably irrelevant in dressage, riflery and car racing. In other sports, the differences between the sexes may be too small to justify separate classes—as in diving and freestyle skiing. In still others, the sexes have compensating differences. In channel swimming, for instance, men are advantaged in strength, but women profit from an insulating layer of fat. Additional sports could be integrated if the abilities characteristic of the two sexes were valued equally. In many areas, such as swimming, it is simply unknown whether the existing differences are due to permanent physiological characteristics or to cultural and social inequalities. Additional empirical research is needed before it will be known where integration is appropriate.

An objection to the use of groupings by sex is that it discriminates against those males whose level of performance is equal to that of the abler females. For example, if we have a girls' football team in our high school, is it unfair to prohibit a 120-pound boy who cannot make the boy's team from trying out for the girls' team? If we provide an additional team for boys under 140 pounds, does that discriminate against girls under 100 pounds? Against short boys over 140 pounds? It is impossible to provide a team for every characteristic that might be relevant to football performance. The objection has force because the differences between the sexes are only statistical. Our 120-pound boy is being penalized for the average characteristics of a major social group to which he belongs, rather than being treated on the basis of his individual characteristics.

The justification for maintaining separate teams for the sexes is the impact on women that integration would have. When there are virtually no female athletic stars, or when women receive much less prize money than men do, this is damaging to the self-respect of all women. Members of disadvantaged groups identify strongly with each other's successes and failures. If women do not attain roughly equal fame and fortune in sports, it leads both men and women to think of women as naturally inferior. Thus, it is not a right of women tennis stars to the scarce benefits, but rather a right of all women to self-respect that justifies their demand for equal press coverage and prize money.

This provides a justification for applying the third account of equal opportunity to the distribution of scarce benefits. It also explains why the "major social groups" have this feature, while arbitrary sets of individuals do not. A group singled out for distinctive treatment and recognized as a class tends to develop feelings of mutual identification which have an impact on the members' self-respect. It also affects the respect and treatment they get from others. In an androgynous society, we might be as unaware of a person's sex as we now are of left-handedness. Then roughly equal attainments would no longer be required, on my reasoning, for unequal attainments would not injure self-respect. Conversely, although there is some evidence of late that blacks have physiological traits such as a longer calf that give them an advantage in jumping and sprinting, I do not conclude that we should form separate track or basketball leagues for whites, since the self-respect of whites is not endangered by this modest advantage possessed by blacks.

III

A different method often used to give the disadvantaged equal access to the basic benefits of sport is to group individuals by ability alone. This occurs when we find second and third string games, B-leagues, intramural meets or special matches for novices or amateurs. Groupings by age, sex, or weight are often just attempts to approximate ability groupings in a convenient and quick way. When convenience is the intent, then, it must not be rigidly imposed to keep talented girls off the first string.

Groupings by ability are much easier to justify than groupings by the specific characteristics just discussed. There is no discrimination against less able members of the dominant group.

Ability groupings take into account all the traits that may affect performance. Competition with those close to one's own ability usually provides the most incentive and satisfaction, except where style of play is very different. It is imperative to make recreational leagues on all levels of skill available to people of all ages, sexes, income levels, and abilities, because everyone has an equal right to sport's basic benefits.

Groupings by ability must not lead to disrespect for those playing in the lower ability groups, however. Sports is an area in which we have tended to confuse respect with what has been called "esteem." I may have a low (and accurate) estimate of myself as a tennis player without losing respect for myself as a person. Although competition does entail winners and losers, it does not entail disrespect for the losers. Much has been said recently about this among other evils of competition. But competition per se is not bad. It offers fun, excitement, entertainment, and the incentive to perform at one's best. The problems arise when losers are scorned or discouraged from playing, and when winning becomes the end rather than the means to basic benefits. It is ironic that sports, long recommended for building character and teaching how to be a good loser and winner, have often taught aggression and elitism. Experts have become idols and millionnaires, while the rest of us watch rather than participate. With effort, the entry of women into sports could foster a reawakening to these values, which are widely shared but have been lost lately in the shuffle of big business sports. Some such reawakening is necessary if ability groupings are to be effective.

IV

So far I have assumed that women are a physiologically disadvantaged group in need of protection or special handicaps. In recent years, women have been making impressive progress in narrowing the gap between male and female performance. But there are apparently some permanent biological diferences that affirmative action and consciousness raising will never change: women are smaller than men, they have a higher percentage of fat, they lack the hormones necessary for massive muscle development, they have a different hip structure and a slower oxygenation rate.

Before we conclude that women are permanently relegated to inferiority, however, let us note that what is a physiological disadvantage in one activity may be an advantage in others: weight is an asset to a Sumo wrestler and a drawback for marathon running; height is an aid in basketball but not on the balance beam. In some sports, women have natural advantages over men. The hip structure that slows running gives a lower center of gravity. Fat provides insulation and an energy source for running fifty-mile races. The hormones that hinder development of heavy muscles promote flexibility. Even small size can be an asset, as jockeys and spelunkers know.

An example of an athletic activity which emphasizes the female advantages is ballet. Some ballerinas can stand on one toe while extending the other leg up into a vertical position where it touches the ear! While admittedly few women can do this, even fewer men can. Men are simply physiologically disadvantaged in the body flexibility that ballet emphasizes. Perhaps the most extreme example of a sport favoring women's natural skills is the balance beam. Here, small size, flexibility and low center of gravity combine to give women the kind of natural hegemony that men enjoy in football.

This suggests a third approach to aiding physiologically different groups. We should develop a variety of sports, in which a variety of physical types can expect to excel. We tend to think of the possible sports as a somewhat fixed group of those currently available. Yet even basketball and football are of very recent invention. Since women have been virtually excluded from all sports until the last century, it is appropriate that some sports using women's specific traits are now developing, such as synchronized swimming.

This method is different from forming handicapped groups or second-string leagues, and it is superior in its impact on the self-respect of the affected groups. It contributes to a woman's self-respect to see or read about the best women golfers. But this pride is tempered by the knowledge that they are "only" the best *women*. The very need for a protected competition class suggests inferiority. The pride and self-respect gained from witnessing a woman athlete who is not only the best woman but the very best athlete is much greater. Perhaps most white male readers have not experienced this sort of identification, characteristic of "minority" groups. But it is clearly displayed in the extraordinary interest in gymnastics among adolescent girls inspired by Olga Korbut, and the pride blacks derived from Jackie Robinson.

V

In calling for the development of new sports, I am suggesting that our concept of "sports" contains a male bias. Historically, this is understandable, because sports were an exclusively male domain, probably based on war and hunting, and actually used to assert male dominance. The few athletic activities permitted to women — mostly forms of dance — were not thought to fall under the *concept* of sport, and are still classified as arts or entertainment instead. Speed, size, and strength seem to be the essence of sports. Women *are* naturally inferior at "sports" so conceived.

But if women had been the historically dominant sex, our concept of sport would no doubt have evolved differently. Competitions emphasizing flexibility, balance, strength, timing, and small size might dominate Sunday afternoon television and offer salaries in six figures. Men could be clamoring for equal press coverage of their champions.

Here it might be argued that our concept of sport cannot be altered to make women equal, because speed, strength, and size are inevitable elements of *spectator* appeal. But it is participating rather than watching that is central to sport. Although speed is exciting, so is precision. Nor do audiences always choose to watch the experts. More important, spectator interest is a cultural product, tending to follow rather than lead media attention.

VI

The just society, in my view, would contain a greater variety of sports than we now have, providing advantages for a wider range of physical types. The primary emphasis would be on participation, with a wealth of local teams and activities available to all, based on groupings by ability. Only where style of play is very different would groupings by weight, age, or sex be recommended. The goal would be to make the basic benefits of health, teamwork, and fun equally available to everyone. Just distribution of the scarce benefits is somewhat more complex. Level of skill, audience appeal, and the self-respect of major social groups all have to be considered.

Current problems of the real world are far removed from such a utopia. Rights to the basic benefits dictate immediate changes in the distribution of our sports resources. Most obvious is the need for equal facilities — everything from socks to stadiums. If this means we must disturb a "Pareto optimal" situation — selling the football team's videotape machine if we are to provide a jogging path for the middle-aged — so be it. More subtle is the need for equal incentives. As well as equal scholarships and prizes, women need peer approval and changed sex-role stereotypes.

In short, I have suggested a division of the benefits of sport into the "basic" and the "scarce" ones. From the assumption that everyone has an equal right to the basic benefits of health and recreation, I have argued that the access to participator sports should not be based upon having the ability to play the sport well. And this ability is only one factor in the attainment of the scarce benefits. Since I believe that the right of women to roughly half of the scarce benefits, overall, stems from the right to self-respect, I have argued that a society which invents alternative sports using women's distinctive abilities and which rewards these equally is preferable to a society which only maintains protected classes for women in sports at which men are advantaged.

B.C. Postow

Women and Masculine Sports: Androgyny Qualified

Supporters of the antiandrogynist, or "vive la différence," ideal of gender identification may understandably find encouragement and reassurance in the contemplation of sports. Sports have traditionally been regarded as an unequivocally masculine endeavor — a training ground for manly skills and attitudes. Nature itself seems to support the antiandrogynist position, for in sports anatomical differences between men and women are undeniably relevant, giving men a very considerable statistical superiority over women. I shall investigate the various senses in which sports may be called masculine, and I shall argue that the fact that sports do qualify as masculine in these senses yields no support to the antiandrogynist ideal. The antiandrogynist position holds that people ought to maintain a distinction between the masculine and feminine either in order to conform to some good natural order, or in order to foster and preserve distinct gender identities for reasons of mental health or social welfare. My investigation will reveal no natural order which is prima

---

For very helpful bibliographical suggestions and other comments, I am much indebted to Mary Vetterling-Braggin, Madge Phillips, William Morgan, and Joan Hundley.

facie worthy of efforts toward its preservation. I shall also argue against the view that the desirability of preserving distinct gender identities justifies maintaining any sort of distinction between men's and women's sports (e.g., by subtly discouraging women's participation, or even by maintaining sex segregation in teams). I shall also argue, on the other hand, that the natural male advantage in most sports must be acknowledged and dealt with in a way not provided for within well-known androgynist ideals of individual excellence.

Joyce Trebilcot distinguishes between two androgynist ideals: monoandrogynism (M), and polyandrogynism (P). According to M, each individual should develop both traditionally masculine and traditionally feminine personality traits, and should engage in both traditionally masculine and traditionally feminine activities.[1] According to P, it is desirable for any individual so inclined to conform to the ideal approved by M, but it is equally desirable for any individual so inclined to develop only "masculine" or only "feminine" personality traits, and to engage only in "masculine" or only in "feminine" activities.[2] With respect to women and sports, M would naturally lead us to believe that it is desirable for women to participate in "masculine" sports; P would naturally lead us to believe that it is equally as desirable for women to participate in "masculine" sports as not to participate in them. Both M and P seem to lead us astray here because they are limited to ideals of individual excellence, and do not deal with the larger social reality. I shall argue that unlike most activities, some sports are masculine[3] in a sense, which I shall call masculine$_d$, which does give women a moral reason *not* to support or participate in them.

Let us first explain the sense in which sports may be called masculine, and then inquire whether the fact that a sport is masculine in any of these senses provides a reason for women not to engage in it, or to engage in it differently or separately from men. There are at least four different features or clusters of features of a sport which someone might reasonably be taken to be referring to in calling the sport masculine. One such cluster of features was isolated by Eleanor Metheny in analyzing those sports (e.g., wrestling, weight-lifting, long-distance running and most team sports) from which Olympic rules have excluded women. She lists these features as follows:

An attempt to physically subdue the opponent by bodily contact
Direct application of bodily force to some heavy object

Attempt to project the body into or through space over long distances
Cooperative face-to-face opposition in situations in which some body
contact may occur.[4]

Perhaps these features are believed to be especially appropriate
physical expressions of aggression, power, and effectiveness,
which are considered to be masculine. Whatever the explanation, however, it does seem that a native speaker would be likely
to call sports which possess these features masculine or even
supermasculine, although there are also other grounds on which
sports may be characterized as masculine. Note that Metheny
has shown that some features which identify a sport as
masculine can be characterized solely in terms of the behavior
required of participants by the rules of the game. To determine
whether a sport has these features, we refer to the rules of the
game rather than to the characteristic attitudes of participants or
to the societal function served by the sport. Let us call mascu-
line$_a$ any sport which requires the behavior depicted by
Metheny's list or some similar list.[5]

A second cluster of features which may prompt people to call
a sport masculine concerns the attitude with which the sport is
characteristically played, and which is thought to be necessary
for playing the sport well. This attitude includes "aggressiveness,
competitive spirit, stamina, and discipline," all focused on winning or setting records.[6] Devotion to a team is also a contributing
factor.[7] These elements of attitude constitute a "mode which is
understood to conform to an image of masculinity no less strong
in contemporary America than in ancient Greece."[8] Let us call
sports which are characteristically played in this mode, and
which it is commonly thought must be played this way to be
played well, masculine$_b$ sports. All sports may be masculine$_b$ to
a greater or lesser degree, but sports such as football, in which
approved aggressiveness includes a readiness to injure an opponent, seem to qualify as masculine$_b$ to an especially high degree.

Another feature which may be thought to qualify a sport as
masculine is its use as a vehicle of masculine gender identification. Let us call a sport masculine$_c$ if participation in it in our
society functions to inspire or reinforce a feeling of identity and
solidarity with men as distinct from women. Baseball and football are two sports which have traditionally served this function
in our society, largely by being designated as activities which are
especially appropriate for boys and men, and inappropriate or
questionably appropriate for girls and women. Swimming and
volleyball would not qualify as masculine$_c$ sports.

There is, of course, some relation between masculine$_b$ sports and masculine$_c$ sports in that masculine$_b$ sports are by definition well suited to socialize males in accordance with the particular ideal of masculine gender identity embodied in the masculine$_b$ attitudinal mode. Nevertheless, an activity which is masculine$_b$ to the highest degree would fail to be masculine$_c$ if it were approved for women and men equally and without role differentiation.[9] Such a sport would socialize both women and men in accordance with the masculine$_b$ attitudinal mode, but it would not socialize men as a group distinct from women. Little League baseball has traditionally been masculine$_c$, but sex-integrated Little League baseball should cease to be masculine$_c$ even if it remains masculine$_b$.

Another reason for which sports may be thought masculine is their definition of athletic excellence in terms of developed capacities, such as strength and speed, in which men naturally have a considerable statistical advantage over women. Let us call a sport masculine$_d$ if it is such that on account of biological factors, most men are significantly better at it than most women, and the best athletes in it are men. Examples of masculine$_d$ sports are football, baseball, basketball, and tennis, which strongly emphasize upper-body strength.[10] Not all sports are masculine$_d$. On the balance beam, "small size, flexibility and low center of gravity combine to give women the kind of natural hegemony that men enjoy in football,"[11] and in long-distance swimming women have the natural advantages of long-term endurance, buoyancy, insulation, and narrow shoulders.[12] Still, the vast majority of our sports, including the most prestigious ones, are masculine$_d$.

Does the fact that a sport is masculine in any of the senses explained above provide a moral reason for women not to engage in it, or to engage in it differently or separately from men? The features which make a sport masculine$_a$ seem generally to be morally neutral,[13] and insofar as they are, I take it to be uncontroversial that these features in themselves provide no moral grounds for women to observe any limitations on participation, or to participate separately from men. Of course sports which are masculine$_a$ are generally also masculine$_d$;[14] and this fact is arguably grounds for sex segregation, but this will be dealt with later.

In my opinion, there is nothing intrinsically immoral in participating in masculine$_b$ sports in a masculine$_b$ way, but if there is a superior ideal there is a moral reason to pursue that ideal rather than the "masculine$_b$" ideal. Mary Duquin depicts a superior ideal of sport which combines instrumental and expressive attitudes and behavior. In ideal sport, "the participant feels a sense of fulfillment when participating, as well as when winning. She feels joy, strength, thrill, competence and control when sporting whether in practice or competition. She performs ethically, drawing her ethics from her own self-conscience. . . . She performs with confidence and comradeship."[15] Now all sports which are masculine$_b$ seem capable of being played in a nonmasculine$_b$ way.[16] Therefore, those with moral objections to the masculine$_b$ attitudinal mode have no reason to refrain from masculine$_b$ sports, but only (at most) to refrain from participation with those who subscribe to that ideal. This might well preclude participation in professional or even subsidized athletics,[17] but it need not preclude mixed teams of men and women, for not all men subscribe to the masculine$_b$ ideal. Nothing that has been said provides support to the antiandrogynist position, for women have not been shown to have any less right than men to play masculine$_b$ sports in a masculine$_b$ way against men. Insofar as Duquin's ideal is accepted as superior to the masculine$_b$ ideal, however, M must be preferred to P, for P would approve of the masculine$_b$ ideal equally with Duquin's ideal.

I shall assume for the sake of argument the positive value of masculine orientation and solidarity for males. It may be thought that women should refrain from participating in masculine$_c$ sports, or at least be relegated to second-class status in them, for we have seen that a sport ceases to be masculine$_c$ if women are fully integrated in it. But sport is not the only way to forge masculine orientation and solidarity,[18] and exclusion from the dominant sport culture is directly and indirectly detrimental to women in many ways.[19] Thus even if masculine orientation and solidarity for males are of undoubted net value, women would betray their own dignity as persons with rights as important as those of men, by accepting limitations on participation or second-class status for the purpose of preserving popular sports as masculine$_c$ male preserves. Those who disagree with me may object that sport is not, as I have alleged, merely one of many possible vehicles of masculine orientation in our society. Arnold R. Beisser argues that sport's emphasis on strength together with its separation of male from female roles makes it uniquely suited to relieve the tensions created by the facts that men have lost much of their fatherly authority and their status of sole breadwinner, and that male strength is almost obsolete, yet "the cultural expectations of masculinity have remained fixed as they were in pioneer days."[20] Notice, however, that the function of sport to which Beisser is here drawing our attention is not merely the formation or reinforcment of masculine gender identity, but rather the relief of a tension generated by the dissonance between reality and the ideology of "pioneer days" that men deserve respect and authority on account of their physical strength. Insofar as sports serve as a safety valve to relieve the pressure caused by the dissonance between this ideology and reality, they help to preserve the ideology. Since this ideology is patently unworthy of preservation, Beisser's observation cannot be used to show that the fact that sports are masculine$_c$ is a good reason for women to refrain from participation in them or to accept second-class status in them.

As I indicated at the beginning of the paper, the fact that a sport is masculine$_d$ does, I think, provide some reason for women not to support or engage in it. The number and prestige of sports in which men have a natural statistical superiority to women, together with the virtual absence of sports in which women are naturally superior, helps perpetuate an image of general female inferiority which we have a moral reason to undermine. An obvious way to undermine it is to increase the number and prestige of sports in which women have a natural statistical superiority to men or at least are not naturally inferior. Thus there is reason, at least where this can be done without undue personal sacrifice, for women to withdraw energy and support from masculine$_d$ sports and to turn instead toward other sports—preferably ones in which women naturally excel. It seems clear to me, however, that it is not obligatory for women who enjoy or are well-suited to masculine$_d$ sports to abstain from them in order to popularize sports in which women excel, for that end can be achieved without such sacrifices.

My moral intuitions become less definite when we turn to a problem of current interest raised in school athletics by the male advantage in masculine$_d$ sports. It seems unfair to bar from men's teams those women who can make the grade, for this would deny those women equality of opportunity to compete, defined as freedom from legal or other socially imposed restrictions. But if women should be free to compete against men, then it seems that men should also be free to compete against women. In masculine$_d$ sports, allowing men to compete against women would expose women to a drastically reduced probability of receiving the moderately scarce athletic resources, such as access to facilities and coaching, that go with making a team. This too seems unfair. Equality of opportunity qua freedom from socially imposed restrictions on one's ability to compete seems to work against equality of opportunity qua probability, given the same level of effort, of actually receiving the benefits of the sport. The first kind of equality of opportunity seems required by the ideal of fair competition; the second kind of equality of opportunity seems required by the students' prima facie equal rights to what Jane English calls the basic benefits of sports, such as health and fun.[21] A scheme supported by Richard Alan Rubin offers a possible compromise. Rubin suggests that there be three independent teams per sport. The varisty team "would consist of the best male and female athletes. . . . The remaining two teams would consist of athletes of lesser ability and would be separated by sex."[22] On Rubin's scheme, women interested in participating on a team in a masculine$_d$ sport would still have roughly half as much probability of making some team (i.e., either varsity or second string) as men have, since men would make up all or almost all of the varsity and all of the men's team, while women would be almost exclusively confined to the women's team. This might be acceptable, however, if Rubin is right that "virtually everyone interested would be able to compete." Preserving one team for women and one for men would, at any rate, avoid the drastic reduction in women's chances of participating that would result from having only mixed teams. Rubin's scheme also avoids the drastic denial of formal equality of competitive opportunity for men that would result if there were a team reserved for women but none reserved for men. Of course one might wish to strike the compromise differently, sacrificing men's rights to formal equality of opportunity in favor of women's rights to equal probability of receiving the benefits of sports. This could be done by having only one second string team which either barred men completely or put a quota on them.

A possible problem with both these compromise schemes is that they are probably illegal under the E.R.A.[23] Another objectionable feature is that they tie probability of receiving the basic benefits of a sport to natural aptitude. Men and women with unsuitable physiques do not have an equal probability of receiving the basic benefits of sports, compared with more athletically gifted men and women. A way to grant fully the prima facie claim of everyone (even those with unsuitable physiques) to an equal right to the basic benefits of participating in the school sports which she or he most enjoys, and still to grant fully the prima facie claim of everyone to equal formal freedom to compete, would be to sever the connection between winning a place on a team and being granted access to moderately scarce athletic resources. In team sports, either enough teams could be available at every ability level to accommodate everyone who wanted to play and who was willing to turn out for practice (with scarce athletic resources simply spread as thinly as necessary to go around), or there could be at least one team for each ability level, with membership on the teams determined by some form of lottery that equalized the probability of being on a team for everyone who wanted to play and was willing to turn out for practice. There would, on these schemes, be no apparent need for sex separation, since women would not be deprived of an equal chance for athletic benefits by being made to compete with men. Of course the best athletes would stand to lose a great deal compared with the usual arrangement which makes access to scarce athletic resources a reward of winning competitions. Perhaps a sound argument could be made that the social desirability of helping the best athletes develop to their fullest potential overrides the prima facie claim of athletically ill-endowed people to an equal right to the benefits of the sports they enjoy. In this case, a scheme like Rubin's would be preferable.

In professional athletics, there may appear to be a special reason for maintaining single-sex teams in masculine$_d$ sports. Jane English argues that "when there are virtually no female athletic stars, or when women receive much less prize money than men do, this is damaging to the self-respect of all women."[24] But this argument is open to several objections. Raymond A. Belliotti seems correct that "we should not respect ourselves because of our own or our group's attainments of fame and fortune in professional sports,"[25] and that "as an empirical matter of fact, these attainments *are not* an important factor in the way the vast majority of women determine their respect for themselves."[26] Furthermore, if women's self-respect were dependent on the existence of female athletic stars, it would seem more helpful to have stars in female-biased sports, where the very best athletes are women, than in masculine$_d$ sports, where the very best athletes are men.

In closing, let me recapitulate the major positions which I have taken in this paper: (1) The antiandrogynist position is incorrect: women do have as much right as men to engage in any masculine sport in any sense of that term, and do not have any duty to accept second-class status. (2) Sex segregation is not morally required in sports on grounds of its usefulness in preserving masculine$_c$ sports, nor is it morally required on grounds of its usefulness in maintaining women's equality of opportunity in masculine$_d$ sports, or on grounds of serving women's self-respect by making possible female stars in masculine$_d$ sports. (3)Because they are ideals of purely individual excellence, both forms of androgynism discussed by Trebilcot lead us astray concerning the desirability of women participating in masculine sports. Neither form of androgynism takes account of the fact that men do naturally have a very considerable statistical advantage over women in performing prestigious activities such as masculine$_d$ sports, or that women have reason to counter the general image of male superiority fostered by those activities by withdrawing support from the activities and promoting activities in which women have a natural advantage over men.

NOTES

1. Joyce Trebilcot, "Two Forms of Androgynism," *Journal of Social Philosophy* 8 (1977): 71, pp. 162–63 in this volume.
2. Ibid., p. 72, p. 163 in this volume.
3. I intend the word "masculine" itself to be neutral between the androgynist and the antiandrogynist ideals. I shall at this point cease to put the word in scare-quotes. This may seem to favor the antiandrogynist position, but it would have favored the androgynist position to use scare-quotes at every occurrence. I have decided that it is fairest to err, if err I must, by allowing my choice of punctuation to favor the position with which I have least sympathy.
4. Eleanor Metheny, "Symbolic Forms of Movement: The Feminine Image in Sports," in her *Connotations of Movement in Sport and Dance* (Dubuque, Iowa: William C. Brown Publishing Co., 1965), p. 49.
5. One suggestion for tinkering with the list is to delete Metheny's third item and to add "the use of deadly force against animals" to capture bull-fighting and hunting.

6. Mary E. Duquin, "The Androgynous Advantage," in *Women and Sport: From Myth to Reality,* ed. Carole A. Oglesby (Philadelphia: Lea and Febiger, 1968), p. 98. Duquin is here speaking of the instrumental orientation (i.e., focus on winning) which she says has characterized sports up to the present. She argues that sports have been regarded this way because they have been regarded as masculine, and "society has traditionally expected males to be instrumental, not expressive" (p. 97).

7. Jan Felshin. "The Dialectic of Woman and Sport," in *The American Woman in Sport,* ed. Ellen W. Gerber, Jan Felshin et al., (Reading, Mass.: Addison Wesley Publishing Co., 1974), pp. 184 and 187.

8. Ibid., p. 184.

9. The fact that females must be excluded in order for a sport to be "masculine$_c$" is also obvious to sports promoters as a vehicle of masculine socialization. Duquin cites the following examples: A. Fisher, "Sports as an Agent of Masculine Orientation," *The Physical Educator* 29 (1972): 120, and P. Werner, "The Role of Physical Education in Gender Identification," *The Physical Educator* 29 (1972): 27.

10. P.S. Wood, "Sex Differences in Sprots," *The New York Times Magazine,* May 18, 1980, p. 96.

11. Jane English. "Sex Equality in Sports," *Philosophy and Public Affairs* 7 (1978): 275, p. 265 in this volume.

12. Wood, op. cit., p. 98.

13. The use of deadly force against animals (see footnote 5 above) seems morally objectionable to me — equally objectionable for men as for women, of course.

14. Possible exceptions are sports in which there is an "attempt to project the body into or through space over long distances," for if the distances are long enough male strength may be countered by female endurance, light weight, and tolerance for heat. See P.S. Wood, op. cit., p. 98.

15. Duquin, op. cit., pp. 101–2.

16. It seems that if soccer can be played noninstrumentally, then any sport can. I know that soccer can from my participation in a series of soccer games played by a mixed-sex faculty group at my own institution. Although we played our best, most of us did not keep track of the number of goals scored, and did not know which team had won.

17 Duquin cites a psychological study which supports the view that extrinsic incentives in athletics may impede a noninstrumental approach: M. R. Lepper, D. Greene, and R. Nisbett, "Undermining Children's Intrinsic Interest with Extrinsic Reward: A Test of the Overjustification Hypothesis," *Journal of Personality and Social Psychology* 8 (1973): 129. (See Duquin, op. cit., p. 102.)

18. Some other ways are the wearing of clothing which is socially defined as male attire, behavior which is demanded of and reserved for males by etiquette, the different roles assigned to men and women in dancing and other mixed-set activities, participation in groups and ceremonies from which women are excluded, and participation in activities in which males and females engage separately (e.g., sex-segregated clubs). I do not wish to defend all of these as morally unobjectionable.

19. This is argued in detail by Iris Young in an unpublished manuscript, "Social Implications of the Exclusion of Women from Sport." Available from Iris Young, Department of Philosophy, Worcester Polytechnic Institute, Worcester, Massachusetts. Drawing on Beauvoir, Merleau-Ponty and Eleanor Metheny, she argues (to put her argument very roughly) that since sport is activity par excellence, to be regarded as an inappropriate participant in sport is to be regarded as less than a human subject or conscious agent. Furthermore, she argues, exclusion from the dominant sport culture carries serious cultural disabilities in business, politics, and everyday life.

20. Arnold R. Beisser. "The American Seasonal Masculinity Rites," in *Sport Sociology: Contemporary Themes,* ed. Andrew Yiannakis et al. (Dubuque, Iowa: Kendall/Hunt Publishing Co., 1976). Excerpted from *The Madness of Sports* (New York: Appleton Century Crofts, 1967).

21. Jane English, "Sex Equality in Sports," *Philosophy and Public Affairs* 7 (1978): 270, p. 260 in this volume.

22. Richard Alan Rubin, "Sex Discrimination in Interscholastic High School Athletics," *Syracuse Law Review* 25 (1974): 566.

23. See Rubin, op. cit., pp. 573–74. Other possible drawbacks of the plan favored by Rubin are expense, dilution of talent, and difficulty of finding schools to compete with at the lower levels. See "What Constitutes Equality for Women in Sport? Federal Law Puts Women in the Running," Association of American Colleges, Washington, D.C. Project on the Status and Education of Women (April 1974).

24. English, op. cit., p. 273, p. 263 in this volume.

25. Raymond A. Belliotti, "Women, Sex and Sports," *Journal of Philosophy of Sport* 6 (1979): 68.

26. Ibid., p. 71.

Jane Roland Martin

Sex Equality and Education: A Case Study

In a remarkably short time a body of literature on Plato's *Republic* has developed which has illuminated his views on the position of women in the Just State. Unfortunately, this literature tends to take Plato's account of education as unproblematic. In this essay I will argue that far from being unproblematic, the education Plato would give his guardians raises serious questions about the extent to which sex equality can be considered a property of the Just State. To document my claim that feminist scholarship has taken Plato's account of education for granted, I will begin with a brief review of the commentary which has grown up around *Republic,* Book V. I will then abstract from that dialogue a set of fundamental assumptions or postulates which constitute what I will call Plato's *Production Model of Education.* In Parts 3 and 4 of this essay I will point to ways in which the postulate which most commentators on Book V have viewed as a guarantee of equal education to males and females can work to the disadvantage of women. Then, in Part

This essay was written while I was a fellow at the Mary Ingraham Bunting Institute of Radcliffe College. I wish to thank Diane Rothbard Margolis and Kathryn Pyne Parsons for discussions of this topic. Ann Diller, Carol F. Gilligan, Charlene J. Langdale, Nona Lyons, Michael Martin, Beatrice Nelson, Janet Farrell Smith and Mary Vetterling-Braggin all made helpful comments on the first draft of this essay.

5, I will examine the role for which Plato seems to provide equal education regardless of sex to see if the claim is justified that in his Just State Plato turns women into men.

Although this essay takes Plato's Just State as its point of departure, my objective is to make clear that educational questions cannot be ignored by those who are interested in achieving sex equality. Thus, my concern here is less with putting forward an interpretation of Plato's *Republic* than with revealing some of the ways in which assumptions about education can have implications for a theory of women's place in society. For this purpose there could be no better case to study than the *Republic*. The Production Model of Education contained therein has dominated Western thought throughout the ages and exerts its influences on us today perhaps more than we realize. The model needs to be made explicit so that we can understand some of the problems which must be addressed if the quest for sex equality is to be successful.

I. FEMINIST PERSPECTIVES ON *REPUBLIC V*

In Book V of the *Republic* Socrates argues to the astonishment of his companions that women can be qualified by nature for membership in the guardian class of his Just State; that is to say, he argues that being female does not *as such* bar a person from being a guardian.[1] The feminist scholarship which has sprung up in the last decade has focused on the apparent inconsistency between this proposal and Plato's disparaging comments about women in Book V itself, in other sections of the *Republic* and his other dialogues. On the one hand, Plato seems to regard women as inferior beings; on the other, he seems to be making sex equality a characteristic of his Just State. Traditional Platonic scholarship has for the most part refused to take seriously Plato's proposals about women.[2] Recent feminist scholarship takes these proposals very seriously, but it is of two minds about Plato's actual commitment to sex equality. For example, Christine Pierce has analyzed the logic of the argument of Book V and concluded that it constitutes an ingenious critique of the main assumptions used in arguments against the equality of women.[3] Plato's negative remarks about women in Book V are in her view to be interpreted as belonging to his rhetorical strategy of granting as much as any misogynist could desire in order to make the argument persuasive. Christine Garside Allen, on the other hand, has argued that Plato *does* consider women an inferior kind of incarnation.[4] However, since for Plato the soul is distinct from the body and bodies do not indicate differences in essential nature, it is not inconsistent for him to admit women into the guardian class: their souls can equip them to be guardians even if their bodies are inferior to men's.

In very different ways Pierce and Allen attempt to show that Plato's account of the role of women in the Just State is coherent. They seem to assume, furthermore, that in allowing women into the guardian class and insisting, as Plato does, that future guardians receive the same upbringing and education regardless of sex, Plato builds sex equality into the structure of the Just State. Julia Annas is not so sanguine about the prospects for sex equality in that State.[5] She argues that there is a serious gap in Plato's argument: he shows that no pursuits are appropriate for women as such, but he never argues the point that none are appropriate to men as such. In contrast to Pierce, who claims that Plato's position is compatible with a guardian class composed preponderantly of women, Annas seems to think that few, if any, women will in fact be qualified by nature to be guardians.

Lynda Lange also believes that few women will belong to the guardian class.[6] She claims that for Plato there is a de facto correlation between femaleness and inferiority. Thus, while some want to call Plato a feminist, what he has done for women in the Just State is simply to allow for exceptions. Both Lange and Annas try to reconcile Plato's seemingly inconsistent remarks on women by denying that he cares about sex equality. They remind us that Plato's reasons for whatever degree of emancipation there is for women in his Just State have nothing to do with fairness and equality, nothing to do with women's rights, nothing to do even with the desires and needs of women. Unity, the smooth running of the State, these are his concerns. If Plato does admit women into the guardian class, it is simply because he believes that to do so is essential for the good of the whole.

Now despite the fact that Lange's essay is entitled "The Function of Equal Education in Plato's *Republic* and *Laws*," she has little to say about Plato's theory of education itself. I take her point to be that although Plato proposes the same education for male and female future guardians, we should not suppose that sex equality is his concern. In effect, she takes equality of education as a given in Plato's system. The problem, as she sees it, is that only a few exceptional females will receive an education for guardianship and, furthermore, that the justification for their receiving it has to do with the unity of the state, not fairness.

The feminist scholar who has devoted the most attention to education in Plato's Just State is Susan Moller Okin.[7] Okin considers the *Republic* to be an extremely radical dialogue because it challenges the most sacred conventions of Plato's time. She argues that Plato's abolition of private property and the family for the guardian class and his attempt at extending kinship ties throughout that class have radical implications for the role of women: once women cannot be defined by their traditional roles in the family, Plato has no alternative but to regard them as persons in their own right.[8] Whereas Christine Pierce attributes Plato's apparent qualms about the capabilities of women to his rhetorical purpose, Okin claims that Plato fails to apply "his own environmentalism" to the case of women in the Just State. If he had kept in mind the central role which he himself gives to socialization and education in the *Republic,* instead of granting that there is nothing which women as a class do better than men, Socrates would have told his companions that women's potential was virtually unknown because of their position in Athenian society.[9]

Although Okin has discussed the role Plato attributes to education in the Just State, there is need for a detailed analysis of the model of education which Plato implicitly adopts. For the sake of argument, suppose that Annas and Lange are mistaken and that Plato did envision a population in which 50 percent of those suited by nature to be guardians were female. It is not at all obvious that the system of education Plato prescribes for his Just State would enable those females to carry out the guardian role successfully. And supposing it did, it is certainly not obvious that Plato has prescribed "an androgynous character for all guardians," as Okin has claimed.[10] Sex equality is not guaranteed by equal access to education, not even by equal access to identical education. Thus, even on those readings of Book V which from a feminist perspective are most favorable to Plato, it is a mistake to assume without study of his account of education that sex equality is a characteristic of his Just State.

II. PLATO'S PRODUCTION MODEL OF EDUCATION

As is well known, Plato arrives at his account of the Just State through a thought experiment. Socrates and his companions think away existing institutions and in their imaginations witness the birth of a city.[11] Their starting point is the principle, enunciated by Socrates, that "Not one of us is self-sufficient, but needs many things."[12] Implicit in this starting point is the assumption that each person is guided by self-interest and that it is in the self-interest of each to share.[13] The question which then arises is whether people will specialize, one person producing enough food for everyone and another making the clothes for each, or whether they will simply help one another when necessary while remaining as self-sufficient as possible.[14] It is at this point in the thought experiment that Socrates introduces an assumption about human nature which is basic to his theory of education.

Each one of us, Socrates says, is born more apt for one task than another.[15] Now this *Postulate of Specialized Natures* must not be understood as attributing to each individual at birth the knowledge how to perform a specific task. We come equipped with a talent or aptitude for one task above all others, but the skill and knowledge and traits of character required for performing that task must be acquired. On the other hand, although Socrates expects a person's natural aptitude to develop over time, he takes it to be fixed and unchanging. Thus, while one's specific nature can flourish or, alternatively, be stunted, a person cannot in mid-life acquire some new aptitude or talent which supplants the original one. Different aptitudes or talents are distributed over the population as a whole, not over an individual's life.

The Postulate of Specialized Natures does not in itself answer the question Socrates asks about specialization. To it, however, he adds an assumption about efficiency. Both production and quality are improved, he says, when a person practices one craft rather than several, that one being the craft for which the person is by nature most suited.[16] Yet even this assumption does not yield the answer he gives to his own question. Specialization is the recommended mode of production in the Just State, not simply because it is on his view the most efficient mode but because Socrates holds efficiency to be highly desirable. Socrates could have witnessed the birth of an inefficient state or of a somewhat efficient state. Without ever making his preference explicit, he chooses efficiency.[17]

As it stands the Postulate of Specialized Natures is purely formal: it does not specify the aptitude or talents people have at birth. Socrates proceeds to give this postulate content in his thought experiment not, as one might expect, through a close inspection of human nature, but rather through an examination of the needs of society. From the beginning a city will need farmers, builders, weavers, cobblers and metal workers, cowherds and shepherds, merchants and sailors. Eventually it will also need warriors and rulers. Socrates creates an imaginary city which, when functioning properly, constitutes his Just State. He then maps its needs back onto human nature. To suppose that he discerns certain natural talents or aptitudes in people and then designs a state which is to fit them is to get things backwards. Socrates discerns the needs of the Just State and designs human nature to meet them.[18]

Given his Postulate of Specialized Natures Socrates could have attributed to human beings talents very different from the ones he does. He could, for example, have said that some people are born above all with a talent for telling jokes while others are more apt doing pushups than anything else. Instead, he assumes a one-to-one relationship between human nature and societal needs. This *Postulate of Correspondence* is crucial for Plato's theory of the Just State.[19] Justice requires that each person do his or her own job and no other, there being three general types of job to be done—that of artisan, auxiliary and ruler. In the name of justice, therefore, it is absolutely essential that each person fit into one and only one category.

The Postulate of Specialized Natures asserts that each person is born more apt for one task than others. The Postulate of Correspondence asserts a one-to-one relationship between the natural aptitude or talent of an individual and a person's role in society. Now, since justice requires that each individual perform his or her own job in society *and* since Socrates assumes that no person is able to do from birth, or simply by maturing, the task for which that person is naturally suited, the role of education in Plato's Just State becomes apparent: education must equip people with the knowledge and skill and traits of character which will enable them to perform the societal tasks or roles for which nature suits them.

Plato's is a *Production Model of Education* par excellence. The human being is the raw material of the educator. Like all raw material, human beings are malleable, but they do have certain fixed talents or aptitudes set by nature. The nature of education is to turn this raw material into a finished product or, more precisely, into one of three finished products, the particular one being for the educator a matter of discovery, not decision, since it is set by nature. The composition of the raw material is from the educator's point of view a given and so are the specifications for the three kinds of end product. In their thought experiment Socrates and his friends have little to say about the good artisan, but the specifications for good auxiliaries and rulers emerge in the course of their discussion.[20] Thus, for example, in a famous passage, Socrates likens those who will be warriors to pedigree dogs: they must be high-spirited and brave, yet gentle with their own people.[21]

Plato sees the task of education as that of producing certain kinds of people. To be sure, he recommends that young children be allowed to play.[22] However, this gesture to freedom should not be interpreted as a denial that the educator's role is to produce certain predetermined products. Children move about freely and play so that their true natures will reveal themselves. Once these natures are discovered, the production of artisans, auxiliaries, and rulers can begin. Plato's is not a Production Model simpliciter, however. The task of education is not simply to produce three kinds of people, but to produce people who will fill certain necessary roles in society. There is, in other words, a *Functional Postulate* implicit in the account of education contained in the *Republic*. Education is a servant of the state which functions to equip the individuals born into it to perform *their* preassigned functions.

Education plays a key role in Plato's Just State: for justice to prevail education must fit people to perform the jobs for which nature suits them. Still, Socrates simplifies the educator's task enormously by introducing in Book V the assumption that to perform the same task, people must have the same education.[23] This *Postulate of Identity* directs educators to ignore individual differences except for the inborn talents by virtue of which people are suited to one societal role rather than another. It directs them to determine one course of study for artisans, one for auxiliaries, and one for rulers: three separate curricula, to be sure, but one and only one version of each.

III. THE IDENTITY POSTULATE: MALE BASED METHODS

As I have said, Plato gives content to the Postulate of Specialized Natures by mapping the needs of his ideal state onto human nature. Now one might expect this mapping to be determined, at least in part, on the basis of sex, but according to Socrates sex is not a determinant of a person's nature. Just as baldness and hairiness do not determine one's specific nature, sex does not. Sex is a difference which makes no difference.[24] Given the Postulate of Correspondence, there is in Plato's Just State then, equality of role opportunity for men and women: it is possible for members of either sex to be suited by nature for the role of artisan, auxiliary, or ruler; since justice requires that each person perform the role that he or she is suited by nature to perform, those males and females who are born to be auxiliaries or rulers must be given the opportunity to occupy these roles.

Lynda Lange believes that despite his apparent sex egalitarianism Plato did not intend the guardian class to be equally divided according to sex.[25] She distinguishes between the possible and the desirable and attributes to Plato the thesis that while it is possible for women and men to function as equals, it is not desirable for them to do so. It is not necessary, however, to attribute either sexist intentions or the belief that nature favors the male to Plato to reach the conclusion that his guardian class might in fact contain few women. Just as there is a distinction to be drawn between the possible and desirable, there is one to be drawn between the possible and the actual. Give Plato the benefit of the doubt and take him to be assuming that as many females as males are by nature suited to rule. If we examine the Identity Postulate we will see that even as Plato provides women with equal *role opportunity,* there is reason to believe that he denies to them equal *role occupancy.*

The Identity Postulate holds that the same societal role requires the same education. Given the Postulate of Correspondence which links natures or inborn talents to societal roles, it follows that people with the same natures will receive the same education. Thus women who are by nature suited to rule will in the Just State receive an education identical to that given men who are by nature suited to rule. For women in the Just State there is, then, both equality of *role opportunity* and equality of access to *identical education.* However, there is no guarantee whatsoever that identical education will yield identical results.

Consider this example. Tennis instructors are fond of saying, "Watch my racket as I serve the ball." I, for one, can watch till doomsday with no apparent effect on my serve, even as my more visually oriented colleagues proceed to hit aces. To be sure, some of these fast learners may have more aptitude for the game than I. But not all. When finally the instructor analyzes verbally the serving motion, introduces a meaningful metaphor, or takes hold of my arm and puts it through its motions, my game will equal my colleagues'. Where education is concerned, natural talent is only part of the story. People with similar talents often learn in different ways thereby benefiting from different modes of instruction.

To the extent that people learn differently they require different educational treatment to attain the same ends. Furthermore, some start with handicaps, having nothing to do with natural aptitude, which must be overcome if a given end is to be achieved. Many female tennis players have difficulty acquiring an adequate serve because they have had little practice throwing a ball. The serving motion is therefore not as natural for them as it is for most males. To give them the same instruction in serving as males are given almost guarantees that they will fail to acquire an adequate serve. To reach *this* goal they must be given special instruction which takes into account their handicap.

In Plato's Just State future rulers engage in intensive physical activity in their teens. At age twenty they systematically study arithmetic, geometry, astronomy, and harmony. At thirty they are taught dialectic.[26] This education comes relatively late in life. If the early socialization of girls in Plato's Just State parallels that of girls today, let alone of girls in the Athenian society of Plato's time, it is unlikely that an identical education for male and female auxiliaries and rulers would yield equal numbers of capable males and females in those roles. Unless they were given special treatment, the likelihood is that many potential female warriors and rulers would simply not be able to finish the obstacle course curriculum in physical skills and abstract thinking which Plato sets for these groups.[27]

It is important to note that when Socrates proposes that men and women having the same natural talents be given the same education, he is extending to women a kind of education which has been designed for future male guardians.[28] However, there is no reason at all to suppose that male-based educational methods will transform most females who are potential guardians into actual ones. Granted, Socrates insists that sex is a difference which makes no difference. But he maintains this in relation to the possession of the natural talents for performing societal roles. Insofar as there is differential socialization according to sex in Plato's Just State and sex-related physiological or psychological characteristics do exist, sex may well make a difference in the *way* females learn, in their motivation to learn, and in the degree of *readiness* they are in when their formal education for ruling begins.

The Identity Postulate holds that to perform the same task the same education is required. Since men and women can, according to Plato, perform the same tasks, they must receive the same education. What Plato and his recent commentators have failed to see is that a property or characteristic of a person which does not make a difference to the *performance* of some role might in fact make a difference to the *learninr* of that role. Differential socialization results in sex or gender being correlated with differences which might make a difference in the way males and females learn.[29] Moreover, there may be physiological differences between males and females which are relevant to learning.[30]

We must conclude that the very postulate which is most frequently cited as evidence for sex equality in Plato's Just State, the Identity Postulate, might itself be the source of sex inequality in that state. I say "might" because we do not know enough details about the socialization of girls and boys in Plato's Just State or about the traits which are physiologically linked to sex in that state to decide the question of whether identical educational treatment will produce identical results.

There are two reasons for believing that in the Just State differential socialization according to sex will not occur. One is that Plato abolishes the family for the guardian class and there might seem, therefore, to be no societal "need" or "reason" for socialization of children into traditional sex roles. We know, however, that differential socialization according to sex begins at birth in our society and permeates every aspect of our lives.[31] Thus, even if young girls are not expected to perform the domestic tasks of society in Plato's Just State, one cannot but suspect that they will have experiences which are systematically different from those of males.

Another reason is that in Book V of the *Republic* Plato speaks of giving males and females destined for the same role in society the same *upbringing* as well as the same education.[32] Does this not mean that he would expose potential male and female guardians to identical experiences from birth so that by the time their formal education begins in their teens the sexes would have had identical socialization? In Books II and III Plato outlines a program of education in literature and the arts for the early years. Let us assume for the sake of argument that it is meant for both boys and girls. However, there is nothing in the *Republic* to suggest that in the Just State people will behave in exactly the same way toward male and female infants and children, let alone that they will speak to them and evaulate them in exactly the same way. Unless a positive program is instituted in Plato's Just State to ensure that sex is irrelevant to socialization, we are certainly justified in doubting that potential male and female guardians will be sufficiently identical when they begin their formal education to benefit equally from identical treatment.

Suppose, however, that there is identical socialization in Plato's Just State in the sense that boys and girls have the same experiences. Plato's program of censorship is based on the assumption that children acquire tastes informally through unconscious imitation; hence his caveats about exposing them to stories which portray the gods quarreling and the lamentations of famous men.[33] One searches in vain in the *Republic* for caveats about exposing children to stories which perpetuate traditional attitudes toward women. Given the way Socrates and his companions speak of women, there is little reason to believe that Plato would recognize sex stereotyping as a factor to be reckoned with in the education of the guardian class.[34] Yet an upbringing which portrays females as irrational, untrustworthy, and generally inferior to males will surely have differential effects on boys and girls. Thus, supposing an identical socialization means *having identical experiences,* we cannot assume that it will produce identical socialization in the sense of *identical results.* In particular, when the identical experiences boys and girls have embody sex role stereotypes, we can expect them to be experienced in different ways.

IV. THE IDENTITY POSTULATE: MALE BIASED DISCIPLINES

When the identical education received by males and females comprises methods of teaching and learning which are determined by what works for males, equality of role occupancy is by no means assured. When that education involves initiating both males and females into fields of knowledge which contain a male bias and transmitting to them subject matter which reflects only the experience of males, then even if an equal number of each sex graduates into the guardian class so that there is equality of role occupancy, women will not be perceived as the equals of men nor will they be treated as such.

Now the fields which future guardians must study certainly do not contain a male bias in the way Nancy Schrom Dye says American history does.[35] Nor do they contain a male bias in the way Naomi Weisstein and Carol Gilligan say psychology does.[36] History has defined itself as the record of the public and political aspects of the past, thus excluding women from historical narratives and providing no insight into their lives. Psychology has, on the one hand, assimilated the experience of females to that of males and, on the other, constructed the female from its own prejudices. The fields to be studied by Plato's guardians do not purport to describe or explain experience. Thus, attributions of sex bias based on the assumption that both male and female experience should be equally reflected in the theories of the field are irrelevant.

The criticism which Catherine R. Stimpson has made of literature and which Susan Snaider Lanser and Evelyn Torton Beck have made of literary criticism, namely that women practitioners of the craft have been slighted, may or may not be relevant to the case at hand.[37] We need to know if in their study of mathematics, astronomy, harmony, and dialectic Plato's guardians are to study the theories of particular individuals and, if so, if theories created by women will be ignored. We also need to know a good deal more about the kind of a guardian course of study to determine if the kind of criticism Kathryn Pyne Parsons has made of contemporary moral philosophy, namely, that there is sex bias in its abstraction from actual experience, is apt.[38]

Whether the issue of sex bias can be satisfactorily answered in relation to the fields of knowledge to be studied by Plato's guardians I do not know. One thing is clear, however. Insofar as these fields of knowledge contain male bias, one must expect to find differences in the way future male and female guardians perceive themselves and one another. If the work of female thinkers in a field is systematically excluded from its subject matter, will not students of both sexes come to believe that males are superior and females are inferior human beings? If the abstraction which takes place in a field is biased in favor of males, will not students of both sexes come to believe that females are abnormal human beings? Disciplinary sex bias, which is something quite different from the bias one finds in individuals or in institutions, surely has destructive effects on both students and practitioners of a field. It is difficult, if not impossible, for women to see themselves as the equals of men, let alone for men to see them as their equals, when women are not accorded *epistemological equality* in the various fields of knowledge.[39]

Recent commentators on the *Republic* have taken the Identity Postulate to be unproblematic. In fact, however, it presents the very real possibility that a male-based pedagogy and subject matter will be imposed on women, thereby making it difficult for sex equality to be achieved. The Identity Postulate is not the only problematic element of Plato's Production Model of Education, however, for if Plato is forcing future female guardians into a masculine mold, the question of equal respect and treatment rises anew.

V. THE FUNCTIONAL POSTULATE: MASCULINE ROLE DEFINITION

According to Arlene Saxenhouse, "Socrates attempts to turn women into men by making them equal participants in the political community."[40] She argues this thesis on the grounds that he ignores the sexual female and, in particular, the peculiar biological qualities of women: women's natural role in the preservation of the city through the procreation of the next generation is left unconsidered; the female is brought into politics through disregard of her body although the thing she can do better than anyone else — hence the thing which should be considered her specific nature — is to bear children.

One need not adopt Saxenhouse's account of the de-sexed female or her conclusion that the appearance of women in the *Republic* must be seen as a means of casting a shadow over the whole enterprise of trying to create the perfect city to agree with her that in admitting women into the guardian class Plato imposes a masculine mold on them. Historically, warriors and rulers have been predominantly male. No doubt this explains why Socrates and his companions never entertain the possibility that members of the male sex might not qualify by nature to be guardians; why it is only females who are problematic in their eyes. To be sure, it does not follow from the fact that females are given entry into roles traditionally occupied by males that a

masculine mold is imposed on them. In principle it is possible
for the entrance of women into traditional male roles to be accompanied by a redefinition of those roles. However, although
Plato does redefine at least the ruler role in relation to the Just
State, the qualities or traits he assigns his guardians were considered in his day and are still considered to be masculine. This is
not to say that males possess these traits and that females do not
or even that males are more likely than females to possess them,
but simply that the traits of Plato's guardians belong to our
cultural stereotype of the male.[41]

The physical qualities of the guardian are clear, Socrates says.
Guardians must be quick to see things, swift in pursuit of what
they have seen, and strong to catch the enemy and fight to the
end.[42] Guardians must also be brave and high spirited since a
high spirit makes the soul fearless, and they must love wisdom.[43]
If they are to be rulers, moreover, they must be rational thinkers
able not only to distinguish the Good by their reason, but to
argue their case according to reality rather than opinion all the
while surviving refutations of it.[44] The capacity for rational
thought is not enough, however. Reason must rule the individuals who are to rule Plato's Just State: his rulers must at all
times exercise self-control.

Susan Okin has called Plato's guardians androgynous because
they are required to be gentle as well as courageous. It is a
mistake to suppose, however, that androgyny is achieved simply
because, as Allan Bloom has put it, Plato sees the need to temper
the qualities his guardians develop in the education for battle
with gentleness.[45] Plato's guardians must be gentle with their
own people so that they do not themselves destroy the city they
are supposed to protect.[46] But when one takes into account the
qualities they need for battle and the kind of thinking they must
exhibit to discern the Good, and when one understands that the
self-control they must exercise at all times involves the subordination in the individual of feelings and emotions to the rule of
reason, it becomes clear that the predominating traits of the
guardians are those which are considered to be masculine.

Now it might be argued that so long as females as well as
males are allowed to occupy a role and that role is defined in
terms of traits which both sexes can possess, then even if it is
defined by traits belonging to our masculine stereotype, sex
equality is achieved. As Elizabeth Beardsley has shown,
however, traits which can be possessed by both sexes are often

appraised differently in males and females.[47] Consider one of Beardsley's examples, the trait of aggressiveness. The authors of a book on assertive training for women report that in the first class meetings of their training courses they ask their students to call out the adjectives which come to mind when we say "aggressive woman" and "aggressive man." Here is the list of adjectives the women used to describe an aggressive man: "masculine," "dominating," "successful," "heroic," "capable," "strong," "forceful," "manly." And here in turn is the list of adjectives they used to describe an aggressive woman: "harsh," "pushy," "bitchy," "domineering," "obnoxious," "emasculating," "uncaring."[48] Thus, supposing that the traits which Plato's guardians possess are judged to be highly desirable ones for males, we must not assume that they will be evaluated as highly when they are possessed by females.

I will call the differential appraisal of traits according to sex, *trait genderization*.[49] The question which remains is whether the traits to be possessed by Plato's guardians are, like aggressiveness, genderized in favor of males. That they are in our society cannot be doubted. The physical courage and the fearlessness which the guardians must display are considered positive virtues when possessed by males. For women to be swift enough to catch and fight the enemy, however, they would not only have to dress in ways which are perceived as unfeminine and hence abnormal, but would have to display a fierceness and tenacity which are considered unnatural for their sex.

Now it might be argued that there is no need for all guardians to be equally fast and fierce; that in the Just State the guardian role will develop specialized functions, with some guardians performing the task of catching and fighting the enemy and others performing less rigorous duties. This position finds support in the allusions of Socrates and his companions to the physical weakness of women and in their apparent willingness to assign the lighter duties of guardianship to women because of this weakness.[50]

It is true that females who failed to acquire the physical traits Plato assigns the guardians would escape the negative effects of their genderization. However, it is far from obvious that one who did not possess those traits could *be* a full-fledged guardian for it is not clear that such a person could possess the soul of a guardian as it is described in Book IV. Moreover, it is not only the physical traits of Plato's guardians which are genderized.

The tragic story of Rosalind Franklin, the scientist who contributed to the discovery of the structure of DNA, demonstrates that when a woman displays the kind of critical, autonomous thought which is an attribute of Plato's guardians, she is derided for what are considered to be negative, unpleasant characteristics even as her male colleagues are admired for possessing them.[51]

The genderization of traits is not simply a function of free-floating stereotypes. Elizabeth Beardsley has pointed out that genderization has its source in both the differential allocation of tasks and responsibilities in society and the differential assessment of the capabilities and abilities of males and females.[52] Theorists have put different labels on the two spheres or realms into which we implicitly divide the social order. Whether one calls it the domestic, private, or reproductive sphere, *that* is where both tradition and the ruling ideology placed Rosalind Franklin. In that sphere — women's sphere — days and nights are devoted to children, home, and family. A woman who lives her life in it must be nurturant and caring, warm and sympathetic; above all, she must put her own purposes and plans aside to help her children and husband carry out theirs. To be an abstract, rational, critical thinker is of little use in that sphere; indeed, one wonders if it might not even be dysfunctional to possess these traits to a high degree in this sphere.

Rosalind Franklin consciously chose the laboratory rather than women's sphere. The traits she possessed were certainly not dysfunctional there, yet she was perceived by some of her scientific colleagues to be a trespasser from the domestic sphere, an alien who simply could not be taken seriously in the public realm no matter what her personal qualities might be.[53] Now in Book V of the *Republic* Plato abolishes the private sphere for the guardian class in his Just State. It might seem, therefore, that his female rulers would not suffer the fate of Rosalind Franklin; that they *could* not be viewed as aliens because there would be no other sphere to which they could belong. The long arm of tradition should not be forgotten, however, nor should we forget that Plato abolishes the private sphere *only* for the guardian class. Given that for the largest segment of society women's place is in the home and that in Athens, in where we presume the founders of the Just State lived, the place of almost all women was the home, then will not the traits of Plato's guardians remain genderized in favor of males?[54]

VI. CONCLUSION

Commentators have assumed that insofar as sex inequality is a characteristic of Plato's Just State its source lies either in the content he gives to what I have called the Postulate of Specialized Natures or else in his abiding concern with harmony and unity rather than with fairness. In fact, however, the Identity Postulate and the Functional Postulate are both potential sources of sex inequality in Plato's philosophy, as they are in any philosophy which adopts them. Sex equality and inequality come in many different guises. Even if Plato does provide equal access to education and equal role opportunity for women we cannot assume that women will therefore achieve equality of role occupancy or, if they do, that they will be accorded equal respect and receive equal treatment.

As far as the Identity Postulate is concerned, the heart of the matter is that identical education is not in every instance equal education. Thus, while potential female guardians in the Just State are to be given the *same* education as potential male guardians, potential male and female guardians will not necessarily receive *equal* education. Imagine two people, one of whom has appendicitis and the other tonsilitis. Perform a tonsillectomy on both and they will each have been given identical treatment. They will not, however, have been given equal medical care for that would be care which was as appropriate for the one illness as for the other.[55] There is provision in Plato's Production Model of Education for differential treatment according to sex; in fact, the Identity Postulate expressly forbids it. His future female guardians might, however, require different treatment from future male guardians in order to arrive at the point at which they can capably carry out their assigned roles in the Just State. If they do, then even if they have equal access to education, they will not have equal educational opportunity for they will not have equal access to equal education.

A Production Model of Education could contain a Postulate of Equivalency instead of an Identity Postulate. Had Plato been aware of the limitations of the Identity Postulate, he might have provided equivalent, rather than identical, education for male and female future guardians. Then, assuming that roughly equal numbers of each sex were by nature suited to be guardians, there would be good reason for supposing that in his Just State there would be equal role occupancy. So long as the guardian role was defined in terms of traits which are considered to be masculine however, in Plato's Just State potential female guardians would be in a no-win situation. They would have to acquire traits thought to be masculine in order to meet the requirements of the guardian role. Yet if they acquired those traits, they would very likely be viewed as abnormal and be derided or belittled for possessing them.

The heart of the matter, as far as the functional Postulate is concerned, is that although traits are attached to social roles, traits can remain genderized even as the social role to which they belong are detached from gender. Give Plato the benefit of the doubt and assume that he sincerely wanted his Just State to have a significant number of female guardians. Then one can say that occupancy of this most important social role is not tied to gender. Yet so long as a role is defined in terms of genderized traits, male and female occupants of the role can expect to receive differential treatment and to be accorded differential respect for possessing these traits.

For Plato's female guardians to escape the fate of a Rosalind Franklin, Plato would either have had to define the role of guardian in terms of traits other than the ones he used or he would have had to sanction measures for changing people's values and attitudes so that these traits would not be genderized in favor of males in the Just State. That he could have defined the guardian role in markedly different terms without radically revising his entire philosophy is doubtful since the traits of rational thinking and self-control, if not all those he attributes to his guardians, are absolutely central to his system of thought. The second alternative would not have serious repercussions throughout Plato's philosophy. Whether he would have wanted to adopt it and whether he actually could have proposed measures for turning around the attitudes and values of the people who would inhabit the Just State are highly speculative questions which I leave open here.

In conclusion, let me stress that the purpose in speculating about the measures Plato could have taken to ensure sex equality in his Just State is not to blame Plato for his failure to guarantee sex equality, but to help us understand what is required if sex equality is to be achieved in our own society. It is unlikely that Plato could have thought to adopt an Equivalency Postulate because it is unlikely that he could have been aware of the limitations of the Identity Postulate outlined here. It is unlikely also that he could have addressed the problem his definition of the

guardian role raises for true sex equality because it is unlikely
that he could have known of the existence of genderized traits.
Thus it does not seem fruitful to condemn him for doing less
than he should have for his female guardians. It *is* fruitful,
however, to take to heart for our own lives the lessons we can
learn from the way Plato's Production Model of Education
functions in his theory of the Just State.

NOTES

1. I use the term "guardian" to refer both to the auxiliaries (warriors)
   and the rulers in Plato's Just State.
2. See Christine Pierce, "Equality: *Republic* V," *The Monist* 57
   (January 1973): 1–11.
3. Ibid., p. 3.
4. "Plato on Women," *Feminist Studies* 2 (1975): 131–38.
5. "Plato's *Republic* and Feminism," in *Woman in Western Thought,*
   ed. Martha Lee Osborne (New York: Random House, 1979), pp.
   24–33.
6. "The Function of Equal Education in Plato's *Republic* and *Laws,*"
   in *The Sexism of Social and Political Theory,* ed. Lorenne M. G.
   Clark and Lynda Lange (Toronto: University of Toronto Press,
   1979), pp. 3–15.
7. *Women in Western Political Thought* (Princeton: Princeton
   University Press, 1979).
8. Ibid., Ch. 2.
9. Ibid., Ch. 3.
10. Ibid., p. 69.
11. At least they purport to think existing institutions away. That they
    succeed in doing so is another matter.
12. Plato, *Republic,* 369b. References to this work will henceforth be
    to *Plato's Republic,* trans. G. M. A. Grube (Indianapolis: Hackett
    Publishing Co., 1974).
13. 369c.
14. 370a.
15. 370b.
16. 370b-c.
17. On this point see Lange, op. cit.
18. Some interpreters of Plato would argue that Socrates discerns cer-
    tain natural talents or aptitudes in people and then designs a state
    to fit them while others would say that he assumes a parallelism be-
    tween human nature and societal needs. However, the account of
    education contained in the *Republic* makes plausible the interpreta-
    tion given here.
19. Nicholas P. White abstracts from *Republic* II a principle of the

Natural Division of Labor which encompasses what I am calling the Postulate of Specialized Natures and the Postulate of Correspondence. For the present purpose, however, it is important to keep these postulates separate. See *A Companion to Plato's Republic* (Indianapolis: Hackett Publishing Co., 1979), pp. 84–85.

20. However, in other dialogues characteristics of the good artisan or craftsman are made clear. See Terence Irwin *Plato's Moral Theory* (Oxford: Clarendon Press, 1977).
21. 375a–e.
22. 537a.
23. 452a.
24. 454b–e.
25. Op. cit., p. 3.
26. 537b–d.
27. On this point see Sheila Tobias, *Overcoming Math Anxiety* (New York: W. W. Norton and Co., 1978), Ch. 3; Eleanor Emmons Maccoby and Carol Nagy Jacklin, *The Psychology of Sex Differences* (Stanford: Stanford University Press, 1974), Ch. 3; *Women and the Mathematical Mystique,* ed. Lynn H. Fox, Linda Brody, and Diane Tobin (Baltimore: Johns Hopkins University Press, 1980). Note that my argument here does *not* rely on the thesis that females would *by nature* be unable to complete the guardian curriculum satisfactorily.
28. See Book VII, especially 540c.
29. For example, with differences in verbal, mathematical, and spatial abilities. See Maccoby and Jacklin, op. cit.; Tobias, op. cit.; Julia A. Sherman, *Sex-Related Cognitive Differences* (Springfield, Ill.: Charles C Thomas, 1978). See also Carol F. Gilligan's findings on moral development in "In a Different Voice: Women's Conception of the Self and of Morality," *Harvard Educational Review* 47, no. 4 (1977): 481–517. Her thesis that female and male moral development proceed differently may have implications for the way males and females learn. Once more please note that my argument does not rest on any claim of biological determinism.
30. Remember that Plato's guardians are to receive education in both physical and intellectual skills. Now it may be thought that for the rulers of the Just State the physical skills required of the guardian class are not nearly as important as the intellectual ones, so that it would not matter to the performance of the guardian role if potential female rulers did not attain the same degree of competence during their physical education as potential male rulers did. Janet Farrell Smith has reminded me that for Plato, however, physical training is not simply a means to bodily fitness: he believes that in training the body one trains the soul (412a). To be sure, a fit body does not guarantee a fit soul, but it is necessary for the kind of soul which all rulers must possess (403d). Thus physical training is not a frill in his Just State as it is often thought to be in our society. On

the contrary, it is an essential component of a guardian's training. Indeed, if potential female rulers do not acquire fit bodies, they will automatically be barred from occupying the role for which they are by nature suited since such occupancy depends on having a good soul.

31. For a review of the literature on this topic see Lenore J. Weitzman, "Sex-Role Socialization," in *Women: A Feminist Perspective* ed. Jo Freeman (Palo Alto, Calif.: Mayfield Publishing Co., 1975), pp. 105–44.
32. 451c.
33. 378c, 388a.
34. See, for example, 388a, 398e, 450c, 469d.
35. "Clio's American Daughters: Male History, Female Reality," in *The Prism of Sex,* ed. Julia Sherman and Evelyn Torton Beck (Madison: University of Wisconsin Press, 1977), pp. 9–31.
36. Naomi Weisstein, "Psychology Constructs the Female," in *Woman in Sexist Society,* ed. Vivian Gornick and Barbara K. Moran (New York: Basic Books, 1970), pp. 133–46. Carol F. Gilligan, "In a Different Voice," op. cit.,; "Woman's Place in Man's Life Cycle," *Harvard Educational Review* 49, no. 4 (1979): 431–46.
37. Catherine R. Stimpson, "The Power to Name: Some Reflections on the *Avant-Garde*" in Sherman and Beck, op. cit., pp. 55–77; Susan Snaider Lanser and Evelyn Torton Beck, "[Why] Are There No Great Women Critics?" in Sherman and Beck, pp. 79–91.
38. "Moral Revolution," in Sherman and Beck, op. cit., pp. 189–227.
39. For a general discussion of the epistemological *in*equality of women (my term, not hers) see Adrienne Rich, "Toward a Woman-Centered University," in her *On Lies, Secrets, and Silence* (New York: W.W. Norton & Co., 1979), pp. 134ff.
40. "The Philosopher and the Female in the Political Thought of Plato," *Political Theory* 4, (May 1976): 196.
41. See Alexandra G. Kaplan and Mary Anne Sedney, *Psychology and Sex Roles* (Boston: Little, Brown and Co., 1980), pp. 3–5.
42. 375a.
43. 376a.
44. 525b, 534c.
45. Allan Bloom, trans., *The Republic of Plato* (New York: Basic Books, 1968), p. 384.
46. 375c.
47. "Traits and Genderization," in *Feminism and Philosophy* ed. Mary Vetterling-Braggin, Frederick A. Elliston, and Jane English, (Totowa, N.J.: Littlefield, Adams & Co., 1977), pp. 117–23.
48. Lynn Z. Bloom, Karen Coburn, and Joan Pearlman, *The New Assertive Woman* (New York: Delacorte Press, 1975), p. 12.
49. Beardsley, op. cit., uses the term "genderization" to refer to language. I use it here to refer to traits themselves.
50. 455e, 456b, 457b.

51. Anne Sayre, *Rosalind Franklin and DNA* (New York: W.W. Norton and Co., 1975). See also James D. Watson, *The Double Helix* (New York: Atheneum, 1968) and Horace Freeland Judson, *The Eighth Day of Creation* (New York: Simon and Schuster, 1979).
52. Op. cit., pp. 119–20.
53. It is important to note, however, that some colleagues did take her seriously as a scientist. See Sayre, op. cit.
54. For an account of the place of women in Athenian life see Okin, op. cit., Ch. 2.
55. On this issue see William K. Frankena, "The Concept of Social Justice," in *Social Justice,* ed. Richard B. Brandt (Englewood Cliffs, N.J.: Prentice-Hall, 1962), pp. 11, 15.

Further References

Parts I and II:

Adler, Alfred. *Understanding Human Nature.* Translated by W. Bean Wolfe. New York: Allen Unwin, 1927. Critique of Freud.

Agonisto, Rosemary, ed. *History of Ideas on Women: A Source Book.* New York: G.P. Putnam's Sons, 1977. Includes nature and nurture theories.

Alpert, Jane. "Mother-Right: A New Feminist Theory." *Ms.* 2, August, 1973: 52–55. Matriarchy does not exist, but if it did, free of male influence, female power could have positive possibilities for the future.

Andreas, Carol. *Sex and Caste in America.* Englewood Cliffs, N.J.: Prentice-Hall, 1971. Nurture.

Aquinas, St. Thomas. *Summa Theologica.* Translated by the Fathers of the English Dominican Province. New York: Berringer Brothers, 1947. Nature.

Ardrey, Robert. *African Genesis: A Personal Investigation into the Animal Origins and Nature of Man.* New York: Atheneum, 1963.

_____. *The Territorial Imperative: A Personal Inquiry into the Animal Origins of Animals and Nations.* New York: Atheneum, 1966.

_____. *The Hunting Hypothesis: A Personal Conclusion Concerning the Evolutionary Nature of Man.* New York: Bantam, 1977. Evolutionary argument to the effect that humans have the same psychological traits as baboons.

Aristotle. *The Politics.* Translated by Benjamin Jowett. Oxford:

---

*For an outstanding summary and critique of many of the works cited in this section, refer to the entry under Warren, Mary Anne.

Clarendon Press, 1885. Nature; women have a "proper sphere."

Astell, Mary. *Some Reflections Upon Marriage.* 1730. New York: Source Books Press, 1970. Nurture; resistance to male rule is a waste of time, but inevitable for the future.

Atkinson, Ti-Grace. "Radical Feminism" and "The Institution of Sexual Intercourse." In *Notes from the Second Year: Major Writings of Radical Feminists,* edited by Shulamith Firestone. New York: 1970. Nature; roots of women's repression are biological.

Bachofen, J.J. *Myth, Religion and Mother Right.* Translated by Ralph Manheim. Princeton, N.J.: Princeton University Press, 1967. Analysis of matriarchy.

Barber, Benjamin R. *Liberating Feminism.* New York: Dell, 1975. Nature/nurture combo. There are innate differences between the sexes, but we can find social and political ways of making life more equal for all.

Bardwick, Judith. *Psychology of Women.* New York: Harper and Row, 1971. Nature/nurture combo; "interactive" theory.

_____, ed. *Readings on the Psychology of Women.* New York: Harper and Row, 1972.

_____ and Douvan, Elizabeth, "Ambivalence: The Socialization of Women." In *Women in Sexist Society,* edited by Vivian Gornick and Barbara K. Moran. New York: Basic Books, 1971, pp. 225–241.

Barker-Benfield, G.J. *The Horrors of the Half-Known Life: Male Attitudes Toward Women and Sexuality in Nineteenth Century America.* New York: Harper and Row, 1976. Nurture. Democracy causes male pathology.

Barnhouse, Ruth Tiffany, and Holmes, Urban T. III, eds. *Male and Female: Christian Approaches to Sexuality.* New York: Seabury Press, 1976. Conservative analysis of the concepts of "masculinity" and "femininity."

Beach, Frank A., ed. *Human Sexuality in Four Perspectives.* Baltimore: Johns Hopkins University Press, 1977. Analyzes sex differences from developmental, sociological, physiological, and evolutionary approaches.

Beard, Mary. *On Understanding Women.* New York: Longmans, Green and Co., 1931.

_____. *Woman as a Force in History: A Study in Traditions and Reality.* New York: Collier Books, 1973. It is a myth that women have been or are subjected to men.

Beauvoir, Simone de. *The Second Sex.* Translated by H.M. Parshley. New York: Knopf, 1953. Nature/nurture; women's biology has led men to classify her as the Other, but this does not force women to stop seeking independence.

Bebel, August. *Women Under Socialism.* 1883. Translated by Daniel de Leon. New York: Schocken Books, 1971. Nurture; socialism would free women from oppression by men.

Bednarik, Karl. *The Male in Crisis.* New York: Alfred A. Knopf, 1970. Nature. Men are by nature more aggressive than women and need more outlets for their aggression.

Bem, Sandra, and Bem, D.J. "Training the Woman to Know Her Place." In *Beliefs, Attitudes and Human Affairs,* edited by D.J. Bem. Belmont, Calif.: Brooks/Cole, 1970, pp. 89–99. Nurture.

Bird, Caroline, with Sarah Welles Vriller. *Born Female: The High Cost of Keeping Women Down.* Rev. ed. New York: David McKay, 1970. Nurture.

Bonaparte, Marie. *Female Sexuality.* New York: International Universities Press, 1953. Freudian.

Borgese, Elizabeth Mann. *Ascent of Woman.* New York: George Braziller, 1963. Nature. The biology of females must be reconstructed so that they have the same biology as males for true equality.

Brenton, Myron. *The American Male.* New York: Coward-McCann, 1966. Nurture; men must adjust to the new roles of women.

Briffault, Robert. *The Mothers.* 1959. New York: Macmillan, 1963. Analysis of matriarchy.

Buck, Pearl. *Of Men and Women.* 1941. New York: John Day Co., 1971. Nurture. Men and women ought to be educated alike and share in domestic tasks.

Bullough, Vern L. *The Subordinate Sex: A History of Attitudes Toward Women.* Baltimore: Penguin Books. 1974. Nature. History of women-hating in western culture. Suggests biological causes.

_____. *The Frontiers of Sex Research.* Buffalo, N.Y.: Prometheus Books, 1979.

Chafe, William H. *The American Woman: Her Changing Social, Economic, and Political Roles,* 1920–1970. London: Oxford University Press, 1972.

_____. *Women and Equality: Changing Patterns in American Culture.* New York: Oxford University Press, 1977. Effect of the women's liberation movement on women's economic status.

Chafetz, Janet. *Masculine/Feminine or Human.* Itasca, Ill.: F.E. Peacock Publishers, 1974.

Collins, Margery L., and Pierce, Christine. "Holes and Slime: Sexism in Sartre's Psychoanalysis." In *Women and Philosophy,* ed. by Carol C. Gould and Marx Wartofsky. New York: G. P. Putnam's Sons, 1976, pp. 112–27.

Cox, Sue, ed. *Female Psychology: The Emerging Self.* Chicago: Science Research Associates, 1976. Collection of nature and nurture theories.

Daly, Mary. *Beyond God the Father: Toward a Philosophy of Women's Liberation.* Boston: Beacon Press, 1973. Patriarchal mind-control is the ruling force of the world: love and friendship between women will destroy it.

304   *Further References*

_____. *The Church and the Second Sex: With a New Feminist Post-christian Introduction by the Author.* New York: Harper Colophon, 1975.

_____. *Gyn/Ecology: The Metaethics of Radical Feminism.* Boston: Beacon Press, 1978.

Darwin, Charles. *The Descent of Man and Selection in Relation to Sex,* 1871. New York: D. Appleton and Co., 1874.

_____. *The Origin of the Species.* 1859. New York: Mentor Books, 1958. Evolutionary theory.

David, Deborah S., and Brannon, Robert, eds. *The Forty-Nine Percent Majority: The Male Sex Role.* Reading, Mass.: Addison-Wesley, 1976. Key elements of "masculine" stereotype.

Davis, Elizabeth Gould. *The First Sex.* Baltimore: Penguin Books, 1973. Women are better off in matriarchal societies. The new age will be a matriarchy in which women's supernatural powers will reign.

de Castillejo, Irene Claremont. *Knowing Woman: A Feminine Psychology,* 1973. New York: Harper and Row, 1974. Jungian.

de Rougement, Denis. *Love in the Western World,* 1939. New York: Anchor Books, 1957. Jungian; calls for a renewal of the "feminine principle" in both sexes.

Deutsch, Helene, M.D. *The Psychology of Women: A Psychoanalytic Interpretation* vol. I: *Girlhood;* vol. II: *Motherhood.* New York: Bantam, 1944; 1945. Freudian.

Dickason, Anne. "Anatomy and Destiny: The Role of Biology in Plato's View of Women." *Philosophical Forum* 5, nos. 1–2 (1973–74): 45–53.

Diner, Helen. *Mothers and Amazons, The First Feminine History of Culture.* Ed. and trans. by John Philip Lundin, intro. by Brigitte Berger. Garden City, New York: Anchor Books, 1973. Defense of matriarchy theory.

Duberman, Lucille, et al., eds. *Gender and Sex in Society.* New York: Praeger Publishers, 1975. Examines various explanations of sex differences.

Encyclical Letter of Pope Pius XI on Christian Marriage. Boston: St. Paul Editions, n.d. p. 32. Nature.

Engels, Friedrich. *The Origin of the Family, Private Property and the State.* New York: International Publishers, 1942.

_____. *The Condition of the Working Class in England in 1844.* 1845. London: George Allen and Unwin Ltd. 1950. Nurture. Capitalism is the root of women's oppression.

Erickson, Erik. "Inner and Outer Space: Reflections on Womanhood." *Daedalus* 93, no. 2 (1964): pp. 582–606.

_____. "Womanhood and the Inner Space." In Erickson's *Identity: Youth and Crisis.* New York: W. W. Norton and Co., 1968. Nature.

Farber, Seymour M., and Wilson, Roger H. L., eds. *The Potential of Woman.* New York: McGraw-Hill, 1963. Collection; examines various casual explanations of sex difference.

Farren, Warren. *The Liberated Man.* New York: Random House, 1974. Nurture. Dominant "masculine" role is self-destructive and should be eliminated.

Fast, Julius. *The Incompatibility of Men and Women and How To Overcome It.* New York: Avon Books, 1971. Evolution is the cause of psychological sex differences; analogues to animal behavior.

Ferguson, Charles W. *The Male Attitude.* Boston: Little, Brown, 1966.

Figes, Eva. *Patriarchal Attitudes.* New York: Stein and Day, 1970. Patriarchy is maintained through the male image of women.

Firestone, Shulamith. *The Dialectic of Sex.* New York: William Morrow, 1970. Advocates elimination of the biological family and replacing it with artificial motherhood.

Fox, Robin. *Kinship and Marriage.* Baltimore: Penguin, 1967. Nature. Basic natural female function is to bear and raise children. This leads to men's assuming a protective role.

_____ and Tiger, Lionel, eds. *The Imperial Animal.* New York: Holt, Rinehart and Winston, 1971.

Freud, Sigmund. "Three Essays on the Theory of Sexuality." In *The Complete Psychological Works,* vol. 7. London: Hogarth, 1953.

_____. "Some Psychological Consequences of the Anatomical Distinctions Between the Sexes." In *Sigmund Freud: Collected Papers,* vol. 5, pp. 186–97. Translated and ed. by James Strachey. New York: Basic Books, 1959.

_____. "Femininity." In *New Introductory Lectures on Psychoanalysis,* pp. 112–35. Translated by James Strachey, vol. 22. 1933. New York: Norton, 1965.

_____. "The Psychology of Women." In *New Introductory Lectures on Psychoanalysis,* pp. 112–35. Translated by James Strachey, vol. 22. 1933. New York: Norton, 1965.

_____. "Female Sexuality." In *Women and Analysis,* ed. by Jean Strouse, pp. 17–26. New York: Grossman Publishers, 1974.

Fried, M.H. "Mankind Excluding Woman." *Science* 165 (August 29, 1969): 883–4. Review of Tiger's *Men in Groups.*

Friedl, Ernestine. *Woman and Man.* New York: Holt, Rinehart and Winston, 1975. Nurture. Domination by men forces women to produce goods usually used in domestic unit.

Fuller, Margaret. *Woman in the Nineteenth Century.* 1845. New York: W.W. Norton, 1971. Nurture. Education will develop women's intellect; each person should have both "masculine" and "feminine" traits.

Gadpaille, Warren. "Research into the Physiology of Maleness and Femaleness." *Archives of General Psychiatry,* 26 (March 1972): 193–206. Critique of John Money's views. Nature's disposition is to produce females. Males result only from the addition of androgen; XX-ness is the primordial substance.

Galt, William E. "The Male-Female Dichotomy in Human Behavior: A Phylobiological Explanation." *Psychiatry* 6 (1943): 1–14.

Gelman, David, et al. "The Sexes: How They Differ—And Why." *Newsweek* (May 18, 1981): 72–83. Hormones "masculinize" or "feminize" the brain, but males and females can overcome hormonal destiny.

Gicles, Janet Zollinger. *Women and the Future: Changing Sex Roles in Modern America.* New York: Free Press, 1978. Nurture. Sex roles shaped by economic factors. In the future, domestic and labor roles of women will converge.

_____, and Smock, Audrey Chapman, eds. *Women: Roles and Status in Eight Countries.* New York: John Wiley and Sons, 1977.

Gilder, George. *Sexual Suicide.* New York: Quadrangle, 1973. Social stability requires patriarchy.

Gilson, E'tienne. *The Christian Philosophy of Saint Thomas Aquinas.* Translated by L.K. Shook. New York: Random House, 1956.

Goldberg, Steven. *The Inevitability of Patriarchy.* New York: William Morrow, 1973. Nature.

Gould, Carol C., and Wartofsky, Marx W., eds. *Women and Philosophy: Toward a Theory of Liberation.* New York: G.P. Putnam's Sons, 1976. Anthology of articles by philosophers, some critiques of nature theories.

Guettel, Charnie. *Marxism and Feminism.* Toronto: The Woman's Press, 1974. Nurture. Oppression of women due to economic exploitation.

Hall, Diana Long. "Biology, Sex Hormones and Sexism in the 1920's." *Philosophical Forum* 5, nos. 1–2 (1973–74):81–96.

Hamilton, Roberta. *The Liberation of Women: A Study of Patriarchy and Capitalism.* London: George Allen and Unwin, 1978. Both economic and ideological roles cause women's oppression.

Harding, Esther M. *The Way of All Women.* New York: Harper and Row, 1970.

_____. *Woman's Mysteries, Ancient and Modern.* New York: Putnam, 1971. Jungian; women should incorporate "masculine," and men "feminine," tendencies into their psyches.

Hays, H.R. *The Dangerous Sex: The Myth of Feminine Evil.* New York: G.P. Putnam's Sons, 1964. Male domination of women is due to male neurotic fear of women.

Hegel, Georg Wilhelm Friedrich. *Philosophy of Right.* Translated by T. M. Knox, 1821. New York: Oxford University Press. 1952. Women belong in the private family, men in public roles.

_____. *The Phenomenology of Mind.* Translated by J.B. Baillie. 1807. New York: Humanities Press, 1966.

Hess, Thomas B., and Baker, Elizabeth C. eds. *Art and Sexual Politics: Women Artists and Art History.* New York: Collier Macmillan Publishers, 1973. Nurture. It has been made institutionally impossible for women to become as successful as men in the art field.

Holliday, Laurel. *The Violent Sex: Male Psychobiology and the Evolution of Consciousness.* Guerneyville, Calif.: Bluestocking Books,

1978. Nature/nurture combination; male supremacy is explained in terms of biological differences yet psychological differences can be eliminated by overriding environmental conditions.

Horney, Karen. *Feminine Psychology.* New York: W.W. Norton, 1967. Critique of Freud's views on women.

Hume, David. "Of Chastity and Modesty." In Hume's *A Treatise of Human Nature,* Bk II, ed. by L.A. Selby-Bigge. 1739. Oxford: Clarendon Press, 1967, pp. 267–70. Female chastity and modesty is a social necessity.

Hutt, Corine. *Males and Females.* Harmondsworth, Engl.: Penguin Books, 1972. Nature; biological explanation of psychological differences.

Hyde, Janet Shibley, and Rosenberg, B. G., eds. *Half the Human Experience: The Psychology of Women.* Lexington, Mass.: D.C. Heath and Co., 1976. Collection. Discussion of several models of sex role development.

Jaggar, Alison, M., and Struhl, Paula Rothenberg, eds. *Feminist Frameworks: Alternative Theoretical Accounts of the Relations Between Men and Women.* New York: McGraw-Hill, 1978. Conservative, liberal, Marxist, radical feminist and social feminist perspectives on sex roles.

Janeway, Elizabeth. *Man's World, Woman's Place.* New York: William Morrow, 1971. Nature/nurture combination; "masculine" and "feminine" differences are socially, as well as biologically, caused.

_____. *Between Myth and Morning: Women Awakening.* New York: William Morrow, 1975.

Jennes, Linda, ed. *Feminism and Socialism.* New York: Pathfinder Press, 1972. Nurture. Women's oppression due to capitalism.

Jung, Carl G. "Concerning the Archetypes, With Special Reference to the Anima Concept." In *Collected Works,* vol. 9, part I, pp. 54–74. Princeton: Princeton University Press, 1954.

_____. *The Development of Personality.* New York: Pantheon, 1954.

_____. *Civilization in Transition.* New York: Pantheon, 1964.

_____. "Woman in Europe." In *The Collected Works of C. G. Jung,* Translated by R.F.C. Hull, vol. 10, pp. 131–33. New York: Random House, 1964. Psychic forces (Eros and Logos) for the most part determine "femininity" in women, "masculinity" in men; however, both males and females can and should come into contact with the force in which they are of short supply.

_____. Psychological Reflections. Edited by Jolande Jacobi. Princeton: Princeton University Press, 1970.

Kierkegaard, Soren. *The Concept of Dread,* 1844. Translated by Walter Lowrie. Princeton: Princeton University Press, 1957. Nature; women are more sensuous than men and lack both intellectual capacity and ethical understanding. All this is due to their childbearing capability.

_____. *Stages on Life's Way,* 1845. Translated by Walter Lowrie. New York: Schocken Books, 1967.

_____. *Either/Or,* 1843. Translated by David F. Swenson, Lillian M. Swenson and Walter Lowrie, vols. 1 and 2. Princeton: Princeton University Press, 1971 and 1979.

Kriegal, Leonard, ed. *The Myth of American Manhood.* New York: Dell, 1978. Collection. Generally in favor of men being "masculine" in the sense of exhibiting "macho" psychological and behavioral traits.

Lang, Theo. *The Difference Between a Man and a Woman.* New York: Bantam, 1973. Nature; women are biologically and intellectually inferior to men.

Leck, Glorianne. "Philosophical Concerns about Gender Distinction." Unpublished. Available from Glorianne Leck, Department of Education, Youngstown State University, Youngstown, Ohio 44555.

_____, and Johnson, Bonnie McD. "Philosophical Assumptions of Research on Gender Difference or: Two-By-Two and We'll Never Break Through." *SISCOM Proceedings,* 1975. Argues against the assumptions in nature theories that a) there are only males and females (and nothing else) and b) gender differences justify differences in treatment.

Lenin, V. I. *The Emancipation of Women.* New York: International Publishers, 1966. Nurture; elimination of capitalism will free women from oppression.

Lewis, Helen Block. *Psychic War in Men and Women.* New York: New York University Press, 1976. Nature/nurture combination; males are more aggressive than women and women are more nurturant than men, but it does not follow that male domination is inevitable. It can be avoided by freeing the culture of the exploitive relationship between the classes.

Lloyd, Barbara, and Archer, John, eds. *Exploring Sex Differences.* New York: Academic Press, 1974. Collection.

Locke, John. *The Second Treatise of Government,* Chs. II, V, VI, VII. 1690. New York: Hafner Publishing Co., 1947. Nurture; domination of the husband over his wife is due to human, not natural, law but this is as it should be.

Lundberg, Ferdinand, and Farnham, Marynia F. *Modern Woman: The Lost Sex.* New York: Harper, 1947. Pro-Freudian attack on feminism.

Lynn, David. "The Process of Learning Parental and Sex-Role Identification." *Journal of Marriage and the Family* 28 (1966):446–470.

_____. *Parental and Sex-Role Identification.* Berkeley: McCutchan Publishing Co., 1969.

McCarthy, Mary. "The Tyranny of the Orgasm." In McCarthy's *On The Contrary,* pp. 167–173. New York: Farrar, Straus and Cudahy, 1951.

Maccoby, Eleanor, ed. *The Development of Sex Differences*. Stanford: Stanford University Press, 1966.

_____, and Jacklin, Carol Nagy. *The Psychology of Sex Differences,* vols. I and II. Stanford: Stanford University Press, 1974. There are some (but not many) psychological differences between the sexes and these are innate. Most prior claims as to the psychological differences between the sexes have not been conclusively shown.

McLennan, John Ferguson. *Primitive Marriage: An Inquiry into the Origin of the Form of Capture in Marriage Ceremonies.* 1865. Chicago: University of Chicago Press, 1970. Matriarchy theory.

Mahowald, Mary Briody, ed. *Philosophy of Woman: Classical to Current Concepts.* Indianapolis: Hackett Publishing Co., 1978. Collection of primarily historical philosophical pieces on sex difference theory.

Mailer, Norman. *The Prisoner of Sex.* New York: New American Library, 1971. Nature; it is in the nature of man that he must dominate women and this serves the sexual pleasures of both sexes.

Maine, Sir Henry. *Ancient Law.* 1861. London: J. Murray, 1873. Patriarchy theory; studies ancient Roman, Hebrew, and Hindu law and concludes that even the very earliest societies were patriarchal, not matriarchal.

Marcuse, Herbert. *Counterrevolution and Revolution.* Boston: Beacon, 1972. Advocates the "feminization" of men.

Marine, Gene. *A Male Guide to Women's Liberation.* New York: Avon, 1972. Nurture; does not follow from woman's capacity that motherhood is women's "natural" function.

Marlow, H. Carleton, and Davis, Marrison M. *The American Search for Woman.* Santa Barbara, Calif.: Clio Books, 1976. Nature; men and women are psychologically and physiologically different, but it does not follow that either sex is superior.

Martin, M. Kay, and Voorhies, Barbara. *The Female of the Species.* New York: Columbia University Press, 1975. Anthropological nurture theory; patriarchy reigns in economically advanced societies.

Martineau, Harriet. *Society in America.* London: Saunders and Otley, 1837. Nurture; education will free women from oppression.

Marx, Karl. *Manifesto of the Communist Capital: A Critique of Political Economy.* Trans. by Samuel Moore and Edward Aveling. New York: Modern Library, 1906. Nature/nurture combination; the oppression of women in the family results from a natural division of labor based on women's childbearing capabilities. The family will remain when capitalism is abolished, but women's oppression will not.

_____. *Economic and Philosophic Manuscripts of 1844.* Trans. by Martin Milligan. New York: International Publishers, 1964.

Mason, J. W. "Psychologic Stress and Endocrine Functions." In *Topics in Psychoendocrinology,* ed. by Edward J. Sachar. New York: Grune and Stratton, 1975, pp. 1–18.

Masters, R.E.L. and Lea, Eduard. *The Anti-Sex: The Belief in the Natural Inferiority of Women: Studies in Male Frustration and Sexual Conflict.* New York: Julian Press, 1964.

Mathieu, Nicole-Claude. "Masculinity/Femininity." *Feminist Issues,* vol. 1 (Summer 1980): 51–69.

May, Robert. *Patterns of Male and Female Development.* New York: W. W. Norton, 1980.

Mead, Margaret. *Male and Female.* New York: William Morrow, 1949.

———. *Sex and Temperament.* New York: William Morrow, 1935. Nurture.

Mencken, H. L. *In Defense of Women* 1922. New York: Time, Inc., 1963. Women are mentally superior to men but physically inferior. Women are too cagey to want the elimination of marriage. Anti-equality of the sexes.

Mill, John Stuart. *The Subjection of Women.* Reprint. Cambridge, Mass.: MIT Press, 1970. Utilitarian arguments for equality between the sexes.

Miller, Jean Baker, ed. *Psychoanalysis and Women.* Baltimore; Penguin Books, 1973.

———. *Toward a New Psychology of Women.* Boston: Beacon Press, 1976. Nurture; women are socially devalued and must take group action to advance.

Mitchell, Juliet. "The Longest Revolution." *The New Left Review* (Nov.–Dec. 1966): 11–37. Pro-Freudian; patriarchy will disappear only after Oedipus complex resolved.

———. *Women's Estate.* New York: Pantheon, 1972.

———. *Psychoanalysis and Women.* New York: Pantheon, 1974.

Mitscherlich, Alexander. *Society Without the Father.* New York: Schocken, 1970. Nurture; education, social organization and thought processes are all imprinted with paternalistic images.

Money, John. "Developmental Differentiation of Femininity and Masculinity Compared." In *The Potential of Women,* ed. by Seymour M. Farber and Roger H. L. Wilson, pp. 51–65. New York: McGraw-Hill, 1963. Nature vs. nurture outmoded; favors current genetic theory which postulates a norm of behaviors for males and females whose boundaries are neither too constricted nor too diffuse.

———. "Psychosexual Differentiation." In *Sex Research: New Developments,* Ch. 1, ed. by John Money. New York: Holt, Rinehart and Winston, 1965.

———, and Ehrhardt, Anke. *Man and Woman, Boy and Girl.* Baltimore: Johns Hopkins University Press, 1972. Nature/nurture combination. Psychological sex differences are caused by differences in the nervous systems of men and women which are in turn caused by the secretion of different hormones in the mother's womb. However, these psychological differences can be eliminated by suitable rearing techniques.

_____, and Tucker, Patricia. *Sexual Signatures: On Being a Man or a Woman.* Boston: Little, Brown, 1975.

_____. *Love and Love Sickness: The Science of Sex, Gender Difference and Pair-Bonding.* Baltimore: Johns Hopkins University Press, 1980. We live in a sexual dictatorship controlled by the Church.

Montagu, M. F. Ashley. *Men and Aggression.* New York: Oxford University Press, 1968.

_____. *The Natural Superiority of Women.* New York: Macmillan, 1968. Nature; women have a biological advantage over men.

Morgan, Elaine. *The Descent of Woman.* New York: Bantam, 1973. Nature/nurture combination. Male hormones make males more aggressive than women, but aggression is not the only way to gain leadership in a society. Anti-Tiger and Goldberg.

Morgan, Lewis Henry. *Ancient Society* 1877. Ed. by Leslie White. Cambridge, Mass.: Harvard University Press, 1964. Nurture; matrilineal clan was the basic social unit prior to patriarchy; women's oppression is thus merely a historically contingent fact.

Morris, Desmond. *The Naked Ape.* New York: Dell, 1969. Nature; because of hunting, males have the dominance drive and territorial drive. Any attempt to eliminate the patriarchal family will clash with these male drives.

Morrison, Eleanor S., and Borosage, Vera, eds. *Human Sexuality: Contemporary Perspectives.* Palo Alto, Calif.: National Press Books, 1973. Collection. Includes discussion of the concepts of "masculinity" and "femininity."

Mozans, H. J. *Women in Science.* 1913. Cambridge, Mass.: MIT Press, 1974. Collection of mostly nature theories; although the great women of science had "masculine" minds, they retained "feminine" virtues; women are better than men at deduction, men are better than women at induction.

Nelson, Marie Coleman, and Ikenberry, Jean, eds. *Psychosexual Imperatives: Their Role in Identity Formation.* New York: Human Sciences Press, 1979. Collection. Psychoanalytic essays on gender identity.

Neumann, Erich. *The Origins and History of Consciousness.* New York: Pantheon, 1954.

_____. *The Great Mother: Ana Analysis of an Archetype.* Princeton: Princeton University Press, 1955. Jungian; the archetype of "the Feminine" is an innate psychological trait in all humans. This trait has a tendency to reign in women but both men and women should come into contact with it.

_____. *Amor and Psyche.* New York: Pantheon, 1956.

Nietzsche, Friedrich. *Beyond Good and Evil.* Translated by Walter Kaufman. New York: Random House, 1966.

_____. *On the Genealogy of Morals and Ecce Homo.* Translated by Walter Kaufman and R. J. Hollingdale. New York: Vintage, 1967.

_____. *Thus Spake Zarathustra.* Translated by R. J. Hollingdale. Baltimore: Penguin, 1967.

_____. *The Gay Science.* Translated by Walter Kaufman. New York: Random House, 1974. Women are by nature inferior to men.

Osborne, Marthe Lee, ed. *Woman in Western Thought.* New York: Random House, 1979. Collection; western philosophers on women.

_____. *Genuine Risk: A Dialogue on Woman.* Cambridge, Mass.: Hackett Publishing Co., 1981. Major positions on physical and psychological sex differences advanced by participants in a Socratic-like dialogue.

Parsons, Talcott. *Essays in Sociological Theory.* New York: The Free Press, 1954.

_____, and Bales, Robert F. *Family Socialization and Interaction Process.* Glencoe, Ill.: The Free Press, 1955. Sex role differentiation in the family is functional.

Petras, John W., ed. *Sex: Male/Gender: Masculine.* Port Washington, New York: Alfred Publishing Co., 1975. Collection of articles on masculine roles.

Pierce, Christine. "Natural Law Language and Women." In *Women in Sexist Society.* Ed. by Vivian Gorneck and Barbara K. Moran. New York: Signet, 1971, pp. 242–58.

Plato. *The Republic.* Translated by F. M. Cornford. Oxford: Oxford University Press, 1941. Nature/nurture combination. Women are by nature inferior to men in some respects, but in others (such as abilities required for guardianship), some women are better than some men. Consequently, all should be educated alike.

Plaza, Monique. "'Phallomorphic' Power and the Psychology of 'Woman.'" *Feminist Issues* (Summer 1980): 71–102.

Pleck, Joseph H., and Sawyer, Jack, eds. *Men and Masculinity.* Englewood Cliffs, New Jersey: Prentice-Hall, 1974. Nurture; men are oppressed in a patriarchal society.

Ramsey, Estelle. "Sex Hormones and Executive Ability." *Annals of the New York Academy of Sciences* 208 (March 15, 1973): 237–245. Anti-Money. Early male embryo is female until fifth or sixth week. Genetic XX-ness is the primordial substance.

Reeves, Nancy. *Womankind Beyond the Stereotypes.* Chicago: Aldine Atherton, 1971. Antinature theories; the presupposition of nature theories about women fail the test of logic and history, yet they continue to be the norm of society.

Reich, Wilhelm. *The Sexual Revolution: Toward a Self-Governing Character of Structure.* Translated by Theodore P. Wolfe. New York: Orgone Institute Press, 1945.

_____. *The Function of the Orgasm: Sex-Economic Problems of Biological Energy.* Translated by Theodore P. Wolfe. New York: Noonday Press, 1961.

_____. *The Invasion of Compulsory Sex-Morality.* New York: Farrar, Straus and Giroux, 1975. Freudian-Marxist; sexual drives in the patriarchal family are repressed and cause the oppression of women. Socialism is necessary for the elimination of patriarchy, but not sufficient for it.

Reitenbeck, Hendrik M., ed. *Psychoanalysis and Male Sexuality.* New Haven, Conn.: College and University Press, 1966.

Reiter, Rayna R., ed. *Toward an Anthropology of Women.* New York: Monthly Review Press, 1975.

Reyburn, Wallace. *The Inferior Sex.* Englewood Cliffs, N.J.: Prentice-Hall, 1972. Nature; women are inferior to men in rationality, creativity, etc. due to menstruation.

Rheingold, J. *The Fear of Being a Woman.* New York: Grune and Stratton, 1964.

Rieff, Philip. "Sexuality and Domination." In Rieff's *Freud: The Mind of the Moralist,* pp. 191–204. New York: Anchor Books, 1961.

Romer, Nancy. *The Sex-Role Cycle: Socialization from Infancy to Old Age.* Old Westbury, N.Y.: The Feminist Press, 1980. Nurture; describes process of sex-role socialization.

_____. *The Sex Role Straightjacket: Becoming Masculine.* Old Westbury, N.Y.: Feminist Press, 1979.

Rosaldo, Michelle Zimbalist, and Lamphere, Louise, eds. *Woman, Culture and Society.* Stanford: Stanford University Press, 1974. Collection; anthropologists on women's roles.

Rossi, Alice, ed. *The Feminist Papers: From Adams to de Beauvoir.* New York: Columbia University Press, 1973. Historical collection of feminist writings.

Roszak, Betty. "The Human Continuum." In *Masculine/Feminine,* edited by B. Roszak and T. Roszak. New York: Harper Colophon, 1969, pp. 297–306.

_____, and Roszak, Theodore, eds. *Masculine/Feminine.* New York: Harper and Row, 1969. Collection; nature and nurture viewpoints and discussion of "masculine" and "feminine."

Rousseau, Jean Jacques. "Sophie, of Woman." In *Emile,* pp. 321–33. Translated by Barbara Foxley. London: J.M. Dent and Sons, Ltd., 1911. Nature; men ought to have total freedom, women ought to become wives and mothers.

Ruth, Sheila. *Issues in Feminism: A First Course in Women's Studies.* Boston: Houghton Mifflin, 1980. Historical and current selections from various feminist perspectives.

Sartre, Jean Paul. *Being and Nothingness: An Essay on Phenomenological Ontology.* Translated by Hazel E. Barnes. 1953. New York: Washington Square Press, 1966. The "female" and "feminine" as obscene.

Scheinfeld, Amram. *Women and Men.* New York: Harcourt, Brace and Co., 1944. Nature.

Schlegel, Alice. *Male Dominance and Female Autonomy: Domestic Authority in Matrilineal Societies.* New York: Hraf Press, 1972.

Schneider, David, and Gough, Kathleen, eds. *Matrilineal Kinship.*

Berkeley: University of California Press, 1962. In matrilinear societies, women are responsible for children, but both women and children are controlled by adult males.

Schneir, Miriam, ed. *Feminism: The Historical Writings.* New York: Random House, 1972. Collection: eighteenth to early twentieth-century feminist writings.

Schopenhauer, Arthur. "Of Women." In *The Complete Essays of Schopenhauer.* Translated by T. Baily Saunders. Nature; women are inferior in every respect to men. New York: Willey Book Co., 1893, pp. 72–89.

Scott-Maxwell. *Women and Sometimes Men.* New York: Alfred A. Knopf, 1957. Jungian. Most women are primarily "feminine" and most men primarily "masculine" due to biology; men should make every effort to come into contact with their "feminine" personality, although women should remain basically "feminine."

Sexton, Patricia Cayo. *The Feminized Male: Classrooms, White Collars and the Decline of Manliness.* New York: Random House, 1969. Classrooms need to be "defeminized" by increasing the number of male teachers. Public workplaces ought to be "feminized" by increasing the number of females at each job level.

Sherfey, Mary Jane. *The Nature and Evolution of Female Sexuality.* New York: Random House, 1966. Anti-Freudian view of female sexuality; denies that the libido is "masculine" in nature.

Sherman, Julia. *On the Psychology of Women.* Springfield, Ill.: Charles C Thomas, 1971.

Simon, William, and Gagnon, John. "Psycho-sexual Development." *Trans-action* 6 (March 1969): 9–17.

Slater, Philip. *The Glory of Hera.* Boston: Beacon, 1968. Ontogenetic experience of matriarchy is universal; we all live under a kind of psychic power our mothers have over us.

Smith, Dorothy E. *Feminism and Marxism: A Place to Begin, A Way to Go.* Vancouver, Canada: New Star Books, 1977. Traditional Marxists mistaken in regarding the demand for sexual equality as a threat to the working class. Advocates combination of Marxism with sexual equality.

Solanas, Valerie. *SCUM Manifesto.* New York: Olympia Press, 1968. Nature. Males are passive, female active. Females are superior to males.

Spencer, Herbert. *The Principles of Sociology,* vols. I and II. New York: D. Appleton and Co., 1897.

_____. *Essays, Scientific, Political and Speculative,* vol. III. 1874. New York: D. Appleton, 1910. Nature; biology makes women psychologically inferior to men and this justifies differences in labor roles.

_____. *The Principles of Ethics,* vols. I and II. 1893. New York: D. Appleton and Co., 1910.

_____. *Social Statics.* 1850. New York: D. Appleton and Co., 1913.

Stacey, Judith, Beraud, Susan; and Daniels, Joan, eds. *And Jill Came Tumbling After: Sexism in American Education.* New York: Dell, 1974. Nurture; school system reinforces sex-role stereotyping.

Stanford, Barbara, ed. *On Being Female.* New York: Pocket Books, 1974. Collection. On women's current attempts to change conditions.

Stern, Karl. *The Flight from Woman.* New York: Farrar, Straus and Giroux, 1965. Jungian; women should shun their "masculinity" and males should come into contact with their "feminine" sides.

Stoll, Clarice Stasy. *Sexism: Scientific Debates.* Reading, Mass.: Addison-Wesley, 1973. Collection. Both nature and nurture theories.

Stoller, Robert J. *Sex and Gender, Volume 1: On the Development of Masculinity and Femininity.* New York: Jason Aronson, 1968.

_____. "The 'Bedrock' of Masculinity and Femininity." *Archives of General Psychiatry* 26 (March 1972): 207–212. The penis is a masculinized clitoris, the male brain is an androgenized female brain.

_____. *Sex and Gender, Volume 2: The Transsexual Experiment.* New York: Jason Aronson, 1975. Freudian; sex and gender can go in separate ways, but in most cases biological forces cause sex differences with mothering also playing a role in gender identity.

Stone, Merlin. *When God Was a Woman.* New York: Dial Press, 1976. Matriarchy theory.

Storr, Anthony. *Human Aggression.* New York: Atheneum, 1968. Aggression is functional in males, not in females.

Stouse, Jean, ed. *Women and Analysis: Dialogues on Psychoanalytic Views of Femininity.* New York: Grossman Publishers, 1974. Collection of Freudian and anti-Freudian views.

Taylor, Harriet. "Enfranchisement of Women." In *Essays on Equality,* edited by Alice S. Rossi, pp. 89–122. 1851. Chicago: University of Chicago Press, 1970. Nurture; subjection of women due merely to physical force, not justice. Women have the right to work outside the home.

Terman, L.M., and Miles, Catherine. *Sex and Personality.* New York: McGraw-Hill, 1936.

_____, and Tyler, Leona. "Psychological Sex Differences." In *A Manual of Child Psychology,* edited by L. Carmichael, pp. 1064–114. New York: John Wiley, 1954.

Thomas, William. *Sex and Society: Studies in the Social Psychology of Sex.* London: Fisher Unwin, 1907. Women and men have the same mental capacities but differ in physiological ones.

Thompson, Clara. "Penis Envy in Women." *Psychiatry* vol. 6, (1943): 123–25.

_____. *On Women.* Edited by Maurice R. Green. New York: New American Library, 1971. Nurture; anti-Freudian. There is penis envy in females, but it is culturally, not biologically, caused.

Thompson, William. *Appeal of One Half of the Human Race, Women, Against the Pretensions of the Other Half, Men, to Retain Them in Civil and Thence Domestic, Slavery.* 1825. New York: Burt Franklin, 1970. Nature/nurture combination; women are inferior but should be compensated by society for the inferiority. Women must have every right males have and capitalism must be abolished in order to attain true equality.

Thurston, Linda. "On Male and Female Principle." *The Second Wave* 1, (Summer 1971): 38–42. Rejection of the positive-negative polarities often presupposed in "male" and "female" principles.

Tiger, Lionel. *Men in Groups.* New York: Random House, 1969. Nature; male aggression is innate and inevitable.

Trotsky, Leon. *Women and the Family.* New York: Pathfinder Press, 1970. Nurture; women must have economic equality with men and share equally in the domestic chores.

Twin, Stephanie L., ed. *Out of the Bleachers: Writings On Women and Sport.* Old Westbury, N.Y.: Feminist Press, 1979. Collection of articles bearing on physiological sex difference theory.

Vaerting, Mathilde, and Vaerting, Mathias. *The Dominant Sex: A Sociology of Sex Differentiation.* Translated by Eden and Cedar Paul. New York: George H. Doran Co., 1923. History has alternated between patriarchy and matriarchy.

Vilar, Esther. *The Manipulated Man.* New York: Bantam Books, 1972. Women dominate men, not vice versa.

Warren, Mary Anne. *The Nature of Woman: An Encyclopedia and Guide to the Literature.* Box 69, Point Reyes, Calif., Edgepress, 1980. Contains fully annotated bibliography of primary readings in sex difference theory as well as detailed philosophical analysis of key terms in women's studies. Highly recommended by the editor of this volume as a valuable guide to teachers of women's studies for use in conjunction with this volume.

Weininger, Otto. *Sex and Character.* London: Heinemann, 1906. Nature; women are purely sexual beings, men primarily rational.

Westermarck, Edward. *The History of Human Marriage,* vols. I–III. 1891. London: Macmillan and Co., 1925.

_____. *A Short History of Marriage.* 1926. New York: Macmillan, 1930.

_____. *Ethical Relativity.* New York: Harcourt, Brace and Co., 1932.

_____. *The Future of Marriage in Western Civilization.* New York: Macmillan, 1936. Darwinian; sexual selection has made women submissive, men aggressive. Male-dominated marriage is necessary for the survival of the human species.

Whitbeck, Caroline. "Theories of Sex Difference." *Philosophical Forum* 5, nos. 1–2 (1973–74): 54–80.

Williams, Juanita H. *Psychology of Woman: Behavior in a Biosocial Context.* New York: W. W. Norton, 1977.

Wilson, Edward O. *Sociobiology: The New Synthesis.* Cambridge, Mass.: Harvard University Press, 1975.

_____. *On Human Nature.* Cambridge, Mass.: Harvard University Press, 1978. Nature/nurture combination; male domination of women is due partly to biological causes, but it is not inevitable; sex differences are eliminable by training.

Wilson, Robert A. *Feminine Forever.* New York: M. Evans, 1966.

Woolf, Virginia. *A Room of One's Own.* New York: Harcourt, Brace and Co., 1929.

_____. *Three Guineas.* New York: Harcourt, Brace and Co., 1938. "Masculinity" in females is caused both by environment and physiology. Lesbianism is more liberating than heterosexuality.

Wolgast, Elizabeth. *Equality and the Rights of Women* (Ithaca, N.Y.: Cornell University Press, 1980). There are sex differences and a just society must take account of them.

Zaretsky, Eliz. "Capitalism, the Family, and Personal Llife: Part I" *Socialist Revolution* 3, nos. 1-2. (Jan.-April, 1973): 69-125. Capitalism is not the cause of women's being forced to stay at home and rear children, patriarchy is. Women's oppression predated capitalism.

_____. "Capitalism, the Family and Personal Life: Part II," *Socialist Revolution,* 3, no. 3 (May-June, 1973): 19-70. Continuation of above.

Zilboorg, Gregory. "Male and Female." *Psychiatry* VII (1944): 257-96.

Part III:

Adkins, Elizabeth. "Genes, Hormones, and Gender." Paper read at the 144th National Meeting of the American Association for the Advancement of Science, Washington, D.C., February 14, 1978. Human comparisons to animal behavior is dubious in the case of sex difference research.

Bardwick, Judith M., ed. *Readings on the Psychology of Women.* New York: Harper and Row, 1972. Contains research papers on the psychology of women.

Beach, Frank A., ed. *Human Sexuality in Four Perspectives.* Baltimore: Johns Hopkins University Press, 1977. Articles critiquing recent research on the psychology of sex differences.

Bem, Sandra. "The Measurement of Psychological Androgyny." *Journal of Consulting and Clinical Psychology* 42 (1974): 155-62. There are feminine males, masculine females, and androgynes of both sexes, so the sexual stereotyping of personality is not a function of biology alone.

Block, J. "Some Reasons for the Apparent Inconsistency of Personality." *Psychological Bulletin* 70 (1968): 210-22.

Broverman, Inge K., et al. "Sex-Role Stereotypes and Clinical Judgments of Mental Health." *Journal of Consulting and Clinical Psychology* 34 (1970): 1–7.

Chodorow, Nancy. "Being and Doing: A Cross-Cultural Examination of the Socialization of Males and Females." In *Women in Sexist Society,* edited by Vivian Gornick and Barbara K. Moran, pp. 259–91. New York: Signet, 1971. Refutation of the claim for universal and necessary differentiation by sex of psychological traits. Admits to statistically significant differentiation and provides a nurture explanation.

Delaney, Janice; Lipton, Mary Jane; and Toth, Emily. *The Curse: A Cultural History of Menstruation.* New York: New American Library, 1977. Women's menstrual cycle is not proof of their physical or psychological inferiority to men.

Ellman, Mary. *Thinking About Women.* New York: Harcourt Brace Jovanovich, 1968. Anti-"masculine" and "feminine" stereotypes. The only significant differences between men and women are that women bear children and men are stronger.

Figes, Eva. *Patriarchal Attitudes.* Greenwich, Conn.: Fawcett World, 1971. Empirical evidence does not support nature theories.

Goy, Robert W., and McEwen, Bruce S. *Sexual Differentiation of the Brain: Based on a Work Session of the Neurosciences Research Program.* Cambridge, Mass.: MIT Press, 1980.

Horner, Matina. "Fail: Bright Women." *Psychology Today* 3, no. 6 (November 1969): 36–38, 62.

————. "The Motive to Avoid Success." In *Readings in the Psychology of Women,* edited by Judith M. Bardwick. New York: Harper and Row, 1972, pp. 62–67.

————. "Toward an Understanding of Achievement-Related Conflicts in Women." In *And Jill Came Tumbling After: Sexism in American Education,* edited by Judith Stacey, Susan Béraud and Joan Daniels. New York: Dell, 1974.

Hutt, Corinne. *Males and Females.* Baltimore: Penguin Books, 1972. Contains studies of humans and animals she believes to show that hormones have sex difference effects.

Kaplan, Alexandra G., and Bean, Joan P., eds. *Beyond Sex-Role Stereotypes: Readings Toward a Psychology of Androgyny.* Boston: Little, Brown and Co., 1976. Contains an article by Anne Constantinople which criticizes the tests for "masculinity" and "femininity" that psychologists have used and an article by Miriam Rosenberg criticizing research thought to favor nature theories.

Klein, Viola. *The Feminine Character: History of an Ideology.* London: Routledge and Kegan Paul, 1946. The conceptualization of "femininity" in various theories has contained bias.

Komarovsky, Mirra. *Dilemmas of Masculinity: A Study of College Youth.* New York: W.W. Norton and Co., 1976. Data showing that college males both accept and reject masculine stereotypes.

Levy, Betty. "The School's Role in Sex-Role Stereotyping of Girls." *Feminist Studies* 1 (1972): 5–23.

Lips, Hilary M., and Colwill, Nina Lee. *The Psychology of Sex Differences*. Englewood Cliffs, N.J.: Prentice-Hall, 1978. Criticizes standard psychological tests for "masculinity" and "femininity" as well as research purporting to show that testosterone causes aggression.

Maccoby, Eleanor E., ed. *The Development of Sex Differences*. Stanford: Stanford University Press, 1966. Includes a survey of research on the possible effects of sex hormones on sex differences.

*_____. *The Psychology of Sex Differences,* vol. II. Stanford: Stanford University Press, 1966. Extensive bibliographies of empirical research done up to 1973.

_____, and Jacklin, Carol Nagy. *The Psychology of Sex Differences,* vol. I. Stanford: Stanford University Press, 1974. Evidence to the effect that females are better than males at verbal skills, males better at visual-spatial perception.

Mill, John Stuart. *The Subjection of Women*. Reprint. Cambridge, Mass.: MIT Press, 1970. Women excel at intuition, men at the intellectual. But there is no justification for claiming that psychological differences are "natural" unless they cannot be explained as a result of educational influences.

Nova Transcript. "The Pinks and the Blues." Available for a prepaid fee of $3.00 from WGBH TV, Box 1000, Boston, Mass. 02215. Review of recent data supporting the view that children are sex-stereotyped from birth.

Parlee, Mary Brown, and Vaughter, Reesa M. "Review of Recent Psychological Sex Difference Research." *Signs* 1, no. 1 (Autumn, 1975) pp. 119–28; 2, no. 1, pp. 120–246.

Phoenix, C.H., et al. "Sexual Differentiation as a Function of Androgenic Stimulation." In *Perspectives in Reproduction and Sexual Behavior,* edited by M. Diamond, Bloomington: Indiana University Press 1969.

Raymond, Janice. *The Transsexual Empire*. Boston: Beacon Press, 1979. Critique of reliance on the "masculine" and "feminine" in psychology.

Roberts, Joan I., ed. *Beyond Intellectual Sexism: A New Woman, a New Reality*. New York: David McKay Co., 1976. Points out distortions in theories of the inferiority of women.

Schneider, David M., and Gough, Kathleen, eds. *Matrilineal Kinship*. Berkeley: University of California Press, 1961. Data on existing matrilineal societies.

Stoll, Clarice Stasy. *Female and Male: Socialization, Social Roles, and*

---

*This is generally considered to be the most complete bibliography available of actual research that has been done.

Social Structure. Dubuque, Iowa: William C. Brown Co., 1974.
Contains data on biological and psychological differences between
the sexes.

Strathern, Marilyn. *Women in Between: Female Roles in a Male World:
Mount Hagen, New Guinea.* New York: Seminar Press, 1972. Data
on a patrilinear society in which women have a relative high degree of
independence but are still not equal to men.

Thomas, A.H., and Stewart, N.R. "Counselor Response to Female
Clients with Deviate and Conforming Career Goals." *Journal of
Counseling Psychology* 8 (1971): 352–57.

Vance, Carole S. "Gender Systems, Ideology and Sex Research," *Feminist Studies* 6, no. 1 (Spring, 1980).

Waber, Debora P. "Sex Differences in Mental Abilities, itemispheric
Lateralization, and Rate of Physical Growth at Adolescence,"
Development Psychology 13 (1977): 29–38.

_____. "Sex Differences in Cognition: A Function of of Maturation
Rate"? *Science,* 192 (May 7, 1976): 572–3.

Weisstein, Naomi. "Psychology Constructs the Female." In *Woman in
Sexist Society,* edited by Vivian Gornick and Barbara K.Moran, pp.
207–24. New York: Signet, 1971.

Williams, Juanita H. *Psychology of Woman: Behavior in a Biosocial
Context.* New York: W.W. Norton, 1977. Available evidence to the
effect that women's psychology is in any way linked to biology is un-
convincing.

Part IV:

Bardwick, Judith M. "Androgyny and Humanistic Goals, or Goodbye,
Cardboard People." In *The American Woman: Who Will She Be?,*
edited by Mary Louise McBee and Kathryn A. Blake, Beverly Hills,
Calif.: Glencoe Press, 1974, pp. 49–64. Defense of monoandrogynism.

Bem, Sandra. "The Measurement of Psychological Androgyny." *Journal of Consulting and Clinical Psychology* 42 (1974): 155–62.

_____. "Androgyny vs. the Tight Little Lives of Fluffy Women and
Men." *Psychology Today* 9, no. 4 (September, 1975): 58–62.

_____. "Probing the Promise of Androgyny." In *Beyond Sex-Role
Stereotyping,* edited by Alexandra G. Kaplan and Joan P. Bean, pp.
48–61. Boston: Little, Brown and Co., 1976. Offers data to support
the view that people with both "masculine" and "feminine"
psychological traits are the most successful and that sexual stereotyping has ill-effects.

Bird, Caroline. "The Androgynous Life." In Bird's *Born Female.* New
York: Pocket Books, 1968.

Chafetz, Janet. *Masculine/Feminine or Human.* Itasca, Ill.: F.E. Peacock Publishers, 1974.

Daly, Mary. "The Qualitative Leap Beyond Patriarchal Religion." *Quest: A Feminist Quarterly* 1, (Spring 1975): 29 ff. Argues against use of the term "androgyny" in feminist theory.

de Beauvoir, Simone. *The Second Sex.* New York: Knopf, 1953.

Dworkin, Andrea. *Woman Hating.* New York: Walton Rawls, 1966.

_____. *Our Blood: Prophecies and Discourses on Sexual Politics.* New York: Harper and Row, 1970. Advocates androgyny which for her means the end of "masculinity" and "femininity" and the end of heterosexuality as we know it now.

Feigen-Fasteau, Marc. *The Male Machine.* New York: Delta Books, 1975. The masculine mystique leads to unhappiness; we need an androgyneous division of labor.

Feldman, Susan. "Trebilcot's Two Forms of Androgynism." *Journal of Social Philosophy,* vol. 10 (May, 1979): 14–16.

Ferguson, Anne. "Androgyny as an Ideal for Human Development." In *Feminism and Philosophy,* edited by Mary Vetterling-Braggin, Jane English and Frederick Elliston, pp. 45–69. Totowa, N.J.: Littlefield, Adams and Co., 1977. Advocates monoandrogynism (expressed in terms of the "human," not the "masculine" or "feminine").

Gelpi, Barbara Charlesworth. "The Politics of Androgyny." *Women's Studies* 2, no. 2 (1974): 151–60.

Harris, Daniel. "Androgyny, the Sexist Myth in Disguise." *Women's Studies* 2, no. 2 (1974): 172.

Heilbrun, Carolyn G. *Toward a Recognition of Androgyny.* New York: Harper, 1973. Advocates monoandrogynism.

Jewitt, Paul K. *Man as Male and Female: A Study in Sexual Relationships from a Theological Point of View.* Grand Rapids, Mich.: William P. Eerdmans, 1975. Antipsychological monoandrogynism. Argues that eliminating sexual polarity would dehumanize all.

Kaplan, Alexandra G., and Bean, Joan P. eds. *Beyond Sex-Role Stereotypes: Readings Toward a Psychology of Androgyny.* Boston: Little, Brown and Co., 1976. Advocates permitting persons to behave in either a "masculine" or "feminine" manner, depending on the situation. Polyandrogynism.

Official Report to the United Nations on the Status of Women in Sweden, 1968. Quoted in Rita Liljeström, "The Swedish Model." In *Sex Roles in a Changing Society,* edited by Georgene H. Seward and Robert C. Williamson, p. 200. New York: Random House, 1970. Example of a monoandrogynistic government policy.

Raymond, Janice. "The Illusion of Androgyny." *Quest* 2 (Summer 1975).

Safilios-Rothschild, Constantina. *Women and Social Policy.* Englewood Cliffs, N.J.: Prentice-Hall, 1974. Polyandrogynism.

Sayers, Dorothy L. "The Human-Not-Quite-Human." *Unpopular Opinions.* London: Victor Gollanz, 1946.

Secor, Cynthia. "Androgyny: An Early Reappraisal." *Women's Studies*

2, no. 2 (1974): 164. Gives eight specific objections to the use of the concept of "androgyny."

Singer, June. *Androgyny: Toward a New Theory of Sexuality.* Garden City, N.Y.: Anchor Press, 1976.

Stimpson, Catherine. "The Androgyne and the Homosexual." *Women's Studies* 2, no. 2 (1974): 237–48. Analyzes the term "androgyne" in its various senses. Argues that the androgyne and the homosexual both offer appealing values, but are significantly different in a number of respects.

Vetterling-Braggin, Mary; Elliston, Frederick; and English, Jane, eds. *Feminism and Philosophy.* Part II. Totowa, N.J.: Littlefield, Adams and Co., 1977. Contains defenses and critiques of both mo-noandrogynism and polyandrogynism.

Watts, Alan W. *Nature, Man and Woman.* New York: Random House, 1970. Monoandrogynism.

Woolf, Virginia. *A Room of One's Own.* New York: Harcourt, Brace and Co., 1929. For a limited ideal of monoandrogynism; there should be cooperation, but not equality, between the "masculine" and "feminine" in each person.

Wolgast, Elizabeth H. *Equality and the Rights of Women* (Ithaca, N.Y.: Cornell University Press, 1980). Anti-androgynist.

JANE ROLAND MARTIN is a professor of philosophy at the University of Massachusetts, Boston. She is the author of *Explaining, Understanding and Teaching* (New York: McGraw-Hill, 1970) and numerous articles in philosophy and education journals, and is a past president of the Philosophy of Education Society. Her current research is on sex bias in educational thought.

JANICE MOULTON currently teaches philosophy at the University of Kentucky. She has written several articles on a variety of philosophical topics. In addition, she is the author of the *Guidebook for Publishing Philosophy* and coauthor, with G.M. Robinson, of *The Organization of Language,* both published by Cambridge Press. She is a founding mother of the Society for Women in Philosophy.

LINDA NICHOLSON received her Ph.D. degree from the History of Ideas Department at Brandeis University. She is now an assistant professor in the School of Education at the State University of New York at Albany where she also teaches in the women's studies program. She is currently at work on a book entitled *Feminism as Political Philosophy.*

ROBERT G. PIELKE is an associate professor of philosophy and religious studies at George Mason University in Fairfax, Virginia. He received his Ph.D. from Claremont Graduate School in 1973 and has taught primarily in the areas of social and political philosophy, ethical theory, and normative ethics. His publications and conference presentations have included a variety of themes from metaethics and political theory to the philosophical analyses of popular culture studies, science fiction and rock music.

B.C. POSTOW is an associate professor of philosophy at the University of Tennessee. She has contributed articles to professional journals on topics in ethics, social and political philosophy, and philosophy of feminism.

FRANCINE RAINONE taught philosophy at the University of Colorado and currently teaches philosophy and women's studies at Colby-Sawyer College, New London, N.H., where she is coordinator of women's studies. She is active in the mid-west branch of the Society of Women in Philosophy and the Marxist Activist Philosophers group. Her philosophical interests include Marxism, value theory, and feminist theory.

ALAN SOBLE is interested in ethical, social, political, and legal philosophy, the philosophy of science, and feminist philosophy. He edited *The Philosophy of Sex* (Totowa, N.J.: Littlefield, Adams and Co., 1980) and taught at the University of Texas (Austin), Wheaton College (Massachusetts), and at Moorhead State University (Minnesota).

JOYCE TREBILCOT works with the women's studies program at Washington University in St. Louis where she is also an associate professor of philosophy. In recent years she has been a visitor in women's studies at Wheaton College (Massachusetts) and at the University of New Mexico. Her work is about feminist conceptions of women and of women's studies.

MARY VETTERLING-BRAGGIN received her doctorate in philosophy from Boston University. Her major interests include the philosophy of natural and social science as well as feminist theory. She edited *Sexist Language: A Modern Philosophical Discussion* and coedited *Feminism and Philosophy,* both published by Littlefield, Adams and Co., Totowa, N.J.

MARY ANNE WARREN received her Ph.D. from the University of California at Berkeley in 1974 and has taught philosophy at Sonoma State University and San Francisco State University. She has published articles on abortion, affirmative action, and population policy. Her book, *The Nature of Woman: An Encyclopedia and Guide to the Literature* is available from Edgepress, Box 69, Point Reyes, California.